SHAMAN INVOCATION TO THE
GODDESS OF THE SPRING

Upon my back my children sitting
pressing my back, protect me!
Upon my shoulders my children
pressing my shoulders, protect me!
Before the Moon is Full
At the sight of the sun
At the beginning of the year
The fruit trees blooming time
At the cry of the she-coocoo
The earth opens and green appears
The trees open and buds appear
I'll be there for you, don't fear!

City of Los Angeles

Mayor's Certificate of Appreciation

As Mayor of the **CITY OF LOS ANGELES**, I am pleased to recognize the outstanding activities of

Z. Budapest

who has contributed to and actively participated in the "Women Take Back The Night" March on April 19, 1980; and

WHO is awarded this **MAYOR'S CERTIFICATE** of **APPRECIATION** for outstanding efforts and accomplishments which have been of great benefit to your community and particularly to the **CITY** of **LOS ANGELES**. **YOUR** community spirit and interest have helped make our City a better place in which to live, and have greatly assisted me in conducting the affairs of this City.

Date: May 1980.

Tom Bradley
Mayor

Sue K. Embrey
President, Commission on the Status of Women

THE HOLY BOOK OF WOMEN'S MYSTERIES
Part Two

by Zsuzsanna Emese Budapest
based on the Dianic tradition passed down through Masika Szilagyi

Inspired by
Masika Szilagyi
Janet Roslund

Artist:
Masika Szilagyi

Contributors:
Mary Farkas
Lhyv Oakwomon
Carol Christ
Chris Carol
Noel Brennan
Starhawk
Annu

Susan B. Anthony Coven Number One
Member of COG
P.O. Box 42121, Los Angeles, Ca. 90042

CREDITS FOR THE CONTRIBUTORS

Starhawk: author and High Priestess, "The Spiral Dance." A rebirth of Ancient Religion of the Great Goddess. Harper and Row Publishers.

Lhyv Oak Womon, Ritual Priestess, Astrologist.

Annu, Manager and part owner of the Feminist Wicca, Therapist, Healer.

Mary Farkas, Feminist Nutritionist, passionate lover of health.

Noel Brennan, author of unpublished work on rituals for children. Sacred poet.

Carol P. Christ, author of "Diving Deep and Surfacing", Beacon Press. Carol P. Christ and Judith Plaskow "Womanspirit Rising", a feminist reader in religion.

Chris Carol, psychologist and Priestess, Musician, Poet. Author of SilverWheel, Songbook One.

Masika Szilagyi, artist and ritual priestess, sacred poet. Folklorist.

Susan B. Anthony Books are available to the trade from Bookpeople, 2929 Fifth Street, Berkeley, CA 94710

ISBN 0-937081-02-7

SONG OF THE HOLY WOMEN

I am singing a shamansong! I am singing a shamansong
Dwelling in seventh heaven
living in the sixth heaven
My Mother created me.
Round formed lakes like water-rings
like heads of the wild rooster-round
I spiritwoman descended.
Into a golden cradle I descend
I Spiritwoman.
Dangling from a golden chain
I descend into the depths,
I Spiritwoman.
Upon a mound built by dippers
I descended, I Spiritwoman.
Upon a sleigh with double corners
I embarked, I Spiritwoman.
The corned sleigh I embarked on,
I Spiritwoman.
The darkest of nights dark center
Of the Crone Spirit
with the hearing divine
I Spiritwoman.
Over to the south of the Ob river
The big shouldered Bear queen
they celebrate her holyday in feasts
I hear, I Spiritwoman.
Black fur-lined rich nest
Red fur lined rich nest
I hold up my white head
my proud hundred locked head
I Spiritwoman.
Upon my five fingered foot
I fasten my reindeer boots
I Spiritwoman.
Upon my six toed foot
I fasten my reindeer boots, I Spiritwoman.
Black wild prayer lucky jacket
Red wild prayer lucky jacket
I threw upon my holy shoulders
I Spiritwoman
My girdle lucky at black prayer
I fastened around my hips,

5

I Spiritwoman
Red girdle, lucky at red prayer
I girded myself with, I Spiritwoman.
My moonbeam spotted magic veil
I placed upon my hundred curled white head
I Spiritwoman.
My sunbeam spotted magic veil
I bound around my hundred locks of hairs
I Spiritwoman.
From the village away
I am stepping away, I Spiritwoman.
From the cities away
Stepping away
I Spiritwoman.
I am the keeper of
a hundred stags and herd
I Spiritwoman.
I am the keeper of a hundred reindeers
I Spiritwoman.
I am the soul of the woods
I step the three steps of the sacred
Nymph spirit girl
I am stepping the four big steps
of the maiden spirits
I Spiritwoman.
My names are:
Black Cat formed priestess
Black Cat formed Priestess
My other names are
Hissing like a she-sabel priestess
Hissing like a she-sabel priestess
Such fame is spread about me
I Spiritwoman.
After all this
The woodspirits girls three steps I step out
I Spiritwoman
The woodspirits Maiden's four big steps I step out
I Spiritwoman
In the fish rich bays of the river Ob
Prosperous bay
I leave behind the seven big cities
I Spiritwoman.
The dwelling of the geese feathered men
the dwelling of the traveling shaman

on the reindeer beaten path
I go there myself, I spiritwoman.
The seven woodbeamed roof
the six woodbeamed roof
Encircle the dwelling
Seven times in the daytime
I encircle the dwelling
six times in the nite time
I Spiritwoman.
This ancient woman built
from redwoods carved door
from forestpine carved door
I open up with my five fingered hands
I Spiritwoman.
I enter the house filled with boys happy noises
I enter the house filled with girls happy noises
I Spiritwoman.
The people there bring me fresh tinder fire and fresh musk
So they welcome me, I spiritwoman.
Bless you women filled with gifts of laughter
Bless you men filled with gifts of laughter
To your daughters I wish long long lives
To your sons I wish long long life
I Spiritwoman!
On my five stringed instrument
I play the lowest string
The lower Crone spirits sing, let them sing!
I play the highest string
The highest Queen spirits sing, let them sing!
What can I leave you with?
I leave you my lucky dance for the rivers fishes
I leave you my lucky dance for the forests wild
When I leave you
No sickness shall touch you!
My wide inner lining of my sacred cape
enfold you with protection!
The sleeves of my sacred cape
bless you all with, bless you all!

Pele, Goddess of Fire by Ulrike

DIANIC GENESIS

In the beginning there was unknowable silence. She had an unknowable name which echoed through the universe, the power of this name, that no one shall utter, filled the universe with action.

Silence broke into its components, lights and shadows. From these lights action made form, and from the shadows formlessness. Visible and invisible, and she created a blend of the two we know today as Nature.

In this blend of form and formlessness, lights and shadows, visible and invisible, she created all the creatures making variations infinitely of herself as the birthing force, and the different form of her, where she is not so clearly visible, the-birthed-in-form.

She intermingled with herself, as she was never divided, and created our solar system, our mother planet, and all the creatures upon it. Among the creatures she ordained, that all species will know her either through instinct or through search, but all she created will periodically return to her holiness, and then again take form inside her.

And ever since the world has a blend of visible forms, female and male, and a blend of invisible forms, self love and self hate. The divine mixing of these creates reality, for her essence is present in all, but her forms don't conform temporary social orders. She is the circle of rebirth, thus we celebrate the moment in our lives as a honor to her, she whose Genesis is still happening, she who has not returned to any comfortable heaven to "watch" over us or forget us.

She who still creates all reality daily, she who is visible and invisible in Nature, she whose name is secret, she who rules the Universe. The Force of Life and Death and all that is in between. She is All.

DEDICATION

I call upon Hecate the Threeformed, Witchqueen, Priestess of the Earthgoddess, to favor this work and bring to light the thoughts; let those who hear, remember, and those who are opposed, be made tolerant.

I thank the Spirit that continues, prospers and grows for the success of the Holy Book of Women's Mysteries Part One and gently place this second volume into her blessed lap for the grace of further reprints and interests in the Goddess.

TABLE OF CONTENTS

1.	Dianic Genesis	9
2.	Dedication	11
3.	Table of Contents	12
4.	Introduction	14
5.	Goddess Religion	16
6.	Laws of the Craft	19
7.	Dangers of the Craft	21
8.	Dianic Affirmations	23
9.	Dianic Tradition	25
10.	Concepts of Womens Mysteries	26
11.	Understanding THEMIS	28
12.	Introduction to the Rites of Life	29
13.	Group Blessing	31
14.	A Ritual of Self Realization	31
15.	Birthday Ritual	33
16.	Dianic New Moon Ritual	35
17.	Rituals for Daily Life	37
18.	Summer Solstice Ritual for Children	39
19.	Spell for Continuance of a Special Request	42
20.	Recipe for Removal of Warts	43
21.	Spell to Stop Enemies	44
22.	Spell for Protection and Peace	45
23.	Ritual Encounter with Selfhood	46
24.	Conception Ritual	51
25.	Menstruation Ritual	53
26.	Celebration of the End of Menstruation	55
27.	Welcoming the New Mother Into the Circle of Mothers	56
28.	Naming Festival	57
29.	Ritual After an Abortion or Miscarriage	60
30.	Croning Ritual	62

31. Dianic Trysting   64
32. Attitudes Towards Death in the Craft   67
33. The Great Rite   75
34. Esotara: Witches Valentines Day   79
35. The Drawing of the Flowers   81
36. The Politics of Food   86
37. Self Blessing   96
38. Weatherwork   101
39. The Story of the Danaids   104
40. Using Dreams   105
41. Past Lifes   109
42. Automatic Writing   112
43. Spell to Appease the Angry Fates   113
44. Possessions by Demons and Devils   114
45. Sacred Sons   118
46. Spell to the Force   128
47. Acceptance of manhood ancient and modern   129
48. Epilogue to the Kouretes   135
49. The Song of Amargin   136
50. Practicing With Others   146
51. Initiation of Shaman Drums   153
52. Dianic Ordination Ritual   154
53. Practicing Solo   156
54. Ten Years Later   161
55. Masika's Book of Life   168
56. Goddess of the Ten Thousand Names   188
57. A Year and a Day Calendar   217
58. About the Author   220
59. About the Artist   222

INTRODUCTION

Many books have appeared about witchcraft in the past few hundred years. Some were presenting the Craft as a curious pastime and highlighted only its "cookbook" aspects (how to get a lover and how to do your enemy in), but missed the dignity and majesty that the Earth religion contained. Some presented the Craft as a highly ceremonious pageantry where you need to invest your life savings to get the proper tools, robes and glittering chalices, as if the power lay in the high quality of objects you needed. Such attitudes missed the humble common sense originating from the Craft, which made it such a desirable religion for peasants and Earth-loving folks. And then again, some books presented the Craft as a fossilized, hierarchical power structure, in which there are those who were "adepts" or "third degree" or otherwise achieved "guruhood". The rest of us folks just weren't fit to tie the laces on their sandals. Reminiscent of another religion or two? Precisely. Such books missed the all-pervading idea of human equality in the Craft. Lastly, there are many books which perverted the Craft to such a degree that in presenting it, they even forgot or "wrote out" the "major deity" concerned with Craft of the Wise, namely the Female Principle of the Universe. Those writers reflected their own sexism and fear of women, no matter how learned their books appeared. Taking out the heart of the theology destroyed people's images of this gentle path.

These were only the "friends" of the Craft! Now for the enemies! Here we have to go back to the very invention of printing. When Gutenberg printed the first book in 1456, it was the Bible! Western culture still holds a cultivated fetish for printed words, regarding them as gospels. If it's printed, it must be so.

This historical invention was turned against women immediately. The *Malleus Maleficarum* by James Sprenger was published in 1485. Like the early years of Television, the Book was widely read and taken as gospel. It was the demented, sadistic fantasy life of the male collective consciousness in the repressed sexuality of two Jesuit priests. It ended up killing eleven million women and men and children. It was a very unholy book. Today, it would fit well into the pornography of our times. The tortures of the women were often sexual, under the pretense of holiness. Some men today get off on such tortures. Imagine what a city must have smelled like when they burned four hundred women at the stake in one day. You KNOW, if your neighbor burns leaves in his backyard blocks away. Why is killing women allowed as a religious document today?

There should have been a Holy Book of Womens Mysteries hundreds of years ago. Ours started as the Feminist Book of Lights and

Shadows, which I wrote in 1975. The Holy Book Collective always knew it was a "dictated book." Our meetings were held on the Malibu mountaintop, breakfasts at "Everybody's Mother" restaurant. We brainstormed about how to resurrect, remember and invent what were women's religious experiences. Every Sunday morning, we were advancing the work in a fabulous speedy fashion, unencumbered by our normal limitations, writing down the ideas concerning Woman's Religion, and what we thought should be communicated. To this date, we have not stopped building, collecting material. It is safe to say, a Woman's Holy Book is never done! Women relate in creativity to religion, in a changing, ever-growing, blooming stream of consciousness. Our Book is always living, not a fossilized unyielding concept from the dark past.

It is a historical book because it contains the memories of the Ancient ways, such as the Women's Festivals, and the Trysting Ritual, and the Sabat celebrations. Yet it is infused with modern practices such as Freeing Political Prisoners, welcoming a new baby into the circle of mothers.

Kramer and Sprenger (the authors of the Witches Hammer) will spin in their graves when women learn about the Great Rite, a sexual rite, and no doubt will think they were right calling all women witches. Most women don't think they're witches because it is too dangerous to think so. It's a horror of ultimate annihilation that is connected to it in the deep mind. But were we not better off as a species practicing a life-affirming religion, acting out life-oriented rituals, regarding each of us as children of the Goddess? Enfolded into a celestial motherlove, would we not spin more healthier dreams, (Monies, literature), societies, relationships, lives? Is the Male principle of the universe not death without the tempering, enfolding force of the Goddess? Ancient religions which everybody practiced universally not too long ago (5,000 years is generous) yielded a planet life saner and more comfortable. All people were more obsessed with life than war. Today's obsession with death is a direct result of the exclusive male value system (they often call 'progress') and degradation of the women of our species. A Woman's Holy Book is but one of the utterances of the awakening Goddess in her many guises. The sense of the prophecy, wonder and sacredness of women articulates through the Mysteries, as the Life Giver becomes more visible in defense of our endangered species, the mothers and their children.

GODDESS RELIGION – HOW IS IT DIFFERENT?

When women or men look at the Goddess religion, they are expecting some if not all the earmarks of the other religions to show, religions they were involved with before. It is confusing for them not to find anything like it, and so it is even debatable if we have a religion or Tradition.

Witches themselves prefer to call it their Tradition. There are many traditions. We are not divided by color (black and white witches, etc.), but rather by traditions, Dianics, Druids, Gardnerians, Welsh traditions, English traditions, Pictish traditions, Nordic traditions, Eclectics, etc. None of the traditions that belong to witchcraft worship the devil. The Devil, poor thing, is a Christian invention, not pagan. Devil worship is a measly 150 years old, and was the backlash result of the witch burnings.

In witchcraft, the first most important cornerstone philosophy is a TRINITY of concept and not DUALITY. This alone colors everything as far as the explanation of LIFE. Since we have no duality, there is no concept of "apartness" of female-male, black and white, good and evil, etc. The Trinity multiplies into three times three as in the nine muses, and from then on explodes into the diversity of nature, accepting the different as a religious concept.

This means there is no division between body and soul. One is not dispised and the other glorified. There is no division of the sexes, both come from the same source, the Mother. There is no division of spiritual and profane, all is interrelated with everything else in the universe, and none stands apart from nature. All is Nature.

Now when you have committed a crime against Life, killed the "enemy's" sons and daughters (because in no war ever were only the men killed), the killers themselves would have to finish the enemy's karma genetically as people. Example: The Vietnam war comes home. Veterans of the war suffering from physical and psychological scars, "ghosts riding on their backs" as they put it. There is a consequence to all sins against Nature. Nothing goes unnoticed. It is not a sin to kill another in self-defense. But there is blame going to war when ordered, because there is a moment in all peoples lives when they can actually and bravely unchoose it, with their free will, which is their Goddess given sense of morality and decency. Of course this moment of choice needs enlightening circumstances to reveal itself, without which the person really could miss her or his destiny. When there is complete ignorance about the choice, the conditions are evil. Deliverance from this evil comes from information. Knowledge. Exposure. Experience. Racial memory. Collective consciousness. The Goddess within all. The Life force manifests in ourselves. So it's never hopeless. But it isn't always easy to tune into ourselves, especially when we are driven with meaningless work and toil, bored to death by repetition and deprived of living teachers who can pass on information about how to live and how to get what you want while in life, how to seek truth in harmony with others (this excluded teachings of "Only We have the Answer, the Others are 'Evil', because they sin against Our God" variety, which covers most the Judeo Christian, Moslem, Krishna, Buddha, Moonies, You Name It Guru, etc.). Does this worry Goddess Religionists? Only to the extent that they may gain political power to OUTLAW others.

Unfortunately, that is happening right now in this country. It is not surprising to me, since now more than ever you can see how they are (the so-called leading religions) militeristic based, and not on their respective Good Books. If Christians would practice their Good Book they would stay out of politics, other peoples bedrooms and stick to their own lives. One wonders where they have the time to care and tend their own qualities of the divine, from all this marching on Washington against the ERA. Organizing like crazy against homosexual rights, keep the blacks down, the browns out, the yellows in (new immigrants are cheap labor), and the War machine drafting. Is this all in the name of Prince of Love???

We have seen four hundred years of systematic killing and torturing of mainly women, who the church decided were witches. We have seen the Good Book waved at us as we were tied to the stake. We know when the conservatives are rising in this country and their lobbyists are busy convincing lawmakers that God wants them to uphold the Good Book values, they can rage into murder any day. We have seen it before.

Women, witches or not, had to live with religious oppression. We experienced it on our skin, some burned, some mutilated. Even today, cutting out the clitorisses of females at the age of six or seven in India, Africa, Moslem countries to be kept pregnant against our will, punished for being poor. Why would a respectable religion be obsessed with woman hatred? Anybody hatred? Well, I don't know. It only makes sense if you look at it as a militaristic effort to set up a social system in which women are controlled with no abortion, and no jobs for equal pay. Sound familiar? When women are controlled the empire is controlled. Women's product is citizens. Consumers. Lovers.

Boldog asszony and daughter by Masika Szilagyi

THE LAWS OF THE CRAFT

Many people are disappointed to find that we have no Ten Commandments, but only one Golden Rule:

DO AS THOU WILT AND HARM NONE

It is a much harder rule to follow than the many rules and regulations, and it requires considerable wisdom. But there are expectations in the Craft and behavior requirements. I will try to sum them up.

1. Honour the High Priestess.

One of the most despised "sins" is "stealing a coven." It means that if a High Priestess welded a group together, nobody should come along and usurp her and take over the coven. Before a NEW High Priestess is chosen, a High Priestess must be absent a year and a day from the activities of her coven. This "rule" comes from ancient times, where obviously the coven leaders had to go and hide from the Inquisitors, and so plenty of time was allowed for the High Priestess or Priest to return.

2. Honour the Succession of Teachers.

This means that if you were lucky to have a spiritual advisor who first opened your eyes to the Goddess and her religion, this teacher counts as a "mother" to your soul, and deserves the attention and gratitude you give your natural mother. If you are taking knowledge without putting something back in energy or services, you earn the same fate. Someday you too will teach somebody who will not give you back anything but take it away. It is not considered noble behavior to take without giving.

3. Relate back to the mother coven on Midsummer when all the tribes are being gathered.

It is custom to return and process, have some fun with the original coven you were hived from. If your path was a lucky one, you were educated and then "hived" with your new coven with the blessings of the mother coven. We honor this connection once a year by returning to celebrate Litha.

4. If there is dissent in the coven, make a new coven.

This has been one of the oldest rules, which gave way to prospering the Craft, instead of disrupting it. Not everybody gets along with everybody, we are witches, not saints. So when trouble comes, just see if it's not a sign to make a new group. Then part amiably and try to maintain respect between the two groups.

5. A coven's loyalty is the coven's luck.

Do not hex anybody within your group, or mess with them psychically, but rather go to the High Priestess or Priest and use regular methods of problem solving. Avoid irrational anger! Then take the advice the coven sees fit and follow it. If it doesn't work, leave the group.

Hexing generally is avoidable.

you attack the innocent, the ban returns tenfold. This is an old
witches take care to come up with imaginative solutions in case
you are sure the person with whom you are angry is really the culprit.
On the other hand, rapists are fair game to hex, witches have to practice
this somewhere.

When you are absolutely resolved to caste a hex, leave the name
out, saying, for example, "He who broke into my apartment," "He who
raped me," etc. The Goddess knows whom you are referring to, and
won't miss her mark, while you may.

When the hex goes out to general purposes, "Enemies of women,"
for example, the Goddess makes historical changes, which you may read
in the news. There is no retribution for standing up for your own, you
need not fear you hurt somebody unnecessarily. For example, Christians pray against Gays, yet more and more Gays come out of the closets.
Obviously, the Goddess has veto power.

    7. You are as secure as your own psyche allows.

If you imagine that some witch can really harm you, you gave a
lot of power to that person. But if you don't, you can just fly above it
all and let the vibes fall back where they came from. Men often tried to
make women "lose" their head, so they can "have" them. It may work
on a noninitiate, but once a woman is her own possession, she is secure
against self-serving kitchen witches and lust on their minds. Manipulating
women by male witches is not much different than society's patriarchal
pig messages, in which Women internalize and participate in their own
slavery. A witch bows to no man. A woman with Goddess consciousness is stronger than patriarchal messages and can change her life and
rid herself of unwanted demands.

    8. The High Priestess is representing the Life Force in the coven,
       and the High Priest her consort and lover.

The High Priestess is supreme, her consort is sacred to her but
never her Master or Lord or Guru.

    9. Many covens have couples in them, other singles.

If you have a consciousness where jealousy is not a threat, sex
within the coven and forming new sexual alliances is a blessed event. But
experience has it that when sexual relationships break up within the
coven, the members also break up with each other all worship as well.
That is not blessed and must be avoided by preplanning and agreements.
For Dianic groups, it's a must that there is a clear understanding of what
to expect. It is the strength of women to bond with each other (we are
so new at it) but worship should not suffer on account of sex. Worship
is a higher form of bonding, and should be respected more than just a
social get-together. The bonds already formed should be protected, not

threatened. Then the coven will stay together for years and form a powerful psychic circle that can take care of the needs of all who participate. (In patriarchal religions, the male celibacy is simply a denial of bonds with women. There is plenty of sex, both homosexual and heterosexual, among priests.)

"DANGERS" OF MAGIC

by Starhawk

There are real dangers to the practice of magic, most of them found within ourselves, particularly before we have a full and deep understanding of how magic works. I have listed here some of the major problems which trip us up, with some suggestions for protection. However, it is a necessary part of everyone's magical education to fall victim to one's own character traits occasionally. We all find ourselves ego-tripping, do-gooding, showing off, and all the rest from time to time, but how else could we learn compassion and tolerance for others who go off on the same tangents? Falling victim to one's own illusions eventually confers a sort of immunity, much like the result of a childhood disease, and with luck, recovery is rapid and complete. Here, then, are the "mumps" and "measles" of magic.

Omnipotence. This is quite common when first discovering that your Will can effect events. You may feel a tremendous rush of power and believe that you can do anything and everything. Experience will cure this fallacy quickly, however, but the condition of omnipotence can lead to . . .

Guilt. You may believe you can do everything, but sooner or later you will fail. Sometimes it is the people you care most about whom you are unable to help. Unless you realize that magic has its limitations and works within the framework of laws (just as standard medical science does), you run the risk of feeling responsible for everything that goes wrong in the universe. Relax. You are not that powerful, nor are you that important.

Paranoia. As your awareness grows and you become more conscious of negative energy and impulses in others, you may become oversensitive and begin jumping at shadows and protecting yourself against dangers that don't exist. There is also the dodge of ascribing every negative thing that happens to you to "psychic attack." A healthy streak of cynicism is a good defense against this one. Remember that magic that is "real," rarely con-

21

flicts with common sense. If you feel beset by evil forces, look within yourself to see what is drawing them.

Saintliness. It is hard to resist the temptation to be more-spiritual-than-thou, to offer unasked-for advice to your acquaintances, and to look down on others who have not "seen the Light," all the while trying to appear humble. With any luck at all, you will come back to earth before you lose all your friends.

Showing Off. This, like Saintliness, is hard to resist. When the fanatic Jehovah's Witness in your Chem class spouts off about religion, how can you NOT tell her you see a hypocritical green spot in her aura? With painful experience, however, you will discover that people will not hear or listen to your advice or commentary unless they have asked for it, and that magic only works when it's real, not show.

Going Half-Astral. When you get so caught up in magic and psychic work that you neglect the earthly plane and your physical body, you will become drained and weakened. In extreme cases, people who lose touch too completely with earth can have what amounts to a psychotic "break." This is easily avoided, however, by making certain you stay grounded and centered when you do any magical work or meditations. Also, it is vital to have a satisfying and rewarding earth-plane life, including a good sex-life and a love of good food.

The Craft should not cause any loss of pleasure or abilities to function in your daily life. On the contrary, pleasure and capabilities in ordinary things should only be heightened by your increasing awareness.

Your very best protection, against all of these ills and any others you may meet physically or psychically, is to maintain your sense of humor. As long as you can laugh at yourself, you cannot head too far down the wrong path, and you always have an immediate ticket back to truth. Whenever you find you are taking yourself too seriously, or whenever you meet someone or some thing who encourages you to do so, beware! Remember, laughter is the key to sanity.

DIANIC AFFIRMATIONS

New age life oriented philosophies often heavily rely on what in another time would be considered witchcraft. Mind control, meditations, thought consciousness are the cornerstones of magic. Imagination plus intensity equals reality, is practiced in spells.

Upon rising:
> I reconnect my soul with the Universal Intelligence, the Goddess Durga! Organizer of the Universe! Multi-armed, ever-ablaze with the fire of life. Let I be led by Durgas power. Blessed be!

When in Traffic:
> My Universe is a safe Universe! It is the Goddess Athena who protects my wheels, I am encircled by a blue light and then a white. I am divinely alert and hold the hands of the Mothers. I am safe. I am blessed. I am safe.

When cooking:
> It is not just dinner that I cook
> but I cook the universal cauldron of change
> I am part of all women who do this every day
> and I cook my own nurturance. I am nourished by my creations.
> I am Goddess of the cauldron. And I cook Health.

Upon signing official papers:
> I call on Themis to lead my pen. All will serve me in the end.

Upon entering your bath:
> It is not just cleanliness I seek, I reconnect myself with the life granting waters of life. I am renewed in body and soul!

When going to a party:
> Play is learning and learning is play. I laugh and dance and keep myself free.

Before singing:
> My voice shall rise to please the Muses!

When visiting friends:
> May friends and foes be gentle with my love.

When falling in love:

> Oh Aphrodite! I felt your sting and now you are on your way. I shall prepare my soul for you with flowers and lack of fear!

When writing:

> Come spirits of my spirit, speak your thoughts through me. I am open as a lotus, and willing as a pet, illumine my mind, imagination lead my path!

When looking for a new home:

> My home is getting near with every step I take searching for it. My home already knows me, and I know my home.

Create your own affirmations.

DIANIC TRADITION

In the True Beginning, before the Judeo-Christian Genesis, the Goddess was revealed to her people as the Soul of the Wild. She was called Holy Mother and known to be a Virgin who lived in wild places and acted through mysterious powers. Known also as Artemis, Her worship took place by moonlight, and young nymphs and maidens were called to serve in Her rituals. It was decreed that the sacred doe of Artemis was never to be shot down. The Holy Mother, Virgin, Artemis was also called by the name Dia Anna, "Nurturer Who Does Not Bear Young." In the hunting and gathering societies Her image was carefully and consistently engraved in stone. She was symbolized by both the Sun and the Moon in recognition of the fact that the torch of life was Hers as was the healing Moon. Images of the Mother were carved everywhere She was worshipped: in caves, in Yoni-shrines, in the woods, in trees. She was the Lady of Plenty, Teacher of Knowledge, Knower of Wisdoms, Sacred Dancer, Inventor of the Wheel, Holy Mother, Virgin, Artemis, Dianna.

In the Dianic Times there were colleges of women who lived according to the spiritual principles of Artemis serving in Her shrines and blessing the sick. Later, when knolwedge of growing foods and domesticating animals was learned, Artemis (Dianna) became connected to all the people through Her Sacred functions as Giver of Bread, Maker of the Loaf, Rainmaker, and Life-Giver.

The worship of Dianna comes to us from these earliest stoneage times. Her names appear on maps of areas throughout the world. The rivers Danube and Don were named after Her. The river Thames was named after Her Mother, Themis, Goddess of Social Instinct. Ancient names for Anatolia, as well as current names for mountains, rivers, and lakes worldwide, when translated, often reveal themselves as Moon Goddess names from antiquity. Mt. St. Helen means Moonmountain. The most astonishing temples ever built (Stonehenge is an example) were created for the Moon Goddess.

Although most of the world's religions originated from the worship of the Moon Goddess, or, "She Who Shines On All," it is a fact that Her worship and service was always carried out by women. In contrast, the Goddess as Giver of Life and Mother of the Sacred Child was worshipped and served by both sexes, but Dianna was not. Dianna was worshipped as Protector and Teacher of the Young, but never as a bearer of children — she did not consort with men. Her service was known as "Women's Mysteries," and ran parallel to worship of other Goddess aspects. Thus it was that many women consciously chose to worship the Goddess with their men, many chose to worship alone, and many others chose to worship with each other. From the dawn of humankind, woman-energy as nurturing energy, expressed through Goddess-worship, has been strengthened through this very holy bonding with each other.

CONCEPTS OF WOMEN'S MYSTERIES

In the Beginning were the women, mothers of the children, and the children belonged to All – to everyone. Mating customs of the women were observed within the sacred marriages and seasons of the religion. On a Midsummer Night women would mate with men, as representative of the male principle. Personalities and preferences were put aside in order to observe and celebrate the sameness of all humanity. Priest as well as priestess participated in the mating sacrament in honor of the the Life Force.

Because of this sacred mating ritual, it was virtually impossible, not to mention irrelevant, to attempt to pair off children with biological fathers. Only motherhood was an unquestionable reality, easily observable, fatherhood was wishful thinking or figment of imagination.

This was a culture in which the breeding of animals was consciously aided for the purpose of achieving stronger or more productive livestock, so the importance of sperm in the reproductive process did not go unnoticed. The women were aware of the female period of "heat" and the male response to it. There was no ignorance concerning the relation of sperm to reproduction, as common scholarly assertions would have us believe. Goddess-cultures acknowledged the "stimulating" effect of the male's contribution to the process, but they did not consider it significant enough to be deserving of worship, as was the Birthing Force, the Female Principle of the Universe.

The period from conception to birth was a lengthy one of intense fetal development. Mothers had to survive many dangers and surmount many obstacles to assure the birth of a healthy baby. Motherhood was recognized as a "warrior's" job. Further, the rearing of the young was not necessarily done by the biological mothers, but was the role of the community "nurturers," both male and female.

Women's Mysteries were concerned with the natural cycles of life, and rituals were designed for specific purposes: to insure good weather conditions for crops; to promote good health among the people; to guard against disease and pestilence; to maintain good fortune by conscious reinforcement of the practice of keeping women in contact with each other as manifestations of the Divine Female.

Traces of Dianic tradition may be found in many modern customs inherent in archery, sports games, weaving, and witchcraft. Examples of ancient tradition practiced today are such things as: prayers said out-of-doors; spells cast using natural forces; the recognition of the Soul of the Wild as friend rather than enemy, as internal deity as well as external manifestation.

Dianics often lived together in small tribes outside of the cities. Such tribes had sacred totem animals: the bear represented Artemis, the wolf, Hecate. Existing legends of children exposed on mountaintops and raised by she-bears or she-wolves are references to these ancient tribes and their practices.

The Dianics were either celibate or lesbian, but they did not consort with men. They made their living independently from men by educating children, hunting and food-gathering, and farming the "wild" for medicinal herbs. It was a common practice for women to leave their homes in the cities for months, or even years, to "join Diana—" that is, to join a Dianic tribe. There was no demand made that these members remain in the tribe forever. Women could leave at any time and return to the city, welcomed by friends and families.

The maximum number of women in a Dianic college at any one time was 50, the number of weeks in the Year of the Goddess.

Famous Dianic priestesses are virtually unknown to us today. The revised (and much-manipulated) story of Atalanta serves as an example of the lifestyle and ultimate fates of such Sisters. Atalanta was left exposed on a mountaintop by her patriarchal father, who wanted a male-child. A she-bear found and raised Atalanta (read: she was raised by the Order of Artemis) until she was old enough to return home, a young woman, and natural heiress to the throne.

In order to keep Atalanta from a power-position, her father decreed that she should marry (a common and very popular patriarchal way to "relieve" women of any power). As a true Dianic of Artemis, Atalanta refused to be wed. Her father threatened her until finally Atalanta set her own conditions: she would agree to mate with the man who could best her in competitive sport. This, too, was Dianic tradition, in that a Dianic's pride was matched only by her prowess in sports and crafts.

The story of Atalanta realistically goes on to relate how she was tricked into defeat in a footrace, thus losing the competition to a male. As agreed, Atalanta mated with the young man in the temple of Cybele, but the act so angered the Goddess that she turned both of them into lions, harnessed to pull the Chariot of the Goddess.

Cybele was not a Dianic Goddess, she was an Asian Goddess, Cybele/Athena did not exclude men from her rituals. As a matter of fact, males celebrated Her worship by castrating themselves during religious "ecstasy" in order to be more like Her. It is probable that Atalanta and her mate joined an Order of Cybele where they both could serve (as priestess and priest). Atalanta never did get her throne back. This record tells us much about the fates of women and life in general, during the "turning" of Goddess-cultures into patriarchy.

Today the Dianic traditions are being revived. Women are becoming more aware of how important it is to develop and share collective energies with each other, and to learn how to transcend personality differences by remembering our unity with the Soul of the Wild. In Dianic witchcraft, Diana and Her earth-daughter, Aradia, still reign supreme.

UNDERSTANDING THEMIS

Themis is recognized above and beyond all gods as the oldest of gods. The goddess as the Wisdom of the EARTH. She is the Oracular power of the Earth. She is Gaia's soul. Gaia the Earthmother.

Themis and Gaia are one in nature, many named. (Aeschylus) Themis is prophesy incarnate, in the old sense, prophesy means utterances, ordinaces, opening of the mouths, as well as oracular, which fortells the future. She is pictured sitting on a tripod in a temple to the Earth-mother, usually over a slope of mountain, over a cliff, or cave. Her shrines are associated with the "Tracker" the Furies when angered. She tracks things down, she cannot be evaded. In her hand she holds a spray of laurel. Laurel was chewed by priestesses to go into trance (I tried to do it here in California and all I got was a mouthful of aromatic dry leaves that didn't want to go down). Laurel was given to poets as well, as a prize for their further inspiration from the Goddess.

In her other hand is a phiale, a pretty shallow holder of liquids, water perhaps from the sacred well. In a deep trance the priestess would say her stream of consciousness and the person listening to it would apply it to herself. Interpretation of such utterances were done by others, not the ones who said them. It was considered proper to separate the source of information from the interpretation thereof.

In Homer's time, Themis holds fast in the new patriarchal pan-thenions. It is she who convenes an assembly and dissolves the assembly; she is still the head of the banquet tables, over which she presides. The entire idea of interacting people in an agreed fashion where there is agora (rules and regulations) social order is Her Domain.

In such troubled times as new fledged patriarchy among the Greek, the idea of the concept Themis still is placed above that of Zeus.

Themis is very deep, her name means Doom, which is a thing set, fixed, settled. "Doom begins in convention, the stress of public opinion, it ends in statuary judgment," said Jane Harrison. One's public opinion is one's doom. So is one's private opinion. Out of these components comes Law. Themis is then the goddess of the Law. Matriarchal law, where women's values are dominant.

Later even the very name becomes Themistes, what society compels what must be, and will be, the prophesies of what shall be in the future. These qualities are the domain today of men, kings, presidents, and dictators, but they spring from the sacred wells of Themis.

Themis is the force that binds nations together, the herd instinct, the collective consciousness is manifest in her image. She is not yet religion, but she is the stuff good religions are made of.

Religions are made out of three major parts according to Jane Harrison, social custom, collective consciousness, and the representation and emphasis of this same collective consciousness. These three factors are interdependent and make up one whole concept. Ritual, collective action, and myth and theology, which is but the representation of the of the collective consciousness, they are binding, incubent and interdependent on each other. There are sister concepts to this, representations of social consciousness in art and morality. Morality is different from religion because its rules apply only to conduct and leaves thoughts free. Art has no such imposing effect. There is no obligation on action or thought. Her goddess is Peitho not Themis, said Harrison. Prof. Durkheim advanced a theory about the religious animal; humanoids. What is religious, is binding. Human body is bound by natural law and the spirit is bound by social imperative. The moral constraints upon humans is of Themis not Physis, and because of this bond, humans are religious animals.

Religious faith and practice is extremely obligatory but it is also eagerly, vividly chosen, it is a great collective of hereness said Harrison.

"Religion sums up and embodies what we feel together, what we imagine together, and the price of that feeling together, imagining together and concessions, the mutual compromises, are at first gladly paid."

INTRODUCTION TO THE RITES OF LIFE

If you have not read Holy Book of Womans Mysteries Part One, our section on Dianic Rites of Life would look very incomplete. All the Major Sabbats, Esbats, and Women's Festivals have been discussed in detail in Part One. This section is to provide further stimulation towards communities (individuals, tribes) attending to their own ritual needs (priestesses themselves) by following the Rites of Life according to inclination and imagination.

We are trying to illustrate that many traditional Rites of Life have been politically suppressed and pushed into oblivion. Upon examination many seem to have been glorifying the female experience, female participation and female deities. So partake, remember and invent! Thou art Goddess!

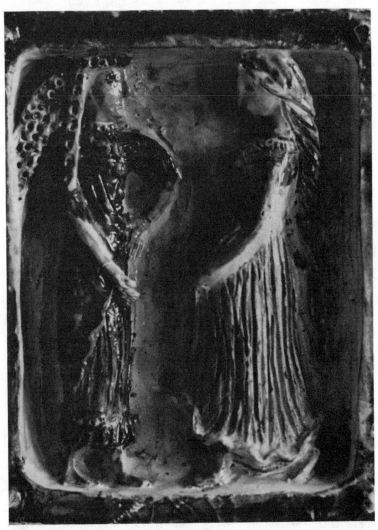

Persephone and Demeter by Masika

GROUP BLESSING

When in the company of your dearest and nearest friends and lovers, a family occasion or just feeling good, try this ritual in which all participate.

Gather into a circle holding each other by the small of the back with your hands and start humming. When you feel relaxed and steady with the sounds you make, take a step inside the circle one by one and lay in the middle. All the rest of the people stroke your aura, touching without touching. This feels very vulnerable but works so simply and naturally. I used this ritual in my Feminaries on the beach as a parting ritual.

There is a song that goes with it from the Indians (substitute your own names):

> Z will be well
> Z will be well
> All manner of things
> shall be well.

Now you wait until the next person has layed down in the middle of the circle and again all bless her the same way. If there is one person who is so moved to pronounce blessings over each person in words, just let them ride along with the music.

After all went through the process you can hug and be silent a little while and to suck in the energy you raised by making believe you suck through a straw. Somebody says: "It is done." All answer: "Blessed be"!

If lying down in the circle is impossible, let the woman stand with her eyes closed as the others lay hands on her. Yet another technique is the woman leans against the hands of the group, trusting herself to be supported by them, while chanting of her name continues.

A RITUAL OF SELF-REALIZATION

Self-Love is where liberation begins. A woman who loves herself makes good choices for herself; a woman who hates herself will make choices that are good for others only. In order to grow in this precious commodity, Self-Love, you yourself must cultivate your own company in this candlelight ritual.

Take a ritual bath or shower. Prepare on your dresser which has a mirror, an altar to yourself. Two white candles on the two sides of your mirror, a little incense (a favorite of yours) in your thurbile.

Now begin by making a list of all the qualities you love yourself for and another list with all the qualities you think are bad in you. Things you are not proud of (actually you should have this list before the bath or shower, so you can dwell on it more and correct it if you think of new things to add).

Then looking into your own eyes in your mirror, after lighting your candles (Blessed be thou creature of fire!), inhale the incense and start saying to yourself:

I. . . (name). . . have come to commune with my soul

Look into your own eyes and see when the soul changes the expression, you will know when, and say the first negative quality on your list. I use my example:

I love you, Z, because you can't balance your checkbook.

Watch for reactions, if any, then go on and say something you are proud of:

I love you, Z, because you are a great ritual Priestess.

Now keep saying the negative qualities until they sound more convincing and you start feeling that what you say is not only words but emotions as well. Integrating into one personality your "lights" and "shadows," you extend divine compassion to yourself. When you feel tears dwelling up in your eyes from love and tenderness towards yourself, the exercise is working well. If you feel that you are convincing yourself surely, if slowly, keep doing it until you feel the emotional breakthrough. Alternating the negative with positive qualities will also help you to see into your integrated being. When you have managed to unblock your own compassion from yourself, and direct it back into the parts of you that you originally despised, you have freed the entire stock of psychic energy that was all along yours but not available to you because of self-hatred.

When I did this exercise for the first time it took two hours, because I got so involved in having sobbing interruptions. After my crying ebbed, then my face started to change rapidly in the mirror taking up all kinds of other faces, all myself from other lifetimes.

It was rapid and with the feeling of zooming, falling into the image, almost television-quick, the faces changed ages, outfits, hairdos, wrinkles, etc. If this happens to you it too is a sign of breakthrough. The self is giving you a rare insight of all the people whose genes you carry within you. Don't panic or be afraid. Just keep steady and say "My spirit is a free and safe spirit" (to keep your cool).

Perform the self-love exercise every Friday (Venus' day), until you have a sense that you indeed Love yourself more than ever before!

This is not a "Me Generation" game, this is an ancient Witchcraft exercise to increase psychic power, which happens to depend on your own self-approval. If anybody tries to discourage you from loving yourself, tell them to stuff it. In the so-called "me generation" somehow the ME that got explored and glorified was mostly male. Women yet have to have their own decade of self-love. And may it come soon! So be it. It is done.

A BIRTHDAY RITUAL

"Happy Birthday!" This expression triggers many smiles, as all of us young and old get to review our lives on our birthdays. Patriarchy has not failed to "borrow" pagan elements for this event. The white candles on the cake are all that's left from the witchy approach. Let's see if we can make more memorable birthdays for ourselves knowing what the Wise Ones did.

On your birthday, as part of your own ritual, write a card for your mother, thanking her for having done such a great labor of bringing you over to the side of the living. This makes you feel your own life's continuity. You have not come from nowhere. Your mother created you. If she is nearby, certainly invite her to your party. Publicly acknowledge her part of your creation. Mothers rarely get honored by younger people. Mother's day does not count, as it is a band-aid on the injustice perpetrated against women. Give us ERA, and then we know you love us! If you are close to your father, invite him too.

Gather your friends together at sundown, after having spent the day meditating on your life. When the sun has set, light your incense, rebirth incense is the most appropriate, but of course, you can never go wrong with frankincense and myrrh. Avoid the usual guru smells, like banana, or blackberry. Those have no occult properties.

In your home, set up a white candle to represent every year you have lived. Put them everywhere, and light them one by one, meditating on the years they represent. If you had something special happen on a certain year, you can use a different color candle for it. If you fell in love, use a pink or red one. If you lost your parents, use black. If you formed a friendship, use blue. If you were sick, use orange to build up your health. And use yellow if you are full of dreams, purple if you have achieved a high goal, green if you made money, brown if you bought property. But all this is optional.

Form a circle with your friends and step in the middle of it. Your best friend should take a leading part here.

The best friend says: "Who do we honor today?"

The rest answer: "A friend who journeyed from birth to here."

The best friend says: "What do we do to a friend we love?"

They answer: "We bless her/him for the seasons to come!

Now all take the candles that represent all the years, and holding them aloft, they shout: "Long life to you . . . (name)"

You answer: "Long life is sent to me by you."

All: "Long life with love and health!"

You: "Love and health is to me from you."

All: "Long life and golden luck!"

You: "Long life is mine, and golden luck!"

Now the candles can be placed back where they were. The cake can be brought out with or without candles. You can now proceed according to regular birthday customs as you like.

If you are isolated, or have no time to organize a whole party for your birthday, you should ask at least one person to perform this blessing for you. Don't skip on your birthday. It is important to re-affirm your origin, your process, and your future. People who hate birthdays, still remember that it is a holy day for you and your mother. The gift of life is worthy to recall and celebrate. So honor yourself with a candlelight ceremony, a treat with friends.

Happy Birthday!

DIANIC NEW MOON RITUAL

Time: In the first quarter of the moon, just when a clear sliver crescent
is shown in the afternoon sky.

Gather together, singing and chanting:
> We all come from the Goddess,
> And to her we shall return,
> Like a drop of rain,
> Flowing to the ocean.

While you gather, pick some green stalks and flowers, if there are any
at hand. Then sit around and make yourselves wreaths for crowns. When
you have finished, admire each other's creations, and feeling thusly adored,
you begin.

Three women take responsibility here. One for the Maiden, one for
the Nymph and one for the Crone. Position yourselves in the circle, with
the Nymph to the East, the Maiden to the West, and the Crone to the North.
Have each of them holding sticks of incense as wands. Frankincense and
Myrrh are a good choice, but regular temple incense will do.

The women of the circle begin to hum low, without strain on the
vocal chords, until the tops of your heads begin to vibrate. The moon should
be in sight above the women, as you gaze upon her crescent shape. When
the hum has unified and you are making one chord, start making it varied
and different, like a tapestry of sounds. Give it texture, harmonize and allow
the divine to flow through you while you listen to the others, and sing yourselves at the same time.

When the time is right, the three priestesses drop a name into the pool
of sound. "Maat" (truth), "Diana" (Holy Mother), "Hecate" (threefold).
The group chants these names, not necessarily in order, but as it flows
through.

Then the Nymph steps out and encircles the circle with her incense
wand, starting from the East, then to the South, then to the West.

> I am the beauty of the Green Earth
> and the White Moon amongst the stars.
> Come into this circle spirits of the east!
> Come into this circle, spirits of the South!
> Hear us, see us, protect us Mother Maat.

She reaches to the West, and hands her incense stick over to the Maiden.

> I am the mystery of the Waters,
> and the desire of human hearts.
> Come join us Love, come join us from the West.
> End all sorrow, and come and protect.

She takes her stick, and the Nymph's stick to the Crone. The Crone takes all three incense sticks and walks around the entire circle only once, landing in her place saying:

> Come call to your soul.
> Arise and come unto me.
> For I am she who gives life to the Universe.
> From me all things proceed, and to me all things shall return.

Then she announces the closing of the circle, saying:

> The Goddess blesses her children.

Now begins the heightened power-raising hum, picking up where it was at the beginning of the gathering.

While this is happening, three white eggs (preferably fresh) are brought out in a basket and placed in the middle of the circle. These eggs will represent the month ahead. New moon to new moon is the time space where you project yourselves.

In a chalice, pure water is placed, along with a small container of salt, in the middle of the circle. Extend your hands over the chalice, eggs, and salt saying:

> Mother darksome and divine, bless our tools, and bless our lives.

The Nymph picks up the eggs and takes them, one by one, in her hand, and projects into it her wishes for the future:

> I name you luck! I name you love! I name you money!

She puts the eggs back into the basket, and hands them over to the next woman on the East side of her. She also takes the eggs, and names them as her life requires, always passing towards the South, West, and North.

The Crone keeps the eggs at her side. The chalice is picked up by the Maiden, and she gazes into it, saying:

> This is health. As I drink this pure water, I will be healed, purified, and nurtured. This is the Goddess gift.

Before she drinks, she holds the chalice up to the moon so that she appears right above the rim of the chalice, catching the moon's reflection in the water.

The chalice is passed around, and the women drink to her health.

The Crone picks up the salt and goes to each woman and sprinkles it on their heads saying:

> This is wisdom which I shower upon you. May you be smart, wise, enduring, and successful. So be it.

Each woman receives it and says: "Blessed be." When all this is finished, a moment of silence is observed to hear omens. The Crone digs a hole in the ground with the Nymph and Maiden's help, and buries the eggs, saying:

> Mother Moon, and Sister Earth, I return these eggs to you for safe-keeping. It is forever, and for our good luck, wealth, and health. As you enclose these eggs, so will your grace enclose our lives. As you hold these eggs so close to you, so shall you hold us all in your heart.

The eggs are covered by earth. "Blessed be " say all. The left-over water is sprinkled over the eggs, along with the left over salt. It is done.

Afterwards, you may sit down and eat the food you have brought. Enjoy free-flowing company, and mingle with each other while playing instruments and dancing. When you are ready to go home, the three priestesses open the circle counter-clockwise, and thank the spirits for coming into the circle (from the East, North, West, and South).

"Merry-meet, and merry-part."

RITUALS FOR DAILY LIFE

by Carol Christ

As I begin to celebrate the presence of the Goddess in my life, I find it important to create rituals which will become part of my ordinary daily life, rituals which will give me strength when I feel weak and which will strengthen the powers I have when I feel strong.

My favorite spell is a very simple one. After cleaning up my house I go around from room to room and purify the space. Sometimes I open a window and direct the bad vibes out with hand motions, while encouraging the good ones to come in. Then I take my chalice (a longstemmed wine glass) from my altar, fill it with fresh water, add salt, and face the east wall of my room. I dip my fingers into the water, raise my hands and say:

Powers of the East
Powers of the daystar rising
And all fresh beginnings
I purify you with salt and with water
For good vibrations of friendship, warmth, and love.

I sprinkle some extra water in the east for good measure and proceed to the south where I say:

Powers of the South
Powers of the summer sun
Which warms our bodies and our minds
I purify you with salt and with water
For good vibrations of friendship, warmth, and love.

I repeat in the west:

Powers of the West
Powers of the purifying and cleansing waters
From which all life comes
I purify you with salt and with water
For good vibrations of friendship, warmth, and love.

and in the north:

Powers of the North
Powers of the earth, the ground
On which we stand
I purify you with salt and with water
For good vibrations of friendship, warmth, and love.

I then proceed around the room sprinkling water over all the thresholds, windows, and doorways and in all corners, while visualizing the things I would like to have happen in the room — love, passion, or good dreams over the bed; creative working space vibes around my desk; friendship and good conversation in the living room, etc. I sometimes repeat the ritual with incense in each direction, threshold and corner when I feel the need for an extra strong spell.

I keep a vial of rose oil on my altar for use in rituals. On days when I wake up and feel I just can't face the world, I light orange or yellow candles on my altar for energy and draw a flower or pentacle on my forehead with rose oil on my fingertip, saying to myself:

This invisible sign is the seal of your
Protection by the Goddess
As you smell Her sweet scent you will remember
Her presence within you.

The idea that the sign of the spell is invisible to everyone but me seems to add to the power of the spell.

I do a lot of candle spells, choosing colors to symbolize the energy I need or want to increase. After lighting my candles I move my hands in circles, directing the energy from the flame toward me while visualizing the qualities I associate with each candle color. Then I stretch my arms and lift my head upwards and say, "Oh Lady Goddess, all power is yours." Then I repeat the circling motions with my hands and place my hands on myself saying, "All power is in me." I find this spell beautiful because it stresses the "life-flows-on-within-you-and-without-you" quality of Goddess religion.

SUMMER SOLSTICE FESTIVAL FOR CHILDREN

By N. Brennan

This can be performed in the afternoon, evening, or night, depending upon how old the children are. It can be performed with anywhere from one to many children. The only tools necessary are flowers, fire, and party food. The food should be baked goods, things that had to be finished by fire (cakes, cupcakes, etc.). If performed outside you can build a small fire, with the children gathering sticks for it, or you can use candles. Candles are also good if you must celebrate indoors.

Bring the children together in a group. An adult leader says:

We are all friends here.
There are no fights now,
And no one is afraid.
We trust each other here
In the presence of the Goddess.

Join hands. If there is more than one child, make a circle, as large as possible. The leader says:

> We are here in the circle of your creation, Lady,
> The circle of your universe.
> It is around us and we are part of it,
> Never separate.
> The protection of the Mother
> Folds around us
> Like magic and wind.
> Celebrate with us, Lady of Summer!

Now the children may drop hands. The leader says:

> The Lady returns in fire,
> Wrapped in flames and fragrance,
> Hearthstone of the universe,
> The nurturing warmth,
> The passion of life and singing summer,
> High Queen of the seasons,
> Turning the slow and starry wheel.

The children may sit down while the leader describes the symbolism of the wheel, the turning and returning of all things, the snake with its tail in its mouth, the cycles of the Goddess — birth, death, rebirth — and also, simply, the turning of the seasons. The children can talk about cyclical things with which they are familiar. Make a wheel out of the flowers you have brought. The children may decorate themselves and each other with flowers. Then ask for silence again. Leader says:

> Fires from the heart of the earth
> Leap forth,
> Reflecting in the sun,
> Rekindling.
> Deep-banked fires
> Flaming in buds,
> Flaming in blossoms,
> Primeval nurturance,
> Copper blood of life,
> Ancient and subtle,
> Returning and present,
> Here now, within us.

Now light the fire or the candles. The leader should do this, not the children, unless there are older, more responsible children who can. Contemplate the fire and discuss its symbolism. Tell about the bonfires that were built for the Goddess in the past, and about the celebrations that went with them. Let the children ask questions if they want, and have them look for pictures in the flames. Then ask for silence again. Tell the children to lie down on their backs and close their eyes. If you are outside, fine, if not, tell them to imagine being in a summer field, in the long, sweet-smelling grass, hearing the crickets and feeling drowsy. Tell them to relax. When they are quiet, the leader says:

Mid-season fires reach high,
The fruitful earth blossoms
Like flames;
Warm summer,
Height of the season,
The dreamy stand-still
Of the year.
Insects drone their song of life
Among the heavy scents,
Winds are laden
With bird-songs,
Woven like tapestries
In leafy branches.
Across the pale sky
The faint moon drifts,
Sudden and pure,
A whisper and a mystery.

The children lie still for a while. Before they begin to get restless, the leader says:

Lady of flowers,
Mother of life,
Bless this food
And bless us, your children,
That we may be strong
And live fairly with one another.

Now the children sit up. Food is passed around. They can eat, and afterwards play games, if time allows. Before they leave, have them thank the Goddess in words of their own. Happy Solstice! Blessed be!

SPELL FOR CONTINUANCE OF A SPECIAL REQUEST

By N. Brennan

Place a white candle on either side of your Goddess representation. You will also need a candle in your own astral color, a brown candle, a blue candle, and a green candle. Anoint the candles with Rose oil. Patchouli and Rose incense are nice.

Invoke the Goddess and seal the circle with your wand, calling on the essence of the Goddess in the four directions. Light the white candles with the following:

> Lady of fire,
> Of sunlight and moon,
> Of stars
> And all light,
> Bright Lady of flame,
> Be with us.

Light the incense and perform a self-blessing. Light the astral candle and say:

> This is my candle. It represents me, . . . (name),
> Child of the Great Mother,
> Daughter of Life.
> I call on you, Lady,
> By your many names.

Next, light the brown candle. Say:

> For the spell successfully begun,
> for the power growing,
> I thank the Mistress of Life.
> The spell will continue,
> Its power grow stronger, stronger,
> Irresistible,
> By the power of the Triple Goddess,
> Maiden and Mother and Crone.

Light the green candle and say:

> With this candle I draw to me
> All I need,
> Resources to accomplish my will.

Light the blue candle and say:

> Peace and prosperity
> With desire fulfilled,
> Attend me now
> With the blessing of the Lady.

Meditate a while. You can write your desire on paper and burn it to ashes in the candle flames if you want, thinking of the success of the spell. When you are done say:

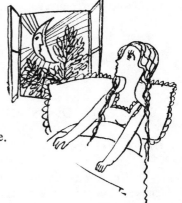

> When the candles are out
> The spell will continue,
> Waxing greater, greater, greater
> Until my purpose is accomplished,
> My purpose is complete.
> It will be so.
> Blessed be.

Thank the Goddess and dissolve the circle.

RECIPE FOR REMOVAL OF WARTS

By N. Brennan

I have used this successfully. Use a base of rose water (make your own, or buy it already prepared). Add a little fresh milkweed sap, crushed from the stems of the plant, some dry crumbled mint leaves, sage, and sassafras leaves. Warm gently over a low flame. DO NOT BURN. Write on a piece of paper, and read aloud:

> Mother of seasons
> And the changing moon,
> Lady of light
> And giver of Spring-time,
> Give health to . . . (name) . . ., our friend,

And in the secret places of the night
Make her/his warts dissolve,
Not to return.
Be with her/him
And with us,
Mother of the universe.

Burn the paper to ashes and add it to the mixture. When the mixture is warm and fragrant, BUT NOT HOT, put it in a small jar to cool. The patient should apply some at night before retiring, and let it dry. Leave it on all night and wash it off in the morning. Use faithfully each night until warts are completely dissolved.

SPELL TO STOP ENEMIES

By N. Brennan

Time: waning moon or dark of the moon. Use a dark altar, or an image of Hecate, Avenging Goddess, on your altar. Place the two usual candles on either side of the image. You will need a black candle, juice from the diffenbachia plant (which numbs and paralyzes the tongue if you get it in your mouth, so don't; you won't need much of it), and spiderwebs. Inscribe the black candle with your enemy's name. Make your circle. Say the following invocation:

Lady of Darkness,
Dark Isis of spells,
Hecate, avenging Mother,
Hear us and help us.

Roll the black candle in the juice of the diffenbachia to stop the enemy from speaking evil about you or your loved ones. Say:

Let the tongue of . . . (name) . . be numb
And powerless to speak the evil,
To speak the untrue.
Let his/her voice fail and throat close
On the harmful words,
By the power of the Dark Lady.

Then roll the candle in spiderwebs. Say:

> May . . . (name) . . . be caught
> And bound by the webs of his/her own deceit.

Then write the person's name on a piece of paper. Light the black candle and say:

> Here is . . . (name) . . ., alone and helpless.
> (Name), you are friendless.
> Emptiness and failure close around you.
> Your plans are as nothing;
> Frustration is yours.
> Trouble, doubt, and fear are at your side.
> Soon you will cease tormenting (me, Name, etc.).

Burn the paper in the flame of the black candle. Take it and the remnants of the candle after dark and sprinkle it before the residence of your enemy, or where the enemy is certain to walk. Light a blue candle (or white) and burn calming or purifying incense for peace.

SPELL FOR PROTECTION AND PEACE

By N. Brennan

Use blue and brown candles rolled in herbs or anointed with appropriate oils. Invoke the Goddess and seal the circle when the participants are inside. Light white altar candles on either side of the Goddess representation. Light incense. (Frankincense and Rose) Invoke the Lady of Flame. Perform self-blessing of participants. Light brown candle and say:

> Mother of all,
> Protecting Lady,
> Goddess of all things,
> Of grey waters
> And bright stars
> And the brown fruitful earth,
> Here is your favor
> And the protection you give.

Then light the blue candle. Say:

> Lady of blue skies and waters
> And soft rain in the forests,
> Comforting Mother,
> Enter us and be with us
> So that we may be strong
> So that we may be sure.
> Let no harm come to us,
> Within or without,
> Anywhere, anytime.
> In all places
> All times
> Surround us with your protection
> Your comfort
> Your strength;
> Let evil be far from us,
> Your good always near.
> Blessed be!

If you are doing this spell for someone, touch her lightly on the head at this point. Meditate a while on the peace and protection surrounding you. Dissolve the circle.

A RITUAL ENCOUNTER WITH SELFHOOD

by Lhyv Oakwomon

When a woman can unburden herself of crippling guilt, of the morbid fears and restrictive feelings of shame inherent in the Judeo-Christian and related dictums of a patrifocal tradition, it then becomes a matter of consciousness to embrace the Feminist Pagan Way. It is a matter of one's own awareness and insight into the basis in Nature of all religious thought and celebration. No one can give or teach you this. It is literally and genuinely between you and your Goddess.

It is in the overwhelming desire for freedom that the Goddess addresses Herself directly to our womansouls — directly, without mediator or intercessor. When we one day experience the profound knowledge that we are, in fact, our own saviors, is the day we begin to priestess our own souls. An empathetic awareness of the miracle of

Nature is achieved through experiences such as: the knowledge that we each possess an individual personal power; the working of our first successful spell; the first time we psychically heal a sister or hex an enemy; our first accurate vision of the future; the first time we sense the truth of the past. These and more are given as signs we are travelling the true Path.

This ritual is a deeply dramatic one, reminiscent of the initiatory rites of traditional pagan cultures, and is played out or performed by women who particularly desire to ritualize their spiritual "coming out." It is an initiation of the 2nd-degree. An ideal time to perform it would be during the Grand Sabbath of Candlemas, for women who know that their destiny is priestesshood.

Experienced priestesses form the circle, etc. and play the drums. The woman about to perform the initiatory ritual, places her body in the yogic "rest" position. She has blindfolded herself to symbolize her state of unawareness before her birth of spiritual consciousness. She may also wish to symbolize other ways in which she has felt unaware. For example, if she felt deaf to spiritual teachings, she could insert earplugs, or if she felt bound and restricted she could bind her wrists (not painfully). If she felt particularly unaware in many areas, or generally, she might choose to symbolize this state by covering herself up completely.

When the music from the drums moves the initiate, she begins to rise. Slowly as she rises, she begins to struggle against her condition, signifying her internal struggles. While she dances she verbalizes her actions. She may wander around drunkenly, stomp her feet or shake her body vigorously. When the energy is high, priestesses from the circle who are not playing drums, stand one at a time and call the name of the initiate. Each one calls in such a way as to make the initiate heed the sound of her voice, then when she approaches, stands silent while another sister in the circle calls out to the initiate. When the sisters feel the time is right, five priestesses step into the circle and stand at the five points of a pentagram, that is, as if their bodies were the five points.

At the first point of the pentagram is the priestess representing Survival. She chants:

Heed my voice! Heed my voice!
How will you survive?
Listen to the sound of base desire.
I am Hunger and Thirst; Nakedness when it is cold.
How will you survive?
I am homelessness, I am joblessness.
How will you survive?

47

The initiate has found her way to the first priestess. They struggle ritualistically until their movements blend in a dance. Now the initiate answers the first challenge:

> I hear my body's need.
> I hear you and answer your challenge!
> I have come out of Tiamat,
> She who is Chaos, the Unformed.
> I have wandered with Ixchel and found
> She who is the Source.
> I am creative, innovative, imaginative and skilled.
> Therefore, I will accomplish!

The priestess standing at the point of Wisdom now calls out in a loud, shrill voice:

> Aaaiiiiiii! Can you hear me?
> I call to you, I call to you.
> Come, for I am lonely. Heed my voice!
> (seductively) I am so lonely, I have no lover.
> I can be bought with gold and silver
> But never sold.
> If we are to be lovers, what is my name?
> Who am I?

Again the initiate makes her way to the sound of the voice, and the priestess and initiate struggle briefly, following it with a seductive dance. The initiate says:

> You are Sophia, Goddess of Wisdom
> And you I woo.
> You are the lover of my youth
> And my womanhood,
> My lover in old age of old.
> You are Memory, the Mother of Wisdom,
> Great Mother of History.
> In the Land of Ragno I was saved from ineptness
> By learning
> And all my learning has led me to Wisdom.
> I am the daughter you lead to Power.

The priestess at the Power point of the pentagram now hails the initiate:

How will you take me, for I am the Mighty Thigh.
Do you dare challenge me?
I am the third obstacle.
Heed my voice.
I give you nothing.
Take me on!

The Power priestess gently, but at medium speed, throws punches at the initiate, who must attempt to block them. When she is blocking them pretty well, the initiate steps up to the priestess and asserts:

I build my cone of Power,
I stand in Beauty.
My first point is knowledge great and small,
Second is my daring
For fear has not defeated me.
Third is my will
Sharpened by my need-fire,
Honed through great struggle,
Fourth is my silence.
My spell rests in the quiet of my womb
That my medicine may have great power.

The priestess at the point of Sex is breathing the Breath of Fire. When she is ready, she challenges by saying:

From what source come these fine words?
Who am I? And Where?
What I have is mine to share or naught.
How will you evoke me?
I am the best-known Secret,
Find me if you can.
I hide. I hide in the clear place.
Who am I?

Here the initiate plays out the act of searching, as if for some lost object. She ends this play by touching her body lovingly.

Ah! I know you!
You are hidden in my hood
And guarded by my bones.
You are the knowing woman's soul, my sex.
You are the numbered unit:

Seven you are at rest, uncalled
Six you are blended, in opposition
Five you are awake, yet alone
Ten you are merged with she who binds Hearts together.
Now this riddle I speak is mine to keep!

The priestess on the point of Passion speaks now:

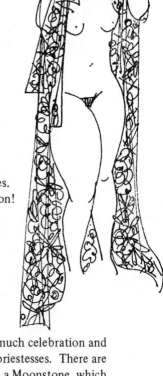

Awaken, awaken! Unstop your ear!
Cast off those bonds! Quickly!
Come you hence, I challenge too!
Who is it, who calls you?

The initiate answers by saying:

Oh! My burning heart
How can I contain you?
Out from me, I say!
You are all that drives me to my goal.
You are the point where my anger shows,
You are the Source from which action comes.
You are the soul of the Goddess of Liberation!
You are Themis, for whom I leap!
You are joy and ecstasy!
No longer am I blind, for I do see,
Nor deaf (my ear is tender)
My hands are free to do their work,
I stand free of the shroud of deceit,
I am whole and ready to meet my fate.

The ritual ends with a womb-hug by all. There is much celebration and feasting, and gifts are given to the initiate by the priestesses. There are three gifts to be given to the woman in this ritual: a Moonstone, which the newly initiated places over her Third Eye with a piece of double-stick tape (this is her meditation stone); a piece of gold cloth in which to keep her new Moonstone; a carved box. The ritual is ended by calling down the Moon.

CONCEPTION RITUAL

Time: When the woman's menstrual cycle is in the most fertile time (check astrological birth control).

Place: Outdoors preferably, but indoors is okay.

To conceive was always one of the major endeavors of women. As creators of the human race, producers of people, women everywhere created many different ways to invoke the goddess of fertility.

The most universal images for conception are the toad and the snake. On one of the Goddess' shrines in Northern India the Goddess is shown in a conception position, which resembles a whole lot of the frogs spread legs. Why the frog, the toad or the snake? These amphibians or reptiles are earlier forms of life, and in fact those stages are repeated in each and every cycle of human gestation, to invoke them is to "start" over again, in other words to conceive. The embryo must swim like an amphibian before it is born, must change and renew like the snake.

Draw on a pink piece of paper your version of this symbol. If you need to, look one up in a book. Draw it in red ink, red for action and the color of blood. Write in the middle of it, "my own child". Then make a doll representing yourself out of some red flannel material, give yourself features, hair, eyes and indicate the nose. Before you sew up the body, sew into it your drawing of the fertility charm, neatly folded into four parts, each time folding it towards yourself, saying:

> Mine is the power of the Goddess
> Mine is the blood that grants life
> I am calling on the new soul to enter
> I am giving the new soul life divine

Repeat this four times each time you fold. Then finish your doll. Now go outside when the Moon is new, after carefully checking the phases of your own birth cycle to determine the sex of your child (see astrology chapter in part one). Take your partner with you with whom you would like to have a child, and make love outside on a blanket in the rays of the moon.

If your choice is artificial insemination, then take your woman friends with you and try to go for an evening swim in the ocean. Ancient women called down parthenogenesis when they honored Dianna the Virgin mother by wildly thrashing around in salt water, during religious ecstasy. If that too is impractical stay at home in your comfortable place and have the insemination happen there, with red candles burning on your altar to call down the goddess action.

Hungarian Madonna with Child by Masika Szilagyi

I talked to women who had this done, and the word is the conception happens in the mind, the mind triggers (or rather the third eye, otherwise known as the pituitary gland) conception. The key is to create an atmosphere when the mind released this energy to the womb.

Yet another version — this I have done to a woman who tried to conceive for two years in vain. I selected a white egg shaped candle in a small shop in the Village for her. We went home and I anointed the egg with my favorite oil, Rosa Lama. Then held it in my hand so to hold it with my thumbs, blessing it over her open hands below mine.

In the name of Isis of a thousand breasts
May your conception be blessed
In the name of the Isis of the thousand breasts
May your pregnancy be blessed
In the name of the Isis of the ten thousand breasts
May the birth be easy and the life you bring forth blessed.

At this point I dropped from my hands into hers the egg that she caught in her own palms. Then I closed her hands over it tightly and said

It is done.

She went home and lit the candle, performed the insemination and conceived of a healthy baby girl.

MENSTRUATION RITUAL

Time: When menses set in.
Place: Home of the woman or friends house.

Gather together the friends of the young woman who already menstruate, and those who don't. Create a party with plenty of food and drinks around; also serve teas that ease the cramping, like Cammomille pennyroyal, comfrey tea. Before your feast begins, form a circle of the women who do not yet menstruate, and have the young maiden stand in the middle of it naked. Take a small dish of earth and water, make it into a paste, and have the young women smear some of this mud on the body of the young maiden saying "Farewell sister of my childhood! I love you as I love the Earth!"

The young woman answers:

> Farewell my childhood! Farewell the nymph I am no more!

When the young maiden is emerged all muddy and dirty looking, she stands between the two worlds, between her childhood friends and between her youthful friends, the other maidens. The Earth is a symbol of maturity.

Then form another circle of young women and older women who do menstruate. The young woman goes with them into a bathroom or bathing place, where they wash away the earth from her body and rubbing her body with scented herbs. They say as they touch her "Welcome, welcome friend of my youth!"

She answers:

> The nymph is gone, but oh, the Maiden is just born! Welcome oh friends of my youth!

The maiden is washed clean and dressed in a gown of her choice, bedecked with flowers that her friends brought. She is led out to face her mother who has a special gift for her, a red stoned ring. This stone can be a garnet, a ruby, red glass, anything that she can afford and convey the message of acceptance to the young one.

Mother to daughter:

> You traveled the road from my breast as a babe to maturity as a young woman. I bless you for the seasons to come! Accept this ring, as a momento for the passage well done!

Mother and daughter kiss each other, Maiden wears her ring. Partying can resume, dancing and sharing of experiences of how other women came to have their first menses, and how different this is from the guilt and shame young women were subjected to before the awakening of the Goddess Consciousness. Sing songs, party until dawn.

CELEBRATION OF THE END OF MENSTRUATION

When a woman knows she will no longer bleed each month it's a time to call your friends together and give a joyous End of Menstruation.

The end of the bleeding means the woman enters the last stage of her Queenhood (individualized independent strong woman) of her life. Her energies are directed towards more spiritual goals, her energies are saved for more achievement. Each time you have a change in your hormonal chemistry, the ancients used to drink Holy Thistle tea, an herb easily available through health food stores. It helps balance out the body and saves you from hot flashes as well.

Form a circle and create an altar in the middle with four red candles and four yellow candles. Prepare it with red roses if you can and white or yellow flowers. Use a Maiden Goddess for your center piece, Athena image, or Dianna , Artemis.

Raise energy through a song or humming. When the energy is raised (you will know when), let one of the friends act as priestess:

> We gather together to commemorate the withdrawal of the flowing bloods from our friend. We ask the Great Mother to bless our sister with good health, vitality and gladness. Let the flow act through the younger women now, let this woman rest, she has finished her part as the Goddess of the Bloods. She is now the Goddess of the Great Achievements.

Celebrant now lights her four red candles.

> I light this first candle for the bloods that are gone. And the second one for the children and health the flow brought me. (omit if not applicable). The third red candle for the flowerings of my womanhood, and fourth for the labors ended in glory.

Priestess:

> I release you, said the Goddess of the Red. I accept you, said the Goddess of the Yellow Ray. I call you into my wisdom to grow in, I call you like a new Maiden, into my sciences, into my knowledge, into dreams to be manifest!

Celebrant lights her four yellow candles now.

> I light this first yellow candle for the release from the Reds. This second one for the flowering of my skills. This third one for friends and support, and this fourth one for the blessings from above!

Now the circle can sing songs, entertain each other, share food and drink, exchange gifts with the celebrant. When the candles reach their natural end, cast them into a living body of water, don't look back.

Blessed Be! It is done!

WELCOMING A NEW MOTHER INTO THE CIRCLE OF MOTHERS

We have baby showers for expectant mothers, bridal showers for young brides, but once you become a mother, nobody cares a hoot. This must change. You, as a mother, now need attention and affection more that ever. You also need new clothes, new ideas, and new friends.

To give birth is as important as the greatest military victory, even more. To take life is easy. The American Indians believed that to go through labor, birthing, is to go down to hell to fetch a new spirit into the light. Society has decided to focus on your new baby more than you. You can change that by starting this new celebration of yourself.

The Ceremony

Time: After the woman has given birth and feels strong enough to do it. This should be the first thing the woman is participating in.

Invite: Women who have had babies, if you can. If not, invite all the women whom you like and cherish the company of.

This event should be planned by your friends. They should present you with three gifts of importance: 1) A new gown, or material for it. This can be any color, but green is preferred. A green-robed lady is the Goddess who gives birth, and then renews herself, becoming a virgin. 2) An herbal tea which is good for the womb, like raspberry. 3) Tickets to a cultural event that you have to go out for. It should be a treat with color and content.

The women establish a time when the new mother is to be in bed with her baby, resting. As a surprise, they enter her room. Three women representing the Fates, a Nymph, a Maiden, and a Crone, come bearing gifts. The women have branches of trees. Use whatever you can provide, but evergreen branches are best, as they are the symbols of rebirth. Do not use ivy, as it is sacred to death, along with being poisonous. Bring flowers too, whatever is in season, and some incense sticks. Sandalwood is best.

56

The first mother greet the new mother, saying: "Blessed be thou . . . (insert name of new mother). We heard in the air that you have returned to the world of mothers. Welcome to the company of creators of humanity!"

The second mother says: "Blessed be thou . . . (the new mother). We have brought you gifts that make you whole. The new gown was sent to thee to clothe you with the beauty of your new life. Blessed be your body, that you will grow strong, to return you to your own after you were gone. Your body and soul fetched a new soul from the unborn." They kiss and exchange the gift informally.

The third mother says: "Blessed be thou . . . (the new mother). I give you an herb that is sweet to your womb. Drink it, and bless it. Be whole. Here are some theater tickets, (invitation to a grand ball, a picnic, a hiking tirp, tennis, a swimming party), to kindle your spirits. You worked hard, and your spirit is tired. Come to this party, and we will all laugh and praise the Goddess!" They exchange the gift informally.

Then the new mother speaks to the three: "I am blessed today as a new mother, and welcomed into the circle of mothers."

The other three say: "We love you. It is done."

Then informal visiting takes place with whatever means you have to pursue it.

NAMING FESTIVAL — Dedication of a New Born Child

Should take place on the first day of a Full Moon, and includes a dedication circle composed of women in the mother's bloodline and extended family. After a purification bath, the mother dresses in white or saffron. The baby should also be dressed in white. Select a tree to represent the Tree of Life: Oak, poplar, willow, alder, or elm is traditional, but any tree available will be fine. The women form a circle around the tree, singing and joyous.

The baby is placed at the foot of the tree with a bowl of corn or barley, a bowl of water, a bowl of salt, and a white garlic bulb. The mother will have chosen the child's Guardian Mother (NOT godmother).

The ritual begins with the Guardian Mother, acting as Maiden, giving the Great Charge:

Aphrodite, Arionhod,
Lover of the Horned God,
Mighty Queen of Witchery and Night;
Morgan, Etoine, Nisene,
Diana, Brigit, Melusine,
Am I named of Old by men;
Artemis and Cerridwen,
Hell's Dark Mistress, Heaven's Queen.
Ye who would ask of me a rune,
Or who would ask of me a boon,
Meet me in some secret glade,
Dance my round in greenwood shade,
By the light of the Full Moon.
In a place wild and lone,
Dance around mine altar stone;
Work my Holy Mystery.
Ye who are feign to sorcery,
I bring ye secrets yet unknown.
No more shall ye know slavery,
Who give true worship unto me.
Ye who tread my round on Sabbat night,
Come ye all naked to the rite
In token that ye be truly free.
I teach ye the mystery of rebirth,
Work ye my Mysteries in mirth.
Heart joined to heart and lip to lip,
Five the points of Fellowship
That bring ye ecstasy on earth.
For I am the Circle of Rebirth.
I ask no sacrifice, but do bow,
No other law but Love I know,
By naught but Love may I be known.
All things living are mine own,
From me they come, to me they go.

The mother, as High Priestess, now moves to the center of the circle, facing the tree. She holds the child in her outstretched hand and says:

Queen Brigit, we have brought you here
The fruit of my womb, for joy, for fay.*
Bless this child with golden luck.

May her/his heart have your silver touch.
Health and wealth shall be her/his lot,
By sickness nor evil shall ever be caught.
Blessed be.

(*fay: magicalness; having magical or fairy-blessed qualities)

The mother places the baby again on the ground and rejoins the circle. One sister now moves forward, takes the bowl of barley or corn, and pours it on the ground in an uninterrupted circle around the baby saying:

Demeter, accept this offering to you.
May this child never know hunger of Body, nor
Heart, nor Soul.

Another sister takes the bowl of water, sprinkles the child, and pours the water on the ground around the child saying:

Marianne, accept this water as an offering to you. May this child have the Life-Force sap always strong within her/him. May fertility of the Moon infuse her/him with love for all living. May she/he know Sisterhood.

A third sister takes the bowl of salt, again making a circle around the child and saying:

Blessed be Sophia, Wisest of the Wise, in the earth and beyond the heavens. Protect and bless this child with wisdom.

All in the circle again, the women unify and raise power, building songs and different patterns out of the sounds. Then the afterbirth and umbilical cord are buried with the garlic under the tree and covered with the leftover water, barley or corn, and salt.

The mother now pronounces the child's name to the women for the first time. There are, however, two names. One is the child's legal name, and the other is the child's Secret Name, and must not be uttered again (not even to the child) until the initiation ceremony of the child. For a girl-child, the initiation ceremony takes place with her First Menstruation ritual; for a boy-child, this will be at his Dedication to the Goddess ritual, at the onset of puberty.

Feastings, dancing and joyousness is in order following the newborn child's dedication.

RITUAL AFTER AN ABORTION OR MISCARRIAGE

When the blood stops flowing, in the evening after the stars appear, friends prepare a bath of warm water. They sprinkle salt, herbs of comfort and cleansing, and rose petals on the water.

The woman enters the warm water saying, "Bless me, Mother, for I am your child!" She immerses herself, lies still and listens to her heart beat and slow breathing.

Friends sing to the beat of the woman's heart, as the woman sees the life she created stir, grow and then leave her to fly up the Milky Way to join the dance of the stars.

1. We are flow-ing wave on wave, from salt sea to salt sea.
2. We are dancing round and round, the Life Tree, the Life Tree.
3. We are leaping higher and higher, like sparks of fire, like sparks of fire.
4. We are flying up along the Milky Way the Milky Way.

The woman bids farewell to the young life. As she emerges from the waters, the woman and friends give each other the five-fold blessing on head, breasts, womb, knees and feet. They share a pot of tea and a cake made with honey.

When the water has drained away, the woman gathers the rose petals to sprinkle onto her garden. Everyone hugs the others and they sing "Deep Peace" together before leaving.

Chris Carol (33)
240 menstrual cycles
Portland, Oregon

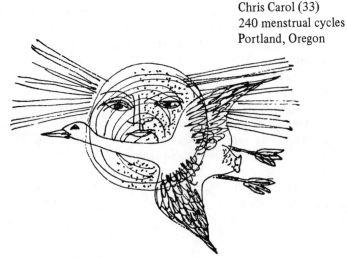

RITUAL FOR HEALING AFTER REMOVAL
OF OVARIES OR WOMB, BREASTS, etc.

Just because a woman no longer has her reproductive organs, she does not achieve Cronehood. Her body changes and it is important to bless this new being and banish the old fears, sicknesses and insecurity.

Prepare a fire, either in a cauldron, or in a pit. Put in it herbs you like; Rosemary and lavender are good smelling herbs.

Form a circle with your friends holding hands and unify either with a hum or a song. When the energy is built, say:

> I . . . (name of celebrant). . . today banish the ills that caused my operation. I banish weakness, I banish sorrow.

Help yourself to this Siberian chant of banishment:

> Into the dark night take away the evil spirit!
> Over the nights mountain scatter the evil spirit!
> Into the Mothers night drive it in banishment!
> Draw   it into the invisible river!
> Drive it further into oblivion!
> Drive it across the threshold of the darkest night!
> All the paths leading back into Life be barred with twice seven arrows barbed with knives!

Now jump over the flames imagining that you are purified by fire each time you jump (minimum of 3 times). The women friends then say to you:

> Renew woman, renew like the sun
> Revitalize and sing the new song
> Your life has not ended
> It has only just begun!
> Renew woman, renew like the sun!

It always helps to receive a momento for the occasion flowers, books, massages, tickets to theater can be given to the woman. Party. Blessed are those who support each other.

CRONING RITUAL/ENTERING THE WISE AGE

This ritual occurs when a woman has reached the point in her life when her Saturn has returned twice to her natal point. This happens to everybody at the age of 56. Saturn is the teaching planet, slow and complete; we celebrate the effects of this celestial event on the womans life by the Croning ritual.

Call a party for the young Crone, friends and relatives can cooperate with the invitations. Try to have some entertainment as well; invite a woman who plays an instrument or recites poetry. When all arrive, the group holds hands in a circle and sings a song to unify the group soul.

> Lady Lady listen to my hearts song
> Lady Lady listen to my hearts song
> I will never forget you, I will never forsake you
> I will never forget you and I will never forsake you!

After a couple of rounds of this, when the time is right, the priestess of the event steps out to ddress the rest. This priestess can be anyone who loves the new Crone.

Priestess:

> We gathered together to celebrate . . . (name) . . . becoming 56 years old, and entering the Wise Age.

> Her proper title is from now on among women 'Young Crone.'

Who is the Crone you ask? A Crone is a woman who has reached wisdom in her heart, who is called on in disputes to arbitrate, who is called on in despair to sooth the wounds, a young Crone is a woman who is everybody's older sister.

Who else is the Crone you ask? A young Crone is the Goddess in her third aspect, she is Magera, she is Hecate, she is the Goddess of unbound power.

Folklore has it that Crones bring good luck when you see them on the streets, if they smile on you, you will have a very good day. They appear in important times to show the grace of the goddess. Crones' wishes must be respected for the Goddess demands this from the younger generation.

Crones enjoy special favors, their magic is stronger, their spells are faster, their loves are stronger.

All: Bless you . . . (name of the new Crone) . . . with good health, happiness and long life!

Now the youngest of the group starts lighting a circle of white candles, previously set out in the middle of the room; 56 of them, one for each year of the Crone's life. Others can help after the Nymph starts. The woman priestess has a bell with which she will ring out 56 times again for each year that has passed. If the Crone would like to give a speech, here is a good place to do it.

When the circle of light is done, the Young Crone steps into it and the bell tolls out 56 times, after which a round of applause from everyone is heard. Congratulations and good wishes are showered on the woman in the circle. As a special feature, the young Crone receives her Crone Jewel. This jewel can be a broach, a necklace, a ring; as long as it has a nice purple stone in it. The color of purple is that of synthesis. It is royal color, a learning color, and a powerful color.

Priestess:

> I present you with your Crone jewel, to remind you that you are our teacher, our beloved sister, and Crone of the Goddess.

Young Crone:

> I traveled the road from my mothers breasts to Cronehood. I thank the Goddess for the good seasons that passed, and, oh, I toast the good seasons to come! Blessed be!

All enjoy the party, dance, perform, enjoy.

DIANIC TRYSTING

Trysting, or handfasting, or Promising Ritual is an ancient way of bonding which we as women and woman loving men need to reestablish. The so called Marriage ceremonies, where mothers always cry and grand-mothers faint — isn't that a give away for its ominous meaning — are but recent institutions geared primarily to sexual ownership. The Promise is Monogomy and in the case of the woman involved 'giving up their maiden-head' , which means loosing your name, social status and identity (try to find a married lady in a city through the phone book if you don't know her husband's name!)

We approach trysting from a universal point of view. The bonds called down on the couple are Loyalty forever which has nothing to do with sex. The words exchanged are promises to take care of each other as long as they live and even after death. It's a moving bond, which should be done not only for couples but as many people who feel this undying bond with each other. Especially in times of threatening ecological disasters, we must form tribes to survive. But we must form love-bonds in order to thrive!

Requirement: The trystees have been friends at least six months. If for some reason they want to be trysted anyway, they should not be stopped.

Time: Full and New Moons

Place: Outdoors under beautiful trees, by the ocean, in groves or indoors in some nice big space. Decorate with yellow and white flowers, yellow for manifestation and white for blessings.

The women dress in robes or gowns or tuxedos or whatever. But they are barefoot for the ceremony.

In preparation the women prepare a tray of green things, something from the roots, from the stems, something from the leaves, flowers and fruits, (carrots, celery, cauliflower, dates, salad, almonds, oranges, etc.).

This is to invoke the Goddess of Life over the tray (food is Life). Also present on the altar are the two chalices, that the women bought for themselves as symbols of their union. The wedding rings were not as much used to signify marriages as chalices were. They are symbols of pleasure. In gold, silver or ceramic, they may have the date engraved on it, for momento.

Lastly two flower crowns for each woman, a wreath for their heads made of fresh flowers preferably yellow and white roses. The high priestess gets one too (yellow for manifestation, white for blessings).

The couple waits barefoot outside the circle while the one priestess goes from east to south then west and north, invoking the goddess accord-ing to ancient rites. Usually with an incense burner held aloft in her hand she pauses in each corner of the circle saying her own invocations or this one:

East: Hail to thee Goddess Isis, bringer of new life and feelings, come into this circle where lovers await your blessings! (If it's not lovers, say friends).

South: Come to this circle firery goddess Heartha, Vesta, Pele! Bring your energy to fuel this bond to be formed here today. Come bring your excitement and joy and ecstacy, blessed be!

West: Hail to thee Aphrodite! Love goddess, water goddess! Come to us into this circle and bless the lovers who ask for it in your name, come and bless this union with love!

North: Come, oh beautiful Earth Goddess Demeter and your daughter Persephone! Come and nourish us with your love and presence. Blessed be!

Then closing the circle two priestesses who facilitate walk over to the trystees and anoint them with either a sacred oil (Rosalama, priestess oil, frankincense and myrrh) or blessed water.

Anointing the forehead: I purify you from all anxiety, I purify your mind from fears (anointing the eyes and nose) I purify your eyes to see Her ways, your lips to speak Her names, (breast) your breast formed in strength and beauty, (touch on the genitals) your genitals I bless for strength and pleasure, and your feet to walk in Her path. Finally, she anoints the palm of the hands saying I bless your hands to do the Goddess' works!

This happens to both trystees. Now they are led in by the hand by the two priestesses. High Priestess holds her hands over the tray of food and all follow her example.

High Priestess:

> I invoke you Goddess of All Life, I invoke you by the foods here present, the roots, to make a strong foundation for this relationship, stems for standing firm and proud by the leaves, to grow and prosper together, by the flowers for joy and laughter, and by the fruits for a long and enduring time together.

Now the Priestess turns to one of the trystees:

> Do you (name) take this woman (name) for your friend and lover for this life time, promise to care and love even if you love others in addition or not?

> I do.

> Do you (name) promise to take (name) as your friend and lover for this life time, to care and to be loyal to, to love even if you love others as well?

> I do.

65

Priestess hands them the tray of food now from which they each select something to offer to the other. Trystee: (offering food and feeding into the mouth of the other):

May you never hunger!

The other person repeats this in a reciprocal way. Then the priestess hands them over their chalices and fills them with wine, champagne, perrier, etc. Trystee offering to each other:

May you never thirst!

Now finally the priestess hands over the crowns of flowers and they crown each other saying:

Thou art Goddess!

Z Budapest trysting wimmin at the Michigan Women's Music Festival

High Priestess:

> Now to mark the first moment of this commitment, I ask you to jump over the broom, which is made of Myrtel tree, and is sacred to the goddess of love (from West to East).

She places the sacred broom in front of them, and holding each others hands, the trystees "jump the broom" together, when they land on the ground again they are pronounced lovers in trust!

After this ceremony often the women want to read a statement, or a poem, dance a dance. General merriment can ensue, eating, drinking, congratulations echoed. After jumping the broom, rings can be exchanged, because the ring in this case is a later development, the chalices are the true symbols of this ceremony.

The corresponding Tarot card to this event is the two of cups, where lovers exchange pleasures in an equalitarian relationship blessed by the Great Spirit.

ATTITUDES TOWARD DEATH IN THE CRAFT

Death is considered a revolving door leading into a new life. From earliest times the representations showing what happens around death in Goddess religions conspicuously lacks terror. This is because the Goddess of Life, the Goddess of Death, and the Goddess of Beauty (Isis, Hecate, Astarte) are three in one — the same. The same Mother who gives life also mourns. Even the sorrowful Maria, Pieta, is but the Goddess's image in Her death-aspect, mourning the passing of favorite sons. The son is dead; She however, is very much alive. She is at hand to perform the burial rites; She is there to accompany the soul of the departed into the promised "certainty while in life, and after death peace unutterable, and reincarnation if desired." She is, in other words, immortal.

The preparation for death included meditations on the best qualities of the person about to pass on. This is shown on tombstones as being a matter between the woman and her priestess, who helps her gain insight into her own gifts. Selection of jewels was part of the woman's preparation for death, because stones stand for human qualities: jade, for steadfastness and smoothness of conduct; moonstone, for psychic clarity and quick passage; bloodstone, to absorb fear; gold, for the healing sun.

Paint was added to the tombstones. Ocher was found all around the graves of Stone Age women, still staining the ground with red. It symbolizes rebirth, and was believed to quicken the process of a new bloodline. Amazon graves were adorned with horns of animals, in particular stags, to denote the Dianic tradition of the Amazon even in death. The Mighty Huntress of the Night collected Her maidens and hunted with them the forces of oppression.

The color of mourning among ancient peoples was not black, but white. The white robes symbolized the White Light and the guiding Moon Goddess, who appears to the dead to attract them to Her domain, Rebirth. Red as a color of mourning was also used to suggest the color of blood for a stimulation of a fast rebirth.

WHEN ABOUT TO DIE

The worst possible thing which can happen is for the dying woman to be in fear. Fear produces terrible dreams and distracts the soul from its natural flight back to the Mother Goddess. Imagine death as a ball that has been bounced against the floor. The first up-bounce is the highest and strongest. This is the chance, when dying, for the most "direct" or conscious exit of the soul from the physical body. This is considered the most evolved way to go through this transition. This is the reason that the last thoughts and surroundings of the dying woman are all-important.

Establish a tranquil environment around the loved one. Do not let families intrude with anxious waiting, fear and grief. It is not the dying woman's job to console the family. Her job is to consciously exit into the peaceful Lap of the Goddess.

Light yellow candles around the room, and maybe throughout the entire house. Put at least two white candles on both sides of the woman. Gather cut flowers and stock up the vases, so that everything looks pretty. A feast should be prepared for the "Rite of Passage," to be celebrated after death with games, laughter, and memories of good times. Dialogue with the dead is the focus here, not the drunken venting of a family's insecurities.

The job of guiding the woman toward rebirth, or peace and rest unutterable, is strictly a woman's job. Only the family's female members should be present at the woman's side, unless she requests otherwise. One ALWAYS, and under all circumstances, honors the wishes of the dying woman.

It is important that friends of the dying woman talk to her while she appears unconscious. The truth is that the spirit isn't "gone," and can hear. In ancient Tibet this was used as a form of guiding the spirit toward final liberation. Tibetans believed that those close to the dying person would know whether that person wanted final "liberation" or another physical incarnation. Final liberation was considered the higher state of spiritual evolution to be achieved be a soul, and it meant that physical rebirth of the soul of the dying person would not occur. Not every spirit chose liberation, meaning that a physical rebirth could occur instantly, or within an appointed period of time; the soul moving instead to inhabit the body of a newly-conceived baby.

While the person who is dying is lying unconscious, the women's friends can chant this very old chant to her, to ease her mind and diminish fears:

I call to mind the Mother of the Universe
Who has created this world, both real and unreal,
And who, by Her own power with Her three aspects,
Protects it, and having destroyed it, She then plays.
Commonly it is said that god created the universe;
Yet the learned of ancient Mysteries
Speak of this birth from the navel lotus, the Mother.
Although it is said he creates,
Yet he, himself, is dependent on Her
Even the water of Ocean, which is liquid in substance
Cannot exist without a container, therefore
I take refuge in Her, Mother of all beings,
Who exists in all things in the form of Power!
Queen of the Universe are Thou, and its Guardian;
In the form of the Universe Thou art its Maintainer;
By all the women Thou art worshipped,
As Thy daughters, they have great devotion to Thee.

While chanting, visualization is the reality that a spirit about to depart understands. All who are present should imagine themselves becoming the Goddess of all-fulfilling Wisdom, all performing Wisdom, by those powers they are endowed to help their beloved attain liberation of the highest kind, or happy reincarnation if desired. Visualize the Goddess as red in color; very beautiful, dressed only in jeweled girdles and a necklace of emeralds, holding to Her heart a skull filled with blood in one hand, while leaning on a white staff of leadership that is balanced in the crook of Her arm. Her other holds aloft a silver bolo. She dances the dance of the Five-Pointed-Power, from east, to south, then west and north, and at last the center, where you visualize Her with the beloved dying person.

Now dwell on this image. All the women who can hold this in their minds, experience the bliss that goes with the merging of the Mother and the child.

Priestesses:
You are the Earth, Creatrix of the World.
You are Water, and in the form of Diana preserveth the world.
You are Fire, and in the form of Pele destroyeth the world.
You exist in the form of Isis,
You are the Air of the world.

You are the Primeval and Auspicious One;
Mother of all men, refuge of your women,
Who ever move in the changes of the world.
The Supporter of all, yet yourself without support,
The Only Pure One in the form of Ether.
Oh, Mother Kali, be gracious to me!

You are Intelligence and Bliss, and Light-Herself.
How, then, can I know you?
Oh, Mother Kali, be gracious to me!
You are that which supports and yet is not supported,
You pervade the world.
You are in the form of the world
Which is pervaded by Thee.

You are both Negation and Existence.
Oh, Mother Kali, be gracious to me!
You are the atom, and ever-pervading,
You are the Whole Universe.
No praise is sufficient, yet your qualities prompt me
To praise you!
Mother Kali, be gracious to me!

70

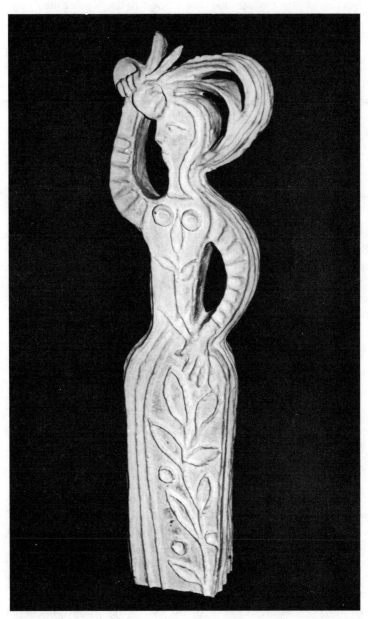

Mageara – Goddess of Death by Masika Szilagyi

Now visualize a white navel cord, red inside, extending from the lotus navel of the Goddess and connecting into the navel of the dying woman. See Kali assimilate the essence of the Prana (Life Force) from the woman into Herself.

Abide in the bliss of this conscious transference. Sing, hum, meditate. Those who can play musical instruments should do so at this time. Ring bells rhythmically, nine times, after this chanting. Then pause, and ring another nine times. When the bells are silent, all the relatives surround the person with fresh-cut flowers. Camphor is kindled in the Cauldron of Rebirth.

THE FEAST OF THE DEAD

This is the same as All Hallows Eve, except that this time one celebrates with a particular soul, and not with all ancestors. Set aside the woman's favorite plate, with her favorite food, and invite her to partake in this last supper. After the feast the priestess whispers in the woman's ear: "Come, Sister, and leave all worldly attachments behind. You have no more worries about us. We bid you good-by."

BURIAL RITES

Ancient women were buried in the earth, and men were put into sacks and exposed in trees for the Bird Goddess to assimilate. This, of course, is impossible for modern use, today. There is a good argument for earthen burial, because "from earth we came and to earth we return," but it is expensive. Cremation was also used in ancient matriarchies, and it was the Fire Goddess who took back the bodies for recycling. If a successful and conscious transfer takes place, it doesn't really matter which type of burial is chosen. It must be left to the preference of the dying person.

In case transference did not occur and the soul is still lingering in the body, a lengthy and careful guiding job must be performed so that the Prana, the essence or soul, can find peace.

72

If the dying person wanted to return immediately, and was very close to a couple who desire children, the two should make love in the same house where the woman is dying, so that she can enter the new cell of the baby at conception. If the person doesn't want to take a body for a while, burial by water is recommended. The soul would then merge with the Great Goddess of "all that is glistening and wet," and exist in the form of water, rain, rivers, clouds. This is a nice possibility. Cremation and then dispersion into the ocean is also used for this reason; the soul merges with the cosmic elements and permeates Nature.

BURIAL PROCESSION

The walk to the burial place must be very, very slow. No loud noises must be allowed around the dead, such as wailing, crying, or loud displays of grief. All those entities could blow the poor soul miles away from the procession, and cause unnecessary fear. You must remember that the Prana without the body is but a thought-form, without resistance to sound vibrations or winds of emotion; like a fallen leaf, one is easily blown about, without the protection of a sister's wisdom.

Even as the procession is moving on, the priestess maintains a continual dialogue with the dead person, explaining to her that it is necessary to let go of all earthly attachments. This is a hard thing to do because the spirit, having no more pain, might really like to stay around and see what is going on. She might have left children behind, and blood-lines are very strong ties which are never successfully broken. A child can call on the spirit of the dead mother for help at any time, and the mother would respond. Basically, if a woman is satisfied about the fate of her children without her, she would be more willing to leave.

A last realization must be dealt with for the spirit to be able to transcend the physical plane, and that is the reality of "death" as the woman once understood it. Following death, the woman experiences a new mobility, depending on her inner emanations of thought, and she is able to see and hear everything. A good imagination now becomes her ship. She might reject totally the fact that she is "gone" from the physical plane. Grief would set in then, when she notices that nobody responds to her when she speaks to them, and nobody sees her when she approaches. This is the last fear that must be overcome, and the priestess must help here by guiding the woman to a realization of the reality of death-separation. Using mental images here is necessary.

THE ART OF REBIRTH

Burn meditation incense on the grave or at the site of burial, and light a white candle as well. Talk to the deceased in low, unafraid tones. Remember, everything communicates through vibrations. Say to the soul:

Imagine yourself like the Goddess of the White Light,
Maat, who is the ancient Goddess of Truth,
Emanating radiance. You are naked, with a feather
In one hand and a scale in the other.
You are the Unity of all Worlds, the Unity of all
Truths, and All-Encompassing Mother.

Abide in this and feel the White Light emanating from you and through you. Chant: "Me and Maat, Maat and me, are One." Repeat in different ways, helping in the imagery because you will merge with Maat while chanting. After this, frequent the site of the grave under the Full Moon, tending to the white candle, bringing fresh flowers, and chanting.

TO CHOOSE A WOMB

Priestess:
Abondon all feelings of attraction or repulsion, with memories' heedfulness restraining the roving tendencies of the mind. Abide in the pure state of Maat, emanating all the Light. Apply yourself to choosing a womb-door, and when you find the one you judge beneficial and good, imagine yourself emanating from the Goddess's navel connecting you to the chosen womb, and enter.

It is no accident that we are all alive at the same time. That we are all reincarnated at the same time and share life together in time is a very special thing, and extremely important. How often have you recognized someone you've never met, or responded to something in someone you've never seen? That feeling of "deja vu" has a valid basis. I believe that the last women killed are the first ones back, and the Amazons were the last ones. The last always becomes first in the spiraling evolutionary cycle, and I feel that the Amazons and witches have been re-born.

74

It is said that all the possible wombs in the world are visible to you as a spirit in search of reincarnation. You must avoid entering a womb because of the frightening sounds you "hear," because those are emanations from your own mind. There is nothing frighteningly "real" in this dream state; you must fight against accidental reincarnation.

When consciously choosing our parents, we indeed have an opportunity to be born to those who can help us develop our spirit higher. When attracted to a physical womb, we must bless ourselves consciously with ever-present bliss, so that we enter into a lucky lifetime with adoring and helpful parents. Blindly entering a womb without blessing or reflection, must because you are frightened by your own thought-form emanations, cause futile and often difficult paths. Be careful whom you choose. You are the one who must live with it.

THE GREAT RITE

GENERAL SEXUAL PRACTICES

The Great Rite is a feature of the Earth religions which has received little discussion in feminist witches' circles thus far. The reason, generally speaking, is that we have not yet been quite ready to take on the entire concept. At one time, I even offered a promise to the Goddess that if I could salvage my lovelife, sparing myself all the sorrows and tilting the scales to the side of pleasure, I would found and lead a Dianic Great Rite to Aphrodite, thereby honoring the Goddess of Love. Did I do it? No. Instead, I found that I was being jealous, possessive, masochistic and a coward in general. Additionally, the further returns of my lovelife ran toward intensive contemplation of the Life Force as in sex I was faced with my own failings. For the first time in my hedonistic, life-affirming love-style, this High Priestess didn't do very well. I even had a second lesson and a few reruns.

As a High Priestess I must explore what the ancient people have left to us, believing in the heritage of women's sexual modes and practices, especially because a few good working models are still with us. Even a short search sheds a lot of light on the probable causes of much unhappiness. Consider the rampant loneliness of the women who are committing suicide in ever-increasing numbers, and those who seek desperate measures in their drive for survival. Whatever happens to the women of a particular race, happens to that race. Whatever happens to the women of a species, happens to the entire species. The human species is no exception.

What we do know is that, universally, the Goddess is intimately connected with religious sexual practices; when mating and pleasuring are observed in Her honor alone, giving up any and all sexual inhibitions of any current era. The patriarchal sexual mores are direct reversals of this religious sexual enjoyment. All taboos of Judeo-Christianity were made against the values of the Old Religion.

The forcible suppression of the female's basic orgasmic nature, and the intolerance shown women's natural cycles, are perversion and represent a sexual glorification of the male, without the influence of the Great Mother. All this reflects a death-worship so deeply ingrained in our society that we can hardly identify it, even as we exist within it.

The essence of the Great Rite was the fact that ancient women related sexually to more than one man or women during its celebration, often experiencing pleasure with many others. This took place in the fresh furrows of the newly-plowed earth, or in private living rooms, in the woods, on the mountains, in all cultures — in festivals honoring Aphrodite, Ishtar, Isis, Astarte, Hera. The sacred time was calculated according to the cycles and seasons of the Earth, and the women of Earth did as the Goddess did. Nature is not sexually possessive. She is certainly promiscuous by Christian standards, but then, Christians or not, Nature is still at it — unconquerable because She is Divine. When the Great Rite was used liberally in sexual festivals in celebration of life, the communities were more closely bound, happy, and fulfilled. Even crime decreased. There was no time for it. Sex was Divine, violence was not.

People do not change, do not truly experience a revolution, until they are able to come to terms with a healthy, natural sexuality. When sexual standards changed, so did we. Through our sexuality, the Goddess reveals Herself, energizes us, and instills a kind of bond that peacefully holds together sizable communities. Sexual mores of the Goddess are free, open, and inclusive, never discriminating against the slow, the plain, the infirm, the unique. Aphrodite accepts all mergings in Her name and entire communities reap great benefits from it in the form of increased good health, vitality, and tolerance for all.

Pleasure is seen as a Virtue in Earth religions. Oneness of all Nature is much sought after in the sexual union, be it with female-male variations or female with female and male with male. Creativity generally, rather than procreation exclusively, is the object of Tantric, Wiccan, Earth-religion practices.

Tantra, the Science of Ecstasy, teaches the duality of all things. This is hard to hear for Dianic witches, since we have a trinity conceptualization of the world order, and when viewed in its truest sense of origins, we see how the duality-concept is not leading people to freedom of sex but to a forced monogamy. The sexual mores of the Goddess decree that sexual favors be "distributed evenly" and justly, loving more than one partner for Her glory. The oneness of all living creatures, the loving freedom of the Goddess is given to all. The least we can do in return is to transcend our own twentieth-century headset and promote love and freedom with many more than one human being.

Bonding sexually with more than one person is seen as a terrifying threat to couples who have assumed responsibilities together and who fear losing their exclusivity with each other. A bond which cannot hold through a divine sacrifice, expanding in religious sexual rites seasonally for the honor of the Goddess, cannot hope for Her blessings for very long. Our mythology tells us how the Goddess was angered by the exclusivity of patriarchal sexual mores, and how She visited famine and tempests upon the people who refused to "losen their girdles" for Aphrodite in Her rituals. Since the Goddess is recognized by Love alone ("No other Law but Love I know"), it is nearly impossible to argue with Her.

Tantra is concerned with the maintenance of a penile erection for as long as possible. Most of the tantric training for men consists of techniques which reinforce the mastery of mind over penis. With Dianic sexual practices this worry is definitely not one of ours. Between women, sexual tension is not created and held by a particular biological state of a penis. It is born and held solely with the mind — with images of the Goddess as the Goddess of Love. The collective female circle becomes possessed by Her, and unbridles female sexual instincts from the far recesses of the third layer of the brain, diminishing the fears, the guilt and the oppression of female sexuality.

Pleasure is a mental process. Sadly, the minds of most people today are conditioned to pain and suffering. Pleasure makes new connections in the human brain, and is a learned process much like orgasm and pain, the two being interconnected at times. Orgasm in sex will burst the ego, which is the single greatest opposition in our organism, and one which blocks the most basic instincts. But that same ego is quite necessary for survival, holding down a job, getting ahead, etc. Pleasure achieves easily as much as pain. The ego must be consciously relinquished for a short time when we approach loving as Her Goddesses. Current sexual fantasies pale in comparison with Goddess imagery and possession by the Goddess during sex. The healing power of sex as it releases energies to the organism is proof of having tapped a most Divine source of energy.

Resistance to sexual practices in the Goddess tradition comes solely from our conditioning (and historical times). Part of our oppression comes from the great body of sexual mores dictated to us by antiseptic, anti-nature, anti-woman religious forces — virtual latecomers to the world, who brought with them their swords, shame, bloodshed and guilt. We are all imbued with it.

As witches we have a chance to transcend all fears which block creativity. Women who practice the ancient sexual celebrations must be very careful, and must practice them in secrecy. The political climate is such that the burning flesh of witches still lingers in the memory of the male churches without regret. Patriarchy knows well that it cannot survive if the women turn once again to the Old Religion with its powerful and natural lovemaking. Once again no one would be able to fixate on paternity, for example, if women relate to more than one man in one ritual, or in one life. The natural and holy sexual practices of the Wicca (Dianics as well as other traditions) are by far the most dangerous to the structure of the patriarchy and, therefore, suffer from the most intense persecution and hatred. The revival of Aphroditian love and the Great Rite is integral to a real revolution. Sex, like religion, is the highest of politics. Sex is the highest held human experience. How Aphrodite is hunting us down, making us hers once again.

I would like you to know that this information is every bit as hard for me and other women members to follow as it is to you. Maybe it's enough to have the vision now and let it unfold as it may for the future.

ESOTARA: WITCHES' VALENTINE'S DAY

The scent of blooming flowers and the warming sun herald the time in nature when all is opened up for renewal; Flora comes of age, fauna abound, and all is ready for love.

In ancient times we celebrated the importance of this time with processions through the streets, dances and curious "sprinkling" rituals, In Hungary, they still do this in the countryside at Easter — young boys go from house to house with vials of perfumed water, and sprinkle all female members of the home, old and young alike. When this has been done, the women offer the boys boiled eggs, sometimes painted especially for a particular admirer. This is clearly a non-personal mating ritual, very sexual in nature.

In this country, "Valentine's Day" takes the place of Esotara (usually celebrated around March 30th), but at a time when Nature is not attuned to the same vibrations. February 14th, the day currently signified as Valentine's Day, falls during a period when the ancients were celebrating Diasia, a gloom festival. Blooming love is strained when Nature is not yet ready for it. The wooing which goes on today, through gifts of flowers and love messages sent via cards, is a modern mating dance, celebrated too early.

Today a general public ritual could be held, using a circle of flowers. Gather all your friends together, inviting them all as singles. Let them all come to the circle by themselves, bringing flowers from your area. Form a circle while holding the flowers in your hands, and just hum together humming for the power within you. When all are centered, one person says to her flower:

Behold the brave beauty of this bloom!
She teaches us to open with our hearts,
To set aside fear and to risk being vulnerable.
Only then can life regenerate.
The Goddess stirs, and binds our hearts together.
She plays the eternal spinning wheel,
Weaving in beauty, diversity, variety and abundance.

Now each person in the circle makes a wish concerning her love-life. The wishes may be expressed aloud or silently, as each person steps to the middle of the circle to make a wish on a flower while holding it aloft. An example might be: "My heart was lonely, but no more. The Goddess will send love, galore!"

The humming should continue as the members of the circle make their wishes, so that the energy level is kept high enough to launch all desire. Dancing, feasting, exchanging gifts, making dates, renewing love vows, kissing friends and lovers, all this is in order. It is very good luck to share love with more than one person, even if only in token.

The Esotara ritual for witches is bolder and more ancient. It harkens back to times when modesty was unknown and unnecessary — an invention of the patriarchal future. For this ritual, witches come together late at night, wearing only jewelry and flowers. They raise power in the same way (humming) except that the Priestess invokes Kore:

> I invoke you, Kore, Mighty Maiden Bloomed!
> I invoke thee by the roots and by the stem,
> By the leaves and by the flowers,
> By all the goodly fruits!
> Come among us and bless us with your loving signs.
> Let us be merry, happy and well-loved!
> Here I bind us in your Sign.

Now the Five-Fold Kiss is passed, from East to South, then West and North. In the Circle the women (men or both) pass this kiss from one to another. The first kiss is on the forehead, for the thoughts of the Goddess; then the eyes are kissed for visions and clearsightedness in love; then the breasts for beauty and nurturance in love; then the genitals for the pleasures of love.

When the Five-Fold Kiss has come full circle, everyone continues to hold the energies high, visualizing for each person in the circle whatever that person wanted to change. All circle member visualize in great detail how that particular change is to be made. Then, before the energy drops, the Priestess says: "The circle of Love is never broken. The Goddess blesses Her children. Blessed be."

Of course in the old times Diana put all the lights out and the people freely made love in the circle.

THE DRAWING OF THE FLOWERS:
A DIANIC GREAT RITE

The observance of the Great Rite may take place on any Full
Moon or particularly relevant Sabbat. May Eve, Midsummer, Spring
Equinox, all are fine for the celebration of this ritual. Other days
which are holy may be used as well since there is no hard and fast rule
regarding this, but I would caution against using All Hallow's Eve. The
Sacred Crone traditionally is not much involved with sexual ecstasies
on All Hallow's Eve, but this is not a specific rule either. We should look
to our current generation of Crones for guidance in this matter.

Aphrodite is the aspect of the Goddess to be invoked for the celebration of the Great Rite. The circle of women build a stone altar,
including images of Aphrodite and symbols sacred to Her. This altar
is placed in the Western corner of the circle, Corner of Waters and
Rebirth. The ancients took a communal bath of purification before the
Great Rite, so using a pool for this modern ritual would be appropriate.

Frankincense and Myrrh are burned and placed in the Eastern
corner of the circle. To the South is set the customary red candle, and
in the North an offering of grain is laid out for the birds. The altar in
the West should have a bowl of water on it. Wands, instead of swords,
are used for this ritual.

All are sky-clad except for jewelry worn as desired and sacred
cords tied around the waists. Each woman brings a fresh flower to the
circle, representing herself, and hidden from others in the circle. Each
woman must remember which flower is hers, so if two or more flowers
are alike they may be marked in some way as to make them identifiable
to the women to whom they belong. Invoke the Watchtowers, moving
from East to South then West to North.

Priestess of the East:
Powerful Mother, Ishtar!
I invoke thee by your favorite colors of purple and of red.
You who gave birth to the dawn, to civilizations,
You who reveal yourself through Love!
Come and join this circle of friends
As we worship you according to ancient rites!
Keep all enemies and envious eyes from the East
Far from us, and bless this circle.
So mote it be!

Preistess of the South:
Conjure, conjure, Oh Goddess of Love!
Conjure and appear through us!

Firey passions, woman-loving Goddess, come!
Enter the hearts of all here present
As we worship thee in loving!
Keep away all enemies from the south.
Allow no evil to enter from your Corner,
Only the good and the sacred shall come.
Blessed be!

Priestess of the West:
Lovely Goddess, Aphrodite, Sea-born Goddess of Life!
Enter our feelings with your gentle delight.
Let our sexuality rise like the waves on the Sea!
Kundalini, white serpent, rise up through our spines!
Let each of us be you, possessed by your love.
Keep all evil away from the Corner of the West.
Blessed be.

Priestess of the North:
Powerful Mother, Demeter!
Without whom there is no life, no grain, no food for the living.
Fertile Mother of life-giving things,
Enter our hearts and let us feel your earthy passions.
Let us smell and touch and stroke in your name as the sacred
    passions rise.
Keep all evil from the North away from us and bestow your warm
    blessings on our great rites!
Blessed be!

Now the women close the circle with, "This circle is now closed. The
Goddess blesses Her Women." Link arms and begin humming to raise
power. When energies are right the High Priestess says: "The Goddess
is here." She then turns to the woman on her left and says:

All ye assembled at my shrine,
Mother, darksome and divine;
Mine the scourge and mine the kiss,
Here I charge you in this sign.

The High Priestess then kisses the woman once on each of the five sacred
points: her forehead, her mouth, her breasts, her genitals and her feet.
This five-fold kiss is passed on from one woman to another. Since it is
a warming-up for the Great Rite, it should be freer than the normal
ceremonial. Laughter, joking, or playfully intimate remarks are to be
encouraged, and the kissing may be informal, long, ritualistic or simul-

taneous. Make sure each and every woman is given her "sign" of the Goddess in the form of the Five-Fold Kiss.

Now one or many women place a great white, purple or red cloth on the ground in the middle of the circle. The High Priestess then leads the women in the Great Charge:

> Hear ye the words of the Star Goddess
> The dust of whose feet are the hosts of heaven
> She whose body encircles the Universe:
>
> I am the beauty of the green earth
> And the white moon among the stars
> And the mystery of the waters
> And the desire of human hearts.
>
> Call unto your soul, "Arise!" and come unto me
> For I am the soul of nature
> Who gives life to the Universe
> From me all things proceed
> And unto me all things must return.
>
> Before my face, beloved of all
> Let your divine innermost self be enfolded
> In the rapture of the infinite.
>
> Let my worship be in the heart that rejoices
> For behold, all acts of love and pleasure are my rituals
> And therefore let there be beauty and strength
> Power and compassion, honor and pride
> Mirth and reverence within you.
>
> And you who think to seek for me
> Know your seeking and yearning shall avail you not
> Unless you know the Mystery:
> That if that which you seek you find not within you,
> You will never find it without.
>
> For behold, I have been with you from the beginning
> And I am that which is attained
> At the end of desire.

Now the women place their flowers into the middle of the cloth. The four corners are then folded in and the flowers mixed up in the cloth so that nobody knows whose flower is where. The High Priestess holds the gathered cloth high in the air, facing West:

> We dedicate this rite to you, Aphrodite,
> Mother of Good Fortune.
> Allow the power that is in loving
> To flow through all of us
> Regardless of personal preferences
> Or physical attractions
> For we are all you, as you are us.

Each woman reaches into the cloth and draws out a flower. As each flower is held up, the woman who placed it there must claim it by saying, "It is I. I am Goddess tonight." This lets the women know who is their initial ritual partner. The tradition has been one for the Goddess and one by choice, but each woman must actually relate to more than one woman — a trinity-concept is worshipped here in Divine ways. This ritual goes beyond personalities, beauty requirements or any other externally imposed considerations. Sex here is spiritualized — sex as a spiritual experience.

The Great Rite begins with physical stroking. This does not require pairing-off. Massage, relaxation through touch, any pleasurable stroking is fine, and if there is a bath available, each woman can climb in to be bathed and attended to by the others.

The physical stroking is followed by anointing all the bodies with healthful oils. Women need not pair off for this either, since it is preferable that the anointing be done to as many women in the circle as possible. The focus should always remain clear: communal pleasuring. Making garlands for each other is part of the ritual, and flower or feather decorations may be created for the purpose of beholding each woman as Goddess of Love.

The Great Rite feeling must be spontaneous. When it occurs of course, it is a gift and the group must have given itself the inner permission to accept it and follow its lead. Kissing is a good beginning, accompanied by stroking, and if the mood enters the women, the Goddess is there. Lovemaking is then allowed freely, with reverence.

Women who are shy, and who do not yet "feel" the power, should involve themselves in some way with the others who do feel such power. Whether through physical contact, massaging or assisting in some other way, the shy woman will then be touched and made love to as well. As a natural-chance choice, lovemaking should be slow and unhurried. Before the evening is ended the women will make love with the "drawer" of their particular flower, but not first and not exclusively.

Words of sexual scenes or words describing sacred lovemaking could be chanted by the ones who think of such things to say. The Sacred Whore is invoked here with Her holiest meaning — She Who

Shines on All Equally. Music may be applied to the general mood, and dancing around women entwined in sexual ecstasy is fine for keeping the energy high. If and when orgasm occurs for somebody it is treated as a sacred chant and shared by other women in the circle. Orgasm, however, is not the goal of the Great Rite, pleasuring is.

When the mood is exhausted and the women lose interest in the revelries, it's time to give thanks to the Goddess of Love. Pure water is carried around the circle and sprinkled on the ground in gratitude. Birdseed and other grains are poured out for the birds, who are the children of the Goddess. Thanks are given to the Mothers from the East, South, West and North, with wands upheld.

Priestess of the East:
Goddess Ishtar, thank you for your guidance and liberation, for the ability to transcend the personal to the universal, and that we have been able to merge with the great All! Bless us before you leave. Blessed be.

Priestess of the South:
Goddess of Fires, Passionate Lover-Mother, Thank you for fueling our hearts with your energies. Bless us before you leave! Blessed be.

Priestess of the West:
Gracious Goddess of the West, Bountiful Aphrodite,
Great Mother of Lovers!
Thank you for your blessing of grace and power.
Bless us before you leave! Blessed be.

Priestess of the North:
Great Goddess Demeter! We have tasted of the earthy love
    which is your favorite,
We have felt the Divine within us!
Bless us before you leave!
Blessed be.

When all this has occurred, pack up the cloth but leave the flowers for the Goddess. Remember to keep silent about the celebration of the Great Rite since the envy of Judeo-Christians could bring you trouble.

THE POLITICS OF FOOD

by Mary Farkas

Good nutrition is the process of gaining one's autonomy; it is the process by which one can take back control of one's life. The day-to-day decisions involved in what we eat are some of the most essential, difficult, and political decisions that we have to make. The understanding of food in its political context may be a new dimension for some of us. Think for a moment about how our food is grown, how our food is

processed, and how our food is distributed, from the fields to the table. How much do we know about what goes into each process? How much control do we have over each process? How much personal contact do we have with each process? The answer is obvious: very little, or none at all. That answer is political, because politics is power or control, and when we don't have control of the very BASIS of life — food — that makes food a very political issue.

> We believe that just as it is time to fight for the right to control our bodies, it is also time to fight for our sweet womon-souls.
>
> We believe that in order to fight and win a revolution that will stretch for generations into the future, we must find reliable ways to replenish our energies.
>
> (Excerpted from the Manifesto of the Susan B. Anthony Coven No. 1)

Food is one of the most basic ways to replenish our energy, but in the incredibly short span of two or three generations we have lost most of our knowledge of food. Historically, women possessed the secrets of choosing, cooking, processing, and preserving food for the whole community. These food facts were passed from mother to daughter and were as necessary to learn as the ability to walk. These skills meant the survival of the group, and women were respected for this knowledge. The traditional healers were the women of the group, who knew which herbs, plants, and foods would cure an ailment. Patriarchy labeled these women healers, "witches," and they became the feared women of the community. In order to completely control a population, the church and state must have control of the healing processes. The crisis times of birth and death must be controlled. The church and state were threatened by the power of the women healers who were an effective alternative to their sanctioned healers — doctors.

86

In order to gain power for this new breed of doctors, the power of the wise women had to be destroyed. To seek out the women healers meant that you were seeking help from the devil since it was supposed that witches derived their powers from the devil. Not only was a social stigma attached to you, but there was the very real possibility that you could lose your own life as a result of seeking help from a witch. The church and state were as quick to murder the supporters of witches as they were to murder the witches themselves.

After many generations of persecution and witch-hunts, the people slowly lost faith in the natural healers and began to believe the priests and doctors. The respect of the community passed from women, whose secrets about food meant their survival, to the doctors and priests who preached new and wonderful means of curing ailments. Along with this passage of respect from women to men went the respect of the community from food to drugs. They lost their faith in the healing powers of the plants and foods readily available to them. How could something so very basic and obtainable be better than the expensive concoctions and procedures used by the new male doctors? Those men, after all, treated the wealthy and the nobility; surely they knew best. The gradual organic process of healing was replaced by miracle drugs which promised overnight relief. We are still trapped in the world of wonder-drugs. We want whatever ails us to go away — fast. Many of us take vitamins for this reason, thinking that these pills will make us feel better, fast. We often fall into the trap of taking vitamins, while thinking that by so doing we won't have to put any effort into our food. We don't realize that the body will adapt itself to innumerable conditions, but it can only take so much abuse. Pain and other discomforts are warning signs that something isn't working right; the body is letting

us know that it can't adapt anymore. We should learn to feel and listen to our aches and pains and try to get at the root of their cause. Aspirin and modern drugs do not cure the reason for the pain, they merely mask the body's symptoms.

The patriarchy has taken away much that was woman's — we have lost control of our bodies, our psyches, our history, our intellectual growth. Presently we see wise women everywhere taking back control of their lives. In this process of regaining our spirit, we must not forget that the patriarchy has also taken away our food, and our knowledge of food. By the 20th century, woman's faith in herself had become so eroded that she believed that the food prepared by the men of industry was better than that which she could make herself. We must relearn the knolwedge of and respect for food if the process of taking back our bodies, our spirit, is to be complete.

Energy of Life

Most of our planet's energy comes from the sun. The sun's energy is converted into organic matter (through the process of photo-synthesis) and stored by plants. All of our food is ultimately derived from plants. Our food is our daily link with the energy of the universe. Food that is as near to its original plant form as possible is the food that possesses the maximum amount of food value, or universal energy. A case in point is the potato. When we cook the potato whole with its skin intact, it retains the most food value. If we alter its original plant form by peeling, we lose most of the vitamins and minerals (food value) that are a part of the skin. If we cut the potato into cubes or strips, we again lose more vitamins and minerals. If we peel, slice mechanically thin, fry to a crisp, package, preserve, and transport the potato hundreds of miles away from where it was grown, we have an almost worthless food in terms of universal energy or food value — the potato chip.

. This link between food and the energy of the universe was also realized by traditional peasant societies, where female fertility symbols (representing the life-force as universal energy) were worshipped to insure a good harvest. The connection between healthy soil, healthy crops, and healthy bodies was understood. The soil was nurtured and cared for. A balance of nutrients was maintained. They realized that the soil was depleted of nutrients after giving birth to a new crop and so they gave back to the soil what they withdrew. Careful, natural fertilization of the soil was (and is) necessary, and in this way a balance of life energy was maintained. The largest peasant society in the world today, China, with one-quarter of the world's population, has achieved the miracle of self-sufficiency by maintaining the practice of returning to the soil the nutrients, the universal energy, that the soil gives to them. China is one of the few peasant societies where hunger is not a problem. China has not committed the folly of the industrialized nations, who believed that their strength was in their industry and manufacturing. The Chinese recognized that their strength, their very life, depended upon their food base. When people are hungry they cannot work. Food is life, and a factory will not produce life.

People in industrialized, urban societies have lost touch with the soil in fact and in spirit. In our concrete, tree-less, soil-less cities, we are not in contact with the cycles of growth. We have no chance to see and help create the growth process of other forms of life — life which we help to grow so that we may ourselves live and grow. Most urban dwellers are unaware of our dependence upon the plant and animal world. In past societies plants and animals were worshipped. Almost the entire population engaged in agriculture — survival revolved around food. They were well aware of their crops, the weather, and the state of the soil. They knew where their food came from, how it was grown, processed, preserved, and cooked. They had an intimate, spiritual relationship with their food. In the United States today, less than 6% of the population is directly involved in farming. We are totally unaware of the day-to-day realities of plant growth. We think that our green beans and peas come from the Jolly Green Giant, our cereal from Kellogg's, our flour from Pillsbury, our cheese from Kraft, our milk from Safeway. Virtually all involvement with our food, except that final act of chewing and eating, is done for us, and many industrial foods are so extremely processed that we really don't even have to chew.

Women and Meat

The tape mentality of our culture extends to the treatment of our soils, of our food, of our female lives. Meat has been traditionally associated with male virility; if a man couldn't "bring home the bacon," he couldn't provide for his family. The canning and food processing industry employs mostly women, yet all of the butchers and meat packers are men. Meat is so strongly identified with the worst animal attibutes of men, that it is always a wonder to me that feminists still eat meat. But our social and cultural habits die hard. Most of us grew up as meat-eaters — in fact, we could not think of a meal without thinking of that space on our plate (often *half* the plate) which would be filled with meat. There is very little support from society for becoming a vegetarian. Hopefully, in coming to grips with our bodies and our health, we will realize that meat is NOT essential for our well-being; rather, it can be very detrimental to our health. Most third-world people are vegetarians, though not by choice. The amount of meat that they can eat is minuscule compared to us. Meat for them is a luxury, a flavoring for food, something to be eaten only during special times of the year. The staple food for the world has always been grains, legumes and vegetables, not meat.

Meat is a protein food, a fact we are told is "good." But meat is also 25-50% fat, and that ISN'T good. In the last 30 years people in the United States have doubled their consumption of all meat products, especially beef and poultry. In this same time period the numbers of people dying of heart disease and cancer has also increased tremendously. The fat found in meat is called "saturated" fat, which means that at room temperature the fat is solid. All meat and dairy products and one plant food (coconuts) contain saturated fat. In recent studies, saturated fat has been linked to heart disease and cancer of the colon. Most deaths in the United States are officially ascribed to some form of heart disease. In acutality, most deaths are due to poor eating habits; life-long habits of eating too much of the wrong things — sugar, refined grains and flours, alcohol, and saturated fat (meat). The second largest cancer killer (next to lung cancer for men and breast cancer in women) is cancer of the colon. Most of the saturated fat that we eat comes from meat. We have no need for saturated fat, but we do have a biological need for an essential fatty acid found mainly in vegetable oils, linoleic acid. Vegetable fats (oils) are called "polyunsaturated" or "mono-saturated," which means that at room temperature, the fat is liquid. We need to eat more poly-unsaturated and mono-saturated fats, because these vegetable fats have been shown to decrease the amount of cholesterol in the blood and aid in the prevention of heart disease. Safflower, corn, soy, and sesame oils are polyunsaturated; peanut and olive oils are mono-saturated. We can eliminate most of the saturated fat in our diet by simply not eating meat.

All plants contain a carbohydrate, or starch, called cellulose. Cellulose is crucial to our diet because it provides bulk or fiber. This

bulk is needed to help move our food through our intestines. Without bulk or fiber (found only in unrefined plant foods), the food takes longer to pass through our digestive tract. Meat contains absolutely no fiber, and if one eats a lot of highly refined starches (white bread and refined grains) along with a lot of meat, there is no fiber in the diet to push the food along. Food from diets low in fiber moves twice as slowly through the digestive tract than food from those diets which contain enough fiber (fresh vegetables, whole grains, fruit). The increase of colon cancer in this country is due to the fact that our diets are lacking in fiber and are high in saturated fats. Because of our low fiber/high meat diets, the carcinogenic toxins in the meat that we eat pass very slowly through the colon, thus increasing the risk of colonic cancer.

Meat contains some of the most dangerous chemicals being used in and around our food. Pesticides and herbicides accumulate in the fat cells of animals and fish, thereby leaving a very high residue of these poisons to accumulate in our fat cells, if we eat meat and fish. Animals are tranquilized, shot full of antibiotics, painkillers, and growth-stimulants. Their food is treated with preservatives and more antibiotics. All of these drugs are present in the meat that we eat even though the government is supposed to monitor the amount of drugs found in our food supply. There just aren't enough inspectors checking up on the safety of our food, and the cattlemen know this. Additionally, the "tolerance levels" set for the amount of drugs allowed to remain in our meat, are established by the meat industry itself. DES is a growth hormone used by cattlemen. It was found to produce cancer in daughters of women who took the drug during pregnancy. Recently the United States banned the use of DES, but who is going to check up to see that the ban is complied with? Processed meats (bacon, ham, "luncheon meats"), in addition to the chemicals found in the raw meat also contain large amounts of preservatives and coloring agents (so the meat won't look grey) added during processing. Of this group of additives, the carcinogenic nitrates and nitrites, BHA and BHT are the most harmful.

Over 90% of all the corn, barley, oats, and soybeans, and over 24% of all the wheat grown in this country is fed to our livestock. We import protein products (Peruvian anchovies) from third-world countries so that our chickens and livestock can get fat. We force-feed our cattle so that their meat will be marbled with fat in order to be "tender and juicy," yet most of the fat accumulates in layers outside of the muscle, where it is just trimmed off and wasted. In fact, nothing embodies our commitment to waste as well as our meat industry. Cattle do not need to eat good-quality, protein crops. They can convert the grasses and by-products that we humans can't eat, into food for themselves. Most third-world countries are forced to import their food because the huge corporations own the best farmland. The price of the food that they have to import has risen dramatically in the last ten years. In 1961 the island of Sri Lanka, formerly Ceylon, needed to sell 156 pounds of tea to buy one ton of wheat; in 1974 they needed to sell 663 pounds of tea, five times more, to buy one ton of wheat. The reason for this increase is that as the industrialized nations become wealthier, their consumption of meat products increases. Thus the grains that would have gone into the world market for third-world countries to import, are now being sent to the wealthy industrialized nations to feed their growing cattle businesses. The people of those countries of the third-world are literally competing against the industrialized nations' livestock, for food.

While on the subject of the indignities of meat, let us not forget the way in which the animals are treated. The fact that these creatures have souls, have feelings, have their own needs to remain healthy, are totally ignored. The last few months of fattening are sheer torture for the animals. They are force-fed and in a constant state of indigestion. In the slaughter house the fear, the incredible panic that they feel at the sight, sounds, and smell of their own kind dying, permeates their flesh and is then served to us for dinner. No, thank you.

Women and Sugar

Did you ever stop to think about all the women you know who have some sort of problem with their menses? Pain and cramps, headaches, backaches, aching feet and legs, depression, constipation, diarrhea — we have probably had them all at one time or another. Our menses is a constant by which we can check our health. If we are in optimum health, we will experience none of the symptoms mentioned above. If you do not know of anyone who goes through a painless menstrual period, that is an indicator of how many of us are NOT in good health. So, what does this have to do with sugar? Simply that good health is built upon the foods that we eat.

Our bodies are made up of about forty known nutrients. If we eat foods that contain all these known nutrients (whole foods), then our bodies will have what they need to grow, repair tissue and bone, and maintain our health. When we eat food that is only partly complete, because it has been refined and processed, its original plant shape disguised, and its original life energy destroyed, we are not providing ourselves with all that we need to remain healthy. The longer we eat incomplete foods, the longer our bodies will be without all of the nutrients that are known to be needed. We then fall into a state of disease; we are missing some of the necessary links to the nutrient web. There are many different diets and philosophies of food, but most can agree upon some basic *types* of food that are necessary to eat daily in order to insure that you get all of what you need. We continue to need these nutrients all our lives.

The greatest nutrient needs come at different phases of our life: when we are infants; as young children; at puberty; as teenagers; when avoiding contraception by using a pill; during pregnancy; while nursing an infant. There is also one other time in our lives when we have greater nutrient needs, and that is when we have our monthly menses. If we haven't taken in all of the necessary nutrients, this monthly elimination will offset the equilibrium our bodies have established, just enough so that we experience how many more nutrients we need than we are actually getting. At each menses we eliminate blood and other waste from our body. Each month we have a chance to grow and repair tissue, and we will upset our balance the least if we have all the necessary nutrients to make that growth and repair work possible. One of the nutrients needed in large quantity, to replace the monthly loss of blood, is iron. Women need almost double the amount of iron that men do (18 mg. per day). The average diet in the United States fails to provide women with enough iron. It is standard practice to prescribe iron supplements *automatically* to all pregnant women, the assumption being that the woman could not possibly get what she needs from her food. If we are eating white flour products, refined grains, few vegetables of little variety, few and limited variety of fruit, some meat, some eggs, some milk, some cheese, and lots of sugar (usually in the form of soft drinks, sugar in coffee or tea, candy, sweets, and alcoholic drinks), you can be certain that you are NOT getting what your body needs to maintain its health.

When sugar, which has absolutely no nutrients, is being digested, it actually pulls other nutrients away from your body because it does not have its own nutrients to aid its digestion. Not only does sugar lack nutritive value, and rob you of nutrients you need, it adds many unnecessary calories to the diet. Our bodies can handle only a limited number of calories each day (plus or minus 2000 calories a day). If most of our calories (25-40%) come from sugar, which has absolutely no nutrients, and from oils and fats (30-45%) which have a disproportionate number of calories to nutrients, then we are leaving very little caloric room for the foods which do contain the nutrients we need daily.

Take the power of food back from the food industry. There is a politics of food that clearly indicates we have got to stop eating the patriarchy's factory food, and begin once again to eat the foods that women once knew how to make. These foods were simple yet delicious because they were whole, live foods which fed and nourished. The less sugar and fat we eat, the more we open ourselves to eating foods that keep us whole.

Sugar was not a common food one-hundred, or even fifty years ago. Today it is so pervasive that we feel if something isn't "sweet," it "doesn't taste good." We know the taste of sugar so well that we have forgotten other tastes. 98% of all children in the United States today have tooth decay (think of all the money spent at the dentist), and over half of the people in the United States, aged 50 and older, have no teeth. Sugar has been proven to cause tooth decay. We eat more sugar today than ever before. Individuals in this country consume OVER two pounds a week.

Sugar is a death-gift from the patriarchy. Cut down now and eventually (any change will take time, so don't rush it, just do it) eliminate all sugar from your diet. You will see what a difference it will make in your ability to WANT to eat and enjoy a greater variety of food. You will also feel better in many ways, if not every way. One way to begin to cut down on sugar intake is not to eat any processed or refined foods. Read the label on things — the ingredients are listed on the label in order by weight; if sugar is a primary ingredient, do not buy that food. Get to the point where you don't have to buy canned or commercially manufactured food. You will eliminate most of the empty calories in your diet in this manner.

Whole foods contain all of the nutrients essential for life: proteins, carbohydrates, fats, vitamins, and minerals. When industry refines our food they usually take some of these essential nutrients away and add chemicals so that the food will have a long "shelf life." A long shelf life is more important to them than a long human life. Of the 2,000 (plus) food additives currently in use, only a fraction of them have been tested as to their safety. The safety tests that are used are often inadequate to test the full range of effects the additives may have over a long period of time. When we eat these chemicals we eat several at once (read the labels), but the tests are done for only one chemical at one time, and the test of safety is left up to the manufacturer of the additive. He gets to choose which laboratory will do his testing. Actually, the United States' public is the testing ground; we have become guinea-pigs for the chemical and food industry. As yet there is no "scientific" proof that such-and-such an additive, or combination of additives, causes cancer or mental illness or allergies; besides, who has the money to support such research — the government? No, the government has more important things to spend our money on — weaponry and space programs are two examples. Again, it is women who realize that food is EATEN and becomes a part of our lives, part of our life process. The patriarchy is too involved in selling and packaging it.

Along with the Women's Liberation Movement came a feeling among many women that they would no longer do traditional "women's things," like cooking. So, in the name of liberation, many of us have either never learned or have forgotten how to cook. However, it is crucial that we not forget what our mothers and foremothers knew about food. We must learn how to cook, because knowing how to cook means knowing how to take care of yourself. I am not against men learning how to cook, but men have traditionally not taken care of their own nutritional needs, much less someone else's. If women do not know how to take care of themselves, certainly the men won't do it for them. We are the ones who get pregnant and whose bodies become nutritionally drained during childbirth. We are the ones who go on "crash" diets to look "beautiful" or stay "fashion-model slim" like we are told, thereby destroying our health.

In the food industry (infact in all capitalist industry) profit is the primary concern. Sugar is added to almost all industry food, to get people hooked on the sweet taste. Valuable nutrients, the life-energy of food, is processed out. Women who understand that food is to be EATEN, rather than sold or transported or used as a weapon of domestic and foreign relations, are concerned with the nutritional, life-giving value of the food. It is only when we are constantly deceived and lied to by the food industry that we come to believe that their food is better than that which we could make ourselves.

Many women eat out in "fast food" places because it "saves" time and is so "easy." We should remember that the fast-food business is just another aspect of our lives which is under control of the giant corporations. Every time we stop for a McDonald's meal or something from Shakey's, or any other of a dozen high calorie/low nutrition foods, we are giving our money, our support, and our good health away to the patriarchy. No one can cook as well or as cheaply as we can. Remember that the Female Principle symbolizes LIFE. Cook your own food, nourish your body. Don't eat the dead food that patriarchy serves up consistently.

...LESSING

There is a ritual in the Craft called the "self-blessing," which comes to us from centuries of oral tradition. It has not been written down in a very long time, so we really don't know how old it is, but because of the elements involved, it feels very ancient. It is a woman's blessing upon herself, honoring her own Divine in a ritual with her "selves." This is a very powerful affirmation of self; a very private and a very personal ritual. Far from being the product of any clergy, this blessing ritual is folk-psychology, a legacy from the peasants. Peasant women in earlier times performed this ritual whenever "cleaning-out" of the inner spaces was desired. Although it is not necessary for this ritual to be done on a daily basis, it may be performed at least once a month, particularly when the moon is full, and preferably after sundown.

One very important rule is that the mind has to be cleared of all doubts and fears in the performing of this ritual. Earlier witches used to try to do this by reciting certain Christian prayers backwards, but I don't think that's really necessary. I think that when you accept a feminist consciousness, accept the political analysis, and develop a healthy amount of self-love, then you already have a new and unique perspective from which to begin. You do not have to do anything as bizarre or complicated as spells and incantations which are often included in "witchcraft" books commonly found in occult supply stores.

Begin with a ritual bath in which you immerse yourself completely. The purpose of this is to allow all the cares and anxieties you have to simply "flow" away from you. Often it enhances your psychic space at this time to visualize colors and/or indulge in fantasy.

Fantasy is a number-one tool. Fantasy is visualization of that which you want to achieve, and very often is the only thing you have to consistently depend on. Fantasy can be practiced until you are able to visualize, at will, something other than a present reality. Look at an apple. Imagine it half-eaten. Look at a woman wearing summer clothing and imagine her in winter clothes. You can practice anywhere at anytime, as long as you don't harm anyone. Soon you will be able to impose one reality onto another one. Our rituals are exercises in the visualization of change, and women are usually able to do this very well.

In your ritual bath you should place a purifying herb or a purifying oil which is derived from the herb. One of the most commonly used is the natural lemon, squeezed into the bath water. That's sort of a home-made "Van-Van" bath. "Van-Van" is the traditional name for a lemon purification oil. Witches are usually able to recognize traditional names of specific oils in order to buy what they need, but it is my contention that it's the essence of the oil that is important rather than any particular formula.

96

Have your altar prepared with everything you will be using in the ritual: Goddess-image, candles, incense, small bowl of salt, and a chalice containing half-water, half-wine. Arrange your altar in a creative manner, with a white cloth, two white candles on the two sides, and a rose or other Goddess-image in the center. Place your chalice in front.

After preparing yourself, step up to the altar and take the container of salt. Put the salt on the floor in front of your altar and stand on it. The salt here symbolizes wisdom, the Salt of the Earth, so you are standing on your own Wisdom. Contemplate the wine-water mixture in the chalice as symbolic of the Life Force. The water represents Aphrodite. Contemplate the fact that there is no organic life without water. The wine brings ecstasy and is sacred to the Goddess because it represents joy and stimulation. By mixing it with water you are also representing temperance, which is important in women's Wisdom.

Drink from your chalice or "special cup." This cup should communicate something festive to you, something special, something joyful. It should not be used for anything other than this celebrating of the relationship you have with yourself. It should be used to drink from only when you commune with the Divine.

Meditate a moment on the altar and the importance of the psychic space you are creating for yourself. Actually, when you are performing magic, it is much more beneficial if you are able to approach your altar completely naked. This is not for any sexual or erotic reason, but to stimulate and increase the energy-flow. After your bath you are clean. Your blood is pulsing quickly, you have rosy cheeks, your pores are open, and you are not likely to get cold, even naked. This way you can celebrate your ritual in "Truth," and with pleasure.

At this point in the ritual, take time to contemplate what you are going to do. You are about to bless yourself. That's a big step. Usually this blessing is done by male clergy in a patriarchal religion in our society.

Incense should be lit now to awaken the brain cells. Many of them respond to smell. The sense of smell has developed in us from earliest times, from "smelling-out" edibles to "smelling" danger. There is a very large portion of the brain which deals with that sense, though the sense of smell in the modern world is seriously stunted. So, choose an incense you feel personally attracted to. Try to choose an incense which is power-oriented, because after you bless yourself there is no turning back. You must deal with getting Power.

Light the white candles saying, "Blessed be, thou creature of fire," as each flame is born.

Between these candles is an image of the Goddess you have chosen. Objects from nature are good for this, like a new rose for example, which is the personification of Persephone. The Goddess has a few symbols which are always associated with Her because miracles happen with or around them, and the rose is such a symbol. A single rose is a lovely centerpiece; it is an altar in itself, and a very, very good working altar at that.

Take a moment to smell the incense, meditate on the candle flames and contemplate the Goddess-image.

Now dip your fingers into the chalice (the first two fingers is traditional) of wine-water and touch them to your forehead while you address the alliance of the Goddess and You. You may call out Her names or you may simply say: "Bless me, Mother, for I am your child." This is an acknowledgement of where your life comes from; an awareness of how you got here. It also makes a connection with the spirit you are addressing within yourself.

Dip your fingers again, touching your eyes and saying, "Bless my eyes to see your ways." That is a very important blessing, for it means that you can look at facts and really learn from them. You can look at your lifestyle and see if it is life-oriented or not. In other words, you clarify your vision of your selves.

Dip your fingers again, and touch your nose, saying, "Bless my nose to smell your essence." Smell is the most neglected sense we have in the human society today. As noted before, most of the brain cells can be stimulated with a certain scent, which in turn stimulates the deep mind. While your conscious mind is tending to modern life, your deep mind can work for you to straighten out your problems. To smell the Essence of the Goddess is also to be close to Nature; to connect with Her in such a way that you are able to remember the fragrance of the roses, the sea-salt smell of the ocean, or the unmistakable liberating scent of a clear evening.

Again dip your fingers, this time touching your lips and saying, "Bless my lips to speak of you." The lips are an extremely important symbol in the Craft. They represent the Word: utterance, ordinance, incarnation of Themis, Goddess of Social Consciousness. Indeed, words are revolutionary. The mouth is a tool of the revolution. The conscious manifestation of a thought is a word. Once uttered, the vibration of that word never stops but just keeps on going without end. Sound never stops. We have a very real and solemn responsibility to be conscious of what we say, because what we say is magic; it is a ritual. Words have power. Speech is how we touch each other's minds. We influence each other with words. We have to articulate change in order to achieve changes. When you bless your lips, think of all this.

Now that you have blessed your mouth and contemplated your speech, dip your two fingers into the chalice again and touch your breasts with it. Meditate on your breasts as the Source of Nourishment, on nourishment as a part of the Female Principle of the Universe, on how nourishment comes from you, how you are nourished, and how you are part of the Source that has power to give. Think of how Divine that makes you. Now say: "Bless my breasts, formed in strength and beauty."

That is a defination of the Female. A defination of Womanhood: strength and beauty combined. To be strong is to be beautiful. Weakness is not reinforced in the Craft, and no "brownie points" are ever given for being a "ding-a-ling." You must assume adulthood in the Craft. You assume responsibility. You ritualize your responsibilities in the Wicca, especially responsibilities toward your contemporaries.

Again dip your two fingers, touch your genitals and say, "Bless my genitals that bring forth life as you have brought forth the Universe." Touching the genitals and speaking of bringing forth life does not mean that all women must give birth to children. It is simply a recognition of our connection to the Source of Life, the Divine Female. The biological destiny of women, which has been used against us, is actually the basis of our Divine. Think this time about the Source of life. Know that you are part of that. Pleasure and birthing are considered sources of energy. Birthing is a manifestation of re-creation of other human beings. Pleasure is a manifestation of self-re-creation. Pleasure is worship because it replenishes the soul. The nerves like it. It's good for you. Anything that is good for you is a ritual of the Goddess, who says, "All acts of love and pleasure are my rituals." So, as you touch your genitals, contemplate all the things in your life which bring you pleasure.

Lastly dip your fingers and touch your feet saying, "Bless my feet to walk in your paths." Wherever your mind leads, your feet will soon follow, and so you must desire to make a straight path; to follow a life-orientation pattern towards yourself, toward your world, toward your people, toward everything around you. The responsibility you accept is that you are Divine, and you have Power. You are only powerless if you allow a structure to exist which makes you powerless. Once you realize that you don't have to be a slave, and you speak of it, the Goddess of Freedom is evoked.

Think about the way in which you've been conducting yourself. Stroke yourself for developing and strengthening your own interests. Stroke yourself for being surrounded by kindred spirits. Contemplate the path you want to take. Fantasize. Treat yourself to wishful thinking. It can be acted on and made "real" later. Revolution is begun as a thought-form. Then it is multiplied in other people's heads and soon after is translated into action. Everything works like that. Everything in the world is first created in an intangible way, as a thought-form, eventually becoming manifest. Thus, every thought is an act. You bless your feet because walking is very certainly an act born of your thought-forms.

After blessing your feet, stand a while and let all the feelings and thoughts blend. Allow energies to well-up in you and flow through you. When you are finished, extinguish the candles saying, "Blessed be, thou creature of fire. Thank you for your presence." Thank your Divine Selves for attending as well. You are never talking to somebody "Out There," so your voice can be kept low and soft. You do not have to shout or throw yourself into a frenzy, as some of the books on "witchcraft" suggest. Screaming what you want is a male approach. They think that if it's louder, it's better. That's not true. Very strong witches have been known to say very little to very great effect. That's part of having your mouth connected to your brain.

Each time you touch yourself in this ritual, allow the touch and the connection of blessing-to-body to carry and teach you, as you linger on that particular part of your body. The flickering candlelight is a good reminder of the need for psychic meditation and personal psychic space.

All of these steps tie in to "folk-psychology" in a direct way. Each of the processes help actualize a wish which would remain only a wish unless projected outside. However small, you will be able to realize what you want. You really "do" it through ritual; the deed is done. You have created for your "self" an alternate reality in which what you wished for actually happened. As your own Goddess you have created, in small, what you wanted.

This concept relates to one of the basic tenets all witches share: "As below, so above." If you create a small "something" here, it will have a ripple-effect of consequences. "Like" affects "like," and the small eventually affects the larger. That's why spells work. When the witch creates something through a spell, it is done.

The completed spell of self-affirmation serves as a celebration and reinforcement of the Divine within you. This is most important because too many of us have internalized our oppression. It is imperative that we change the influences working in our deep minds. Religion controls inner space; inner space controls outer space. If a woman internalizes her oppression and thinks she is inferior or unclean, then she internalizes her own "policeman." She will then act accordingly. She will not need to be policed by actual oppressors because she will have assimilated their judgements and will be able to "police" herself.

The easiest and most efficient way for a small number to oppress a large number of people is to sell them a religion. If that religion is embraced by the majority, then they will "police" themselves and act in accordance with a value-system which may actually oppress them. Once they have internalized it, they have actually lost. This is what has happened to women under patriarchy.

Self-blessing, self-affirmation rituals are a way of exorcising that patriarchal "policeman," cleansing the deep mind, and filling it with positive images of the strength and beauty of women. This is what the Goddess symbolizes — the Divine within women and all that is Female in the Universe. We MUST NOT underestimate the importance of this concept.

100

WEATHERWORK

The witch's space in society, her value and usefulness, developed out of a basic need for her ability to make rain. Rainmaking always figured prominently in the agricultural matriarchies, and shamans even today are called upon to make rain for their communities. Each country thus developed its own brand of shamanism, and all of these are valid. In Japan, when a shaman wants to make rain, she picks some flowers and then throws them away on the road, so the skies will presently open and weep. In ancient Greece, the priestesses used to make water on a bull hide in order to bring rain. Among Indians, ringing cowbells and performing certain dances to the rain-gods seems to do the trick. Dianic witches work with a circle, where power is raised and the Goddess of all organic life, the Fair Luna, Selene, Helen, Diana, The Moon, is addressed for all the healing rains.

Gather at least five (try) sisters together, and go to a parched and wild place where nobody can see you. Create the circle as usual, but when invoking the Four Corners, call the Goddess of Water and Her clouds from all directions. This is because it may not be known exactly how the Lady will accommodate the circle, and She may have to be called in from all sides.

In weather-work it is very important to remember that rain is made to fill a need. Witches do not go out practicing rain-making just to see whether they can or not.

The Goddess of All Life is apt to defy you if you try to interfere with Her works out of pride. Her real work is not dropping everything (volcanoes, earthquakes, rivers) just because one witch is summoning. Weather-work performed consciously, as a service to the community, is what the job is all about. However, you must still face and accept the possibility of failure, without sadness or getting an attitude. The Lady may have better things to do, or may feel that no rain is a better plan.

But in case of dire need of the people priestesses brought the rains down with enough regularity of success that the Goddess appears to take good notice of the people's wishes.

Understanding all this, take a bath of purification before going to the circle, adding a handful of salt to the bath water. Anoint your body with Priestess oil, sacred to the Moon Goddess. Secure a flower, preferably a white or yellow rose or lily, and place them in the middle of the circle. Take deep-sounding drums, cymbals, cowbells, and if you have cowbones with which you can make rhythm, do it. Use willow wands (willow loves the water best) rather than athalmes in this ritual, especially for drawing the sacred circle and the pentagram of protection in the air. Bring a bucketful of water into the circle, and place the flowers in it to float. Raise power by looking up at the moon and imagining a cone resting on your shoulders which reaches up to Her face. Begin a unifying hum.

Shaman (She-man), turning to the East:

> Hail to thee, Goddess of New Dawn!
> Hail to thee, powers of the East!
> Bring us your protection and blow
> Your clouds here to rain! Blessed be.

Shaman (She-man), turning to the South:

> Hail to thee, Powers of Great Fire!
> Witness our rites and blow
> Your water-laden clouds overhead!
> We need the gentle drops to heal
> Our fields and grow the
> Substance of life. Blessed be.

To the West:

> Hail to thee, great Goddess of Waters!
> Corner of the West!
> Aphrodite, Goddess of Life!
> Lift your heavy clouds,
> Your vast western waters,
> And blow them toward our lands!
> We await your rain as we await rebirth!

To the North:

> Hail to thee, Demeter!
> Whose Earth is parched in this place
> And whose daughter, Persephone,
> Is growing old before Her time.

The greens are yellow and life is thin.
Reach out your mighty brown arms
And embrace your lover, the Winds.
Squeeze from Her arms the life-giving rain we need.
So mote it be!

Now begin to dance around the bucket of water with the flowers in it. Burn Frankincense and Myrrh in your cauldron. These are favorites of Isis.

While the dance is growing in energy (first slowly, but then faster and faster as the spirit is captured, and from East to South to West to North), one of the women chants this very old rain-making rhyme from Asia. I have translated it from the Hungarian.

Kajrakan! Kajrakan! (old names for the Moon Goddess)
Blessings! Blessings! Blessings!
Give a handful of space for waters in the sky!
Give a needle-sized space in the waters of the sky!
I am the daughter of the Sheman!
I am the willow on the river banks!
My people are shouting for you!
Demeter is waiting for you!
Be the earth's navel in the sky!
Be the sky's navel in the earth!
Spirits of our Mothers, I invoke you now!
Open up the shutters of the sky!
Give a handful of opening for the rain,
Give a needle's-point opening in the sky,
Burst forth from the Mountain Mother's back!
Burst forth from the lap of the River Goddess!
Great Luna, manifest yourself!
Waters, waters, waters coming down.
Blessings! Blessings! Blessings!

While the music-making and dancing continue, pick up the bucket of water and splash each other liberally with it. It is best to do this naked, splashing water on each other's fronts and backs, shrieking and hooting and making wild. Let the flowers fall to the ground, and do not pick them up. Now dance over the wet area until you are exhausted. All fall down on the ground, still calling for the rains. Wait until the energy slows, then thank and dismiss the spirits. The rains will come.

PARTING CLOUDS – WHISTLING UP THE WINDS

Weather work, like personal work, is witches work, and parting clouds is a good way to get started practicing it. Pick a nice place outdoors and contemplate what you are going to do. If possible, you should sit with your back against a tree, since your aura is magnified when combined with the tree's energy, and the magnified waves get larger and higher all the time you connect with the tree. Sit in the Goddess-position, preferably.

Choose any cloud you want and visualize it as it separates. Work on this only as long as it feels good and you are successful. Stop before you reach a point of frustration and resentment if it does not work the first time. Just let go of it for a while, and then check later to see how it's doing. Parting clouds can make your whole day.

Another good exercise to do as long as you are outside learning weather work and there is no wind, is "whistling-up the wind." This practice is useful to bring in the clouds or cool the weather if it's too hot. You can whistle yourself, or get a little pipe of some sort, but you must whistle. Think of yourself as the wind, and do a little dance as you identify with Nature. With your hands, make pulling motions as you dance. Reach out for the wind and pull it to you while you whistle and dance.

THE STORY OF THE DANAIDS

At the water festival called Hersephoria, the true story of the lovely Danaids comes to light. This festival was held at any time the rains were needed for the people's food crops. Carefully selected Maidens (who had no death in their families that year, or whose parents both still lived) had the honor to bring in the blessing waters. Large urns with tiny holes all around on it were filled with water and Maidens carried them around the town they were serving. Of course through the holes the water sprinkled on the thirsty ground. These water nymphs were worshipped for making Argos fertile. They had their own temples and their own honoring festivals. Of course they were the daughters of Dianna, the soul of the Wild.

Their story suffered perversion at the onset of the new patriarchy. In order to discourage the further power of the Rainmaking Maidens, a new story was pinned on them. They were the daughters of Danau (masculinized form of Dianna) who were forced to take husbands. They killed their husbands on their wedding nite, and as a punishment they were given leaky urns to carry endlessly around to the wells and back. The story is transparent. The fifty Maidens represent the fifty weeks in the matriarchal year, and the function of the leaky urns was their normal ministry. Listen to their song and understand why the marriage didn't work for them.

"We, the great seed of the Holy Mother, ah me!
Grant us that we, unwed, unsubdued, from marriage of men
     may flee!"

USING DREAMS; PRACTICAL STEPS TO DREAM INTERPRETATION

By Annu

Scientific research has shown that everyone dreams every night. All dreams have meaning, and the meaning is helpful to the dreamer. The purpose here is to give the beginner a practical step-by-step guide to dream interpretation.

Materials Needed

When we want to study our dreams seriously, it is helpful to compile our own personal dream symbol dictionary. Some use a small loose-leaf notebook with alphabetical index; others prefer a card file. A spiral notebook is practical for writing the dreams down as it's flat and easier to handle, but any notebook will do. Keep a pen or pencil handy too. A pencil flashlight is good for writing at night. Improvise in any way you wish.

How To Remember Dreams

Be prepared with notebook and pencil beside the bed so dreams may be recorded immediately upon awakening. Dreams begin to fade within minutes. Eight minutes after awakening, the average person has forgotten their dreams. The use of autosuggestion prior to sleep facilitates recall. If you have difficulty remembering dreams, then just before you fall asleep, repeat to yourself three times: "I will remember my dreams when I awake in the morning." It is also helpful to write key symbols in the notebook immediately upon awakening so that dream pictures do not slip out of consciousness unrecorded. You may not have time to record the whole dream right away. If interpretation is postponed, reviewing key symbols usually aids dream recall.

How To Record Dreams

It is efficient to date the pages the night before and plan to write dreams on one side of a page, leaving the facing page free for work on dream analysis. It's best not to mix them because interpretations may change. Record the dream as fully as possible, including such details as people, setting, actions, emotions, colors, numbers and impressions. What seems to be an unimportant detail could be an important clue to the dream's meaning. Honesty is essential when recording dreams.

The following step is of utmost importance At the top of the page, briefly record important events of the day before, the main strands of thought, activities and efforts. Dreams are usually a comment on what we have been doing, thinking and meditating about recently during conscious activity. Dream content is usually limited by the conscious focus of the dreamer and information and guidance which an individual can use constructively. Rest and physical fitness affect the recall, scope, depth and clarity of dreams.

How To Interpret Dreams

Important symbols should be underlined and then listed separately and interpreted. Each symbol may have several meanings. One of them will best fit the context of the dream. When you cannot think of anything related to the symbol, you can ask yourself how you would describe this symbol to another person and record that description as a possible meaning. Sometimes simple dictionary definitions provide an answer.

Books and symbol dictionaries may also provide a take off point to interpretation if it is kept in mind that the meaning of a symbol may be different than its denotation for each of us.

106

When you find meanings that fit the dream context, it helps to record that meaning in the dream dictionary or file. You are then on your way to learning the language of symbolism.

Another approach to unlocking dream meaning is to ask the purpose of the dream as a whole. "What is the dream trying to tell me?" This may be fairly obvious even though you may not understand every symbol of the dream. Don't forget to take a second look; dreams are sometimes not as obvious in meaning as we first think they are.

When you find the meaning of one dream in one night, that meaning may be a clue to the other dreams of the same night, which often relate to different aspects of the same subject as do successive acts in a play. In order to find the meanings of the symbols, you can think back to the activities, thoughts and emotions of the previous day. The dream is frequently related in some way to yesterday's events unless, as is occasionally the case, the dream is precognitive or an ESP-type dream.

Almost always, each person, animal, house, automobile or other symbol in the dream represents an aspect of ourselves and our own personal situation. The main character in a dream is usually the dreamer.

Remembering what you did or thought about the day before, plus knowing that each symbol is an aspect of the self, helps unlock the meaning of the dream. Dreams are invented by each of us as messages from self to self. Each person is her or his own best interpreter. It is best to remember to interpret the dreamer, not just the dream, to best determine what is important in a particular dream.

An element of practicality is necessary for interpretation. A word of caution: If a dream seems to be telling you to do something you know is not constructive, you have probably misinterpreted the dream. Dreams can be helpful tools only if interpreted correctly.

How To Obtain Guidance From Dreams

Dreams can guide and help you after you have set goals and ideals for your life. Obviously, those goals and ideals need to be chosen carefully. Your choices may not coincide with those set for you by parents, mate or friends. Choices usually require serious self-examination. When the choices have been ill-chosen, your dreams will surely tell you. When wandering through life without goals, your dreams will wander right along with you.

Meditation, practiced regularly, will clear the channels to receive guidance. Working on practical application of all available advice in one's daily life is a helpful goal.

It is also helpful to go back over dreams occasionally after you are separated in time and emotion from them. Sometimes things are seen more clearly in retrospect. Symbols gain depth, and meanings become apparent. It is best to record symbol definitions as you go along day by day in the individual dream dictionary. Most dreams have meaning on several levels at once and should be interpreted accordingly. Determine the purpose of the dream.

Another aid to dream interpretation is a close friend or a group. Sometimes others know us better than we do ourselves. We may think we do not have the unused talent or characteristic that a dream says we have. Sometimes our friends know we do. A friend or group helps, not by forcing interpretations on the dreamer, but by simply asking if the dreamer thinks a symbol or dream could mean this or that. It is the dreamer's dream and, in the final analysis, she/he has the last word.

There are various types of dream imagery. First of all, there is nonsensical or meaningless imagery which occurs when the body is re-acting to it's own stresses during Non-Rapid-Eye-Movement sleep (NREM). In general, such imagery is related to problems of diet, fever, or endocrine secretions. Secondly, there is literal imagery. Much of dreaming serves the same ends as conscious thought, solving problems of outward circumstance. Usually, the literal and dramatic are woven together. A third type of dream imagery is pictured and acted out. Feet and shoes have to do with one's footing in what is being attempted. Dreams of mouth and teeth have to do with what we say, such as speech that harms others. Fourth type of imagery: personal figures. Every dream has its own personal symbols loaded with shades of displayed meaning.

Dreams are intended to change the dreamer somehow as well as to inform. A fifth type of imagery is exhibited as "archetypal" symbols from mythology and ancient history and are almost universal to humans.

Testing the Validity of Dream Interpretation

First, there is comparison within the dream record. Interpreta-tions which fit all parts of the dream together are usually right. If a theme is repeated often, it is likely that the dreamer hasn't yet gotten the point, or acted on it. If a theme shows a progression in successive dreams, the dreamer may conclude that the dream material is bieng interpreted effectively and that progress is being made on the forces within that are producing the dream. A dreamer may validate interpre-tations about the interpretations. A feeling of release from inner panic may signal a sound interpretation. A test of one's life might be how grumpy one is. Examine the quality of your relationships.

If practical daily life skills have improved, interpretations are most likely valid. One is likely to see progress made in the dreams themselves.

The Growth Conclusion Method

This is a method that allows the by-passing of analysis. The experienced user of dreams is aware that dreams can be consciously directed. This means that conflicts can be resolved by applying conscious direction to unconscious events. In a variation, what is bothering the dreamer is identified. The dreamer then directs that particular dream to come to a growth conclusion constructed by the conscious.

Dreams, in general, tailor their content to what the dreamer can effectively handle. Dreams are usually self-regulatory and self-correcting.

As you study to interpret and apply your dreams, you may wish to check out some more helpful books: *The Revelation,* published by A.R.E. (information on the seven gland centers); books by Carl G. Jung; books on numerology, color, Tarot, astrology, etc.

Information of this article has been gotten from the A.R.E. Journal, Vol. III No. 5, November, 1972. Also, thanks is given to Jim Richard who has put together an article from his personal experience and information gleaned from books and articles.

PAST LIFES

I had no idea how much money people pay to hear the stories of their past lifes until I met somebody from the scientology crowd. They used little tin cans to hold in their hands and "measure" the excitement of the person if the past life was not "clear" and for a hundred dollars a session you could squeeze the tin cans in your hands and spin stories about who you used to be. Others read past lives and blame a lot of their present problems on them. Others actually can relax you to have a journey into the old deja vu.

As a Dianic Witch living in the end of the 20th century, I am not surprised people like to spend time with themselves from some area better and more decorative than our Here and Now. Still I resist the seduction. Who knows? I could have been very familiar at home in an old Sumarian temple, being a priestess, but does that help me creating a ritual to march to with ten thousand wimmin against violence on the streets? Yes it does. But no that's not my focus, I focus on the march.

The Here and Now is our challenge, the only part in our lives where we are called upon to act as Goddess. Everything else has been done. We have the past for a reason, IT IS GONE. The Here and Now will soon become the past and while we dwelled in our fantasies we missed making our mark on the moment. The moment of birth and death are karmic dates set before entering this existence, the middle of it, the growth, the changes the richness of our experience is the reason for living.

So let nobody make you believe that we are on this earth to suffer, to toil, to put up with oppression, because then later on after we die we get to be taken care of. I even heard TV preachers say they want to come right back (after the end of the world) and they then wanted to help Jesus to make his kingdom by becoming Mayor of Hawaii. The preacher no doubt would take any lesser jobs too, but notice how the end of the world projection, and after death life included a full staffed patriarchy and its jobs, like Mayor etc, intact! Obviously the christian vision of the end of the world means further male domination of politics and TV. Woe!

This existence is most precious and important as far as we the the living are concerned. The 2 million years of development as humanoids, gave us a nice vehicle, (body) to be goddess in. We have free will, we have politically interesting times (if often painful and terrorized), we have challenge. To be Goddess means acting out your fates, participating actively in your welfare; not following a trail of tears but to devote yourself to a holistic existence. In our case as wimmin, we must work consciously to approve of ourselves, to do the best we can to turn our lifetimes into meaningful role models for the future daughters.

The religion of the Goddess glorifies the living. How much time is appropriate to spend researching our past? If there is a burning desire in your heart to go through centuries of hidden memories, and it is so compelling that you feel there is something in it for you, go ahead! If you are not intense about it, don't waste too much time , but use your resources for improving your lot in the living body you are in now.

Reincarnation theories:

Reincarnation in the different life times is like making a new bead upon a necklace. And you know how different necklaces can be. There is the necklace that features all the same matched pearls. Then there are those which have one pearl and one glass bead, some have apple seeds and some have acorns. Lifetimes can be that varied. There may be no other connection between them than the impulse to live, the thread upon which the beads are strung. Do we need to know what other beads are on the thread? Not really. If we did, Mother Nature would have arranged it, let's say, that on our 31st birthday we could recall the whole thing! Much like menstruation happens to wimmin naturally, so would the reincarnation recall. But it isn't so. Nature shields us blocks out this information so we don't get confused about the importance of our present tense. She is wise to do so.

For artists, the case is different. Those lifetimes could have information that improves their art perceptions. Writers in particular get a lot out of past lives, many interesting books are written about the subject.

A Technique to Recall Past Lives

Gather together with a leader, yes you need a leader or facilitator (you cannot recall and direct at the same time). Lie on the floor comfortably, breathing in and out with the rest, merged in chaotic meditation, which is to say no focus, no reaction; just like staring into fire.

The leader sits up, also comfortable, lights two white candles dedicated to memory. She lights incense; it should be a light one (Frankincense and Myrrh).

Leader:
I . . . (name) . . . am calling the guides to lead us back in time, come Goddess in your aspect of history, come awareness before our birthtimes, come and reveal the pictures in our minds, and not frighten us but heal.

Now the woman who is the leader starts a countback thusly:

We are all going back to a year ago this time, meditate and see what you see a year ago this time, . . .

Each time space she describes with a few events from the papers that we can all identify with. 1980 should definitely be when Mt. Helen erupted. The leader must be very sensitive to the space of going back, hopefully also skilled in hypnosis because you just have to use deeper tools than plain memory in this case. She leads you back next five years ago, ten years ago and finally to your birth . . . each time leaving enough silence to let the mind wander and recall.

After she led you back to your birthtime, there is a strong tendency to rush the process and go to Egypt or Anatolia, where the Amazons roamed, but you must flow, not race, with your soul or you loose it.

> We all go to the 19th century now . . . a time of revolution, a time
> of artistic achievements (something like that, not too much but
> not too little) . Where are you in 1890? 1880? 1870?

Lead back the years and see if any episodes come to mind. At this point
the participants are told to allow their minds to pick up whatever messages may come forth and go with a vision if they get one.

This is a long and patient process (a weekend long at least), so take
a break after each century, and let the people write down on a paper
what they experienced. Talking is forbidden now. The silence is broken
by the leader only. No food should be eaten while this going back in
time continues. Do not push too hard. It flows at one point only if you
managed to remain calm.

After the exercise is complete, the participants should take a nap.
At this time many more things might come to them. A real modern discussion should not happen until the entire process has been done, and
everybody is enriched by the experience.

Leading back process: When you have reached the last back time,
start telling the people it's time to return. You need not take step by
step, century by century, as you did backtracking. You can just say:

> We have reached the end of our journey. Now we turn back to our
> normal selves in the twentieth century. We all become as we were,
> a little smarter, a little more compassionate towards ourselves.

Again, light the incense and the candles and say thanks:

> Goddess of history, thank you for revealing us pictures of our
> older selves, we are returning now to our times. Please bless us as
> we wake. We will all feel refreshed and happy. It is done.

AUTOMATIC WRITING

Automatic writing is exciting and fun; it is also rapport with the
dead and must be taken seriously. It is not an easy means for escaping
reality; used as such, it could set you up as a target for spirits who want
to dominate you. A few simple precautions can help to create a positive
automatic writing experience.

Place some cut flowers in the center of the table or floor where
you plan to work. Purify the space by moving clockwise around the
room holding a censer or cauldron with purification incense (myrrh and

frankincense, or dragon's blood incense are fine) burning. If others are present (3 or 4 is good), unify first by humming, then evoke Sophia, Goddess of Wisdom. Draw a large pentagram on a yellow sheet of paper, place it under the flowers, and light a yellow candle. Now you are ready.

Use a yellow pad and hold a good pen lightly over the paper. Two women can hold the pen at once, but it must be comfortable. Feel for inclinations and go with them. At first, you will probably find yourself drawing circles. This is perfectly normal, and may be all you get for a while. Be patient. After a few moments of "loosening up," one of the participants should call for a spirit to enter the space and communicate. After a little more time, ask questions: "Is anyone here with us?" "What is your name?" How old are you?" "What is your message to us?" "Can we help you?" These are warm-up questions, so don't rush it. Once a spirit presence is established, the circles on the paper will be better formed and less random. However, always allow for large, loopy letters and no punctuation. Continue asking for messages. Tell the spirit to relax and to use your hand freely to communicate with you.

The communication between this reality and that one is small, and it depends on an almost perfect two-way connection. When it happens successfully, when the link falls into place and you can decipher the writing, when you gain wisdom from what the spirit has written, then automatic writing becomes an incredibly moving experience. It is something like knowing you will never be lonely again. Once a spirit has identified herself, you can call on her specifically. She may eventually come to be a close friend and companion. Always remember to respect your relationship with the spirits. Never call upon them for trite or trivial reasons, and never allow yourself to "lose yourself" in the excitement of the experience. Automatic writing should be done at New or Full Moon. During Waning Moons you should rest and meditate.

SPELL TO APPEASE THE ANGRY FATES

This spell comes from chthonic culture, meaning the culture of the Earth Religion, prominent prior to the invention of male gods. Such a culture has been examined by many historians and philosophers, and is mentioned discriptively by Engels as being a matriarchal period, when only communal property and high status for women were known. The spell is good for legal cases, dealing with justice, freeing someone from prison, or averting the "evil eye." It is particularly good to perform this ritual when you have moved into a new space or new area, in order to make friends with the earth spirits abiding there.

Build an altar, preferably low to the ground. It is important to establish this contact with the earth — our home, our Mother. Do this before the sunrise. On the altar, place three very special, beautifully crafted bowls (or cups), and crown them with flowers and the wool from a freshly-shorn ewe (failing that, buy some yarn). Fill all three bowls with a holy drink offering, gathered with your own bare hands from an everflowing, virgin fountain (unpolluted, live water).

At dawn, pour the holy drink offering slowly on the ground as you face the East. Pour the water into three streams. When the last bowl of water has been offered to the Earth Mother, refill that bowl with honey and water to use as a chalice. Drink this, offering some to the Mother as you do.

Now gather three-times-nine olive branches (if there are no olive trees in your area, branches from any sacred tree indigenous to your area will work). Lay these on the spot where the water from your offering was taken into the earth. Say your spell thoughtfully as you place the olive branches down on the ground. Commune a while with the Mother. Say, "Dear Holy Ones, with kindly hearts receive and bless." Whisper your prayer, don't raise your voice. When you have finished, say "Blessed be." Walk away from the spot without looking back. All will be well.

POSSESSION BY CHRISTIAN DEMONS AND DEVILS

In the news recently was a tragic story of a young woman who died of starvation while being "exorcized" by Christian priests. The priests were charged with murder and in their defense produced a tape recording of the young woman, speaking in a male voice and hurling obscenities at them. The possession, not the exorcism was to blame, claimed the defense. The Devil made the woman starve to death. The inquisition was satisfied.

This particular case is only one of many in which we see the emergence of a frighteningly ignorant thought-form, the relatively new idea of a "Devil." Christians, Moslems, even Krishna-people, pay a lot of attention to the concept of evil-incarnate. The Christian devil, like their god, is male. The same holds true for Moslems. Hinduism differs in that it offers female-evil in the person of Kali.

The truth is that duality-religions (something Wicca is NOT) need a "bad guy" from whom their "good guy" can save humanity. Their gods are usually warrior types, fashioned after heroes and military figures. Television reflects this duality in the good-guys-dressed-in-white-catch-the-bad-guys-dressed-in-black theme.

In essence, the patriarchal gods and devils are exact flip-sides of each other. If you have one, you get the other. Patriarchal duality: good-bad, black-white, god-devil, man-woman. There are other ways.

Kali is actually quite different in that She represents a fossilized belief in the ancient Trinity of the Goddess. Within the natural cycles of all life, Kali brought change, transformation, rebirth, and regeneration. In India today, however, Kali's shrines are virtual slaughterhouses. Kali does not "possess" people's minds. In Her cycle She has no flip-side. She is Round. The "Destruction" of Kali is the death necessary for re-birth. Future-oriented death is not evil; it is natural. It is a part of the Round.

Frankly, my cure for "devil" possessions would consist of an inten-sive program of education, prevention, and removal of all the negative and hurtful myths the person may have absorbed.

In case a witch has to attend to a person who is possessed by the Christian devil or patriarchal demons, remember that the Great Goddess is LIFE. She can be stimulated even in the most brainwashed mind.

A trinity of priestesses should first purify the room with Frank-incense and Myrrh, making invocations to the Four Corners of the Universe. Enclose the space in a protective magic circle.

Walk slowly around the room with the censer, holding it up in front of you. Pause at the EAST while the High Priestess says:

Watchtowers of the East — Ea, Astarte, Aurora, Ashtoreth — come into this house. Come through the doors, through the walls, through the ceiling and the windows. Permeate this room with your healing energy. Initiate . . . (name) . . . into your Mysteries. Blessed be!

If, at this point, a new name for the ill person comes to you, accept it and use it. Initiation means a new name, and with it comes a new identity. If no name can be found for your friend, wait until one comes. Cure could depend on whether or not the person absorbs the new name.

The other two priestesses follow each invocation with affirmations:

The Goddess is here. The Goddess has come. She is present in us. Blessed Be!

Pause at the SOUTH and say:

Watchtowers of the South, Spirits of the Fires, Sacred Fires, come permeate this place. Burn away all anti-Life energy. Let your work be done through the heart, through the blood. Come now and heal . . . (name) . . . Blessed be!

The accompanying priestesses:

The Goddess has come. The Mother is here. The healing be done.
Burn away all ills. Blessed be!

Pause at the WEST:

Watchtowers of the West! Goddess of Cleansing, of the Waters of
Life. Come and wash away all ills. Equalize as only the Waters
can. Permeate this place. Flow through . . .(name) . . . Work
through the muscles, through the fluids, blend in the blood. In,
in, comes the good! Out, out goes the ill! Blessed be!

The two other priestesses say:

The Goddess has come. Welcome! The Goddess of Love is here.
Welcome! She washes away the ignorance like rain. So welcome!
Blessed be!

Finally, pause at the NORTH and say:

Watchtowers of the North. Great Earth Mother whose destination
is the darkest of space. Earth-Mother, Earth-Daughter! Make a new
manifestation of . . . (name)'s . . . thoughts. Bind the ills with your
assured hand and take them to the underworld. There lock them up
under seven keys, and seven-headed serpents of Sacred Duties will
keep them there for seven years, only to release them into the VOID.
Blessed be!

All priestesses chant:

The Goddess is present. The Goddess is here. The Goddess is blessing all who here participate. She blesses . . . (name of individual
priestess) . . ., who is fair and strong; She blesses . . . (name of other
priestess) . . ., who is valiant and loving; She blesses . . . (name third
priestess). . ., who is nurturing and generous. Blessed be!

This may be chanted over and over for strength and blessing.
Turn inward and hum to raise inner power. Holding a cup of clear
water, mixed half-and-half with honey, sprinkle it all over the room and
the ill person. This is the Mother's Holy Water. Have everyone drink of it
if possible, but if not, priestesses drink it for good luck.

Invocation of High Priestess:

Harken to me, Old Mother! You who preceded all the gods! Astarte,
Ishtar, Ashtoreth, Lilith, Havla! Come and aid . . . (name) . . . to

116

find the Peace in Thee! Out, out bad thought, imaginary devil, entity of ill-fortune! Come in, come in, Mother of Cure, Mother of Love, Blissful Mother. Blessed Be!

The trinity of priestesses should develop a rhythmical musical tune, using a bell, flute, cymbals, even sticks. The rhythm must be kept together and the invocation chanted over and over. You may change the mantra as you wish, but always keep the emphasis on the Mother-Goddess aspect. Also, tones of "E" are very healing, and might be useful. If you can blow or hum an "E," do so. Don't expect an immediate cure. The mind became ill over a long period of time, subjected to incredibly bad mythology. It may take several times of hearing about the Goddess before the woman is able to see Her, to feel Her, and to have Her reawakened within.

When you notice that the person is calming down (even the toughest cases have "rest periods"), try to give her an acupressure massage. Follow this with a scrubbing, using sponges in lukewarm water, then anoint the body with Priestess oil or a rose-scent, and give a cup of Valerian tea for sleep. Make a circle of salt around the bed where the person lies, and place large pentagrams overhead or underneath the bed. Keep fresh-cut flowers at the bedside for guiding spirits.

If, after receiving such loving care, the ill person is still unresponsive the next morning, bring a big brass horn (the loudest you can find) and blow it into the room where the "possessed" person is. Expose the body to sound-vibrations so strong that the thought-form can undergo change.

Each time a "repeat" performance is needed, first blow the horn as loudly as possible. Repeat purification of the room and continue chanting ancient imagery of the Goddess into the room. Use slide projectors, musical instruments, everything.

Repeat this treatment FIVE times (once for each point of the Pentagram) but no more. If it hasn't worked after the fifth time, save your energies for yourselves and don't absorb any more of the sad madness that comes from an overdose of Christianity. Even witches have their limits.

THE SACRED SONS

Throughout the evolution of Goddess-worship there has been one extraordinary feature setting us apart from other religions — we are Inclusive. This inclusivity is inherent in a religion which reveres the mother rather than the father. A superficial scrutiny might lead one to believe this is simply a matter of opposites. However, upon examination we rediscover the major fact of the miracle which is birth: it is the Mother who carries the children. Male and female in the Mother's womb, male and female in Her religion as well.

There are only two kinds of people in the world: the mothers and their children. Mothers can give life to each other as well as to the men, who are not able to do the same for the mothers. This constitutes a dependency upon the Female Life-Force for life renewed, and was accepted naturally by our ancient forbears as a sacred gift of the Goddess. In patriarchal times this sacred gift was turned against the women, and used to force them to give up roles of independence and power.

All male-god worshipping religions which have no life-force represented in the form of the Female Principle of the Universe, end up being exclusive. They become, essentially, male, homosocial edifices without the redeeming quality of nurturing, maternal love.

Jehovah is an archtype. He is jealous and possessive, and orders the wholesale slaughter of all those who worship other gods. He is nothing more, nor less perhaps, than a warrior. That is not a religion. That is militancy incorporated into moral law by force, not as a result of the inherent, collective feelings of those whose lives are controlled by it. Only the Mother knows how to include, inherently; Her male children must exercise conscious (religious) efforts to do so.

Today in the Craft, male witches are often referred to as "warlocks." This word literally means, "traitor." As such it is unacceptable. Our sons, our Sacred Children, were not raised as traitors, but as lovers of life, lovers of women, brothers or lovers to each other, helpers of the Goddess in the most essential skill of nurturing. Sons of the mothers in Goddess-worship became Kouretes, members of the Goddess-serving priesthood.

The word "Kouretes" actually means "adult male," or "sons of Cronos." Cronos was an old god, consort to the Goddess, Rhea. Even in the Old Times it was Rhea who had to protect newborns from the wrath of Cronos, who would eat the young if left to himself. This mythology symbolized a very real danger — if nurturance were left solely to men, without the civilizing influence of the Goddess, they would destroy each other and their sons as well. Example in today's society, men made enough bad decisions to destroy life on our planet. Kouretes were sons saved by the Goddess, becoming Her helpers to save the rest. They, as protectors and teachers of the young, constitute the Sacred Priesthood of the Mother Goddess.

Hymn of the Kouretes

This ritual poetry was left to us on slabs of stone, found in the Minoan strata of the Birth Cave of Dikte, in Crete. Although incomplete, from it we can receive an impression of the sacred priesthood of Rhea. This is not written to the Olympian Zeus, as some would have us believe, for Zeus had not been invented yet. This hymn celebrates the Kouros, the Kronian — Sacred Child of the Goddess.

Chant:
Io, Kouros, most great, I give Thee hail! Kronian, Lord of all that is wet and gleaming, Thou art come at the head of Thy Daimones to Dikte for the year. Oh, march and rejoice in the dance and the song!
That we make to Thee with harps and pipes mingled together, and sing as we come to stand at Thy well-fenced altar.

Io, Kouros, most great, etc . . .
For here the shielded Nurturers took Thee, a child immortal, away from Rhea, and with noise of beating feet hid Thee away.

Io, Kouros, most great, etc . . .
And the Horai began to be fruitful, year by year, and Dikte to possess mankind, and all wild living things were held about by Wealth-Loving Peace.

Io, Kouros, most great, etc. . . .
To us also leap for full jars, and leap for fleecy flocks, and leap for fields of fruit and for hives to bring increase.

Io, Kouros, most great, etc . . . .
Leap for our cities and leap for our sea-borne ships, and leap for our young citizens, and for goodly Themis!

Kouros with child by Masika

Io, Kouros, most great, etc . . . .

This hymn of the Kouretes begins with the invocation of the god, who is given various titles and instructions as to how and where to come. The Kouretes who are performing this invocation are the matriarchal witches. They are not talking to an Olympian god, nor are they "petitioning" a "Father." Rather, they are commanding spirits to appear! This is internalized to the point where, by doing the commanding, they activate this spirit because they ARE the spirit. Judeo-Christians, by comparison, dare not claim they are gods in and of themselves, but place "Him" as Spirit-Creator "out there" somewhere who will save them rather than within.

The concept of a Sacred Son, held dear in both religions, is here discussed from a Mother's point of view. This is Kouretes, "Young-man-just-come-to-maturity," "The greatest of Youth." This is the independent Male Principle, no longer the babe-in-arms often found (along with the Great Mother) in religious symbology. This Kouretes is a role model for matriarchal manhood.

In the hymn, the Kouretes as high officials are always attended by Daimones — attendants, escorts. These were attached only to matrilinear male gods, never to the Olympians who overturned them. This is a feature which changes during patriarchal times, because it is a very pagan concept of religious impulse, originating in Goddess-worship. Patriarchal male gods, Zeus and Jehovah, do not have attendants, although Jesus does. Had Jesus been a real Kouretes, he would have had thirteen female Meneads (Holy Women) in attendance, instead of twelve men.

The Kouretes themselves are escorts and attendants, as we see in an account by Strabo:

> These attendants are Kouretes. They are certain young men who perform armed movements accompanied by dancing.

This would lead us to conclude that those forms of folk-dance in which arms are used (sword-dancing, shield-danding, and even the great Russian leaping dances) are living legacies of the culture of the Kouretes.

As their theme, Kouretes act out the protection of the young as their sacred duty to Rhea, Mother Goddess. However, with the forced advocacy of patriarchy upon them, their theme stories had to change accordingly (hence, the "Birth of Zeus," "Birth of Dionysus," or "Zagreus.").

Rhea (The Flow), the Universal Mother, is in labor. She attempts to conceal this fact from Cronos, because he eats his children out of jealousy of his power and his access to Rhea. Rhea seeks Her Kouretes for help, and they clank their protective armor loudly over Her, successfully concealing Her cries. As soon as Rhea delivers Her Baby, she turns it over to the Kouretes for further protection. What an obvious, clear ritual for men's maturity!

Elsewhere, other features are attached to this ritual. In one instance, the Titans come with white-chalked faces to take away the Child and destroy him. They succeed in this, the Child dying or becoming a Titan himself. Later, the Kouretes, with the help of the Goddess Rhea, bring the Child back to life, and the whole story repeats. The birth-death-rebirth cycle is thus ritualized.

The story of the male principle in Nature is pretty much the same. Here the Goddess gives birth to a son who grows to manhood and becomes Her lover. He then impregnates Her and dies at the end of the year, only to be reborn of Her again the next Spring. This weaving in and out of the circle of rebirth is symbolized with the Kouretes, where the nurturing aspect of the human male is made sacred.

Because the Kouretes claimed specialized religious function, that of fertilizing the Goddess-incarnate, they were called upon to serve as Her orgiastic priests. This meant meeting with the ritual priestesses during the appropriate seasons (Spring-Midsummer, September) and mating with them in the freshly furrowed fields belonging to the community.

As Divine Lovers and Sacred Sons, as participants and co-actors with the Great Goddess in Her circle of rebirth, the Kouretes were also of practical service as medicine men, seers, metallurgical craftsmen, inventors, builders, bee-keepers, and shield-makers. As medicine men, they never handled altar offerings, but dealt mainly with the spiritual/physical growth of the community's male population. They even presided over the births of community infants, assuring them safe entrance into the world, serving as nourishers and teachers/midwives as well. They lived with each other, worshipped Pan, and considered themselves sons and lovers of the Goddess. They were the initiators of heroes, the magical men of the community. However, at their most Divine, Kouretes were always priests of the Life-Force, performers of initiations and practitioners of nurturance. Clearly, they were magicians, adept in their craft.

Themes of the Kouretes repeat: Mother-saving-Son. Often the Son was represented by a stone, thrown from heaven between the thunder and lightning. This stone was a Holy of Holies, and was used in certain rituals to purify new initiates. The image of this thunder is the image of initiation. The sound of the thunder is a magical vibration of

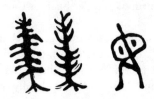

awesome power, associated with the Mountain Goddesses: Kybele, Rhea, Bendis, Kotys. The initiation by thunder of the Kouretes indicates they became members of fraternities dedicated to the continuing worship of Rhea.

The symbols of the Kouretes include: the sacred cup, in which herbs were brewed for curing; the shield of protection; the thundering sounds made with instruments for a religious purification from fear through the energy of sound.

There were stages in between the sacred priesthoods of the Goddess and the patriarchal "priesthoods" to come. The Kouretes did not die quickly or easily. First, they changed all the names, and the Sacred Child became Dionysus. Thus it was that the ecstasy so essential to the Kouretes and all such religious priesthoods could survive into the grim patriarchal periods, where the war-like lifestyle led, predictably, to the practice of a scarcity-consciousness, poverty ridden society.

In a way, the cults of Dionysus were heavily interwoven with both mythological worlds — matriarchal elements stirred the soul of the times, even though the messages were consistently, conscientiously, and forcibly suppressed. Dionysus became a hit in the all-new pantheon of powers. As a hermaphrodite, Dionysus could even be admitted into some circles dominated by Dianics. His attendants were the Satyrs (Priests of Pan) and Kouretes. Dionysus kept matriarchal company.

During this same period, the Dianic priestesses were finding it necessary to become "attendants" to Dionysus, in name, so that they could continue to practice, in modified form, such traditional rituals as dancing on the mountaintops. Worship was so much a part of the lifestyle, so permeated every moment, that the total reality was essentially controlled by it. What we currently recognize as "culture" originated from religious instincts — from worship — and continues to control our lives.

Another stage through which the Kouretes (korybantes) passed was becoming "Bacchi." As counterparts of the Bacchanalians, they recede more and more into secret fraternities, usually living together in the seclusion of the mountains.

The birth-theme so prominently featured in Kouretes' ceremonies, was the first to be co-opted by the male god Zeus, who declares, "Come, O Dithyrambos, enter this, my male womb." This obvious attempt to transform the initiation rites into rituals of male loyalty to each other (to the exclusion of the Female Principle of the Universe) failed miserably. True priests hid away in the wild, rather than change their matriarchal worship of Mother and Child.

There in one pure stream
My days have run, the servant I

Initiate of Idaen Jove
Where midnight Zagreus roves, I rove
I have endured his thunder cry

Fulfilled his red and bleeding feasts
Held the Great Mother's mountain flame
Enhallowed I and named by name
A Bacchos of the mailed priests

Robed in pure white I have borne me clean
From men's pained birth and coffined clay
And exiled from my lips always
Touch of all meat where life has been.

Invocation to the Kouretes

Come O Dithyrambos, Bacchos, come . . .
Bromios, come, and coming with thee bring
Holy hours of thy own holy spring.
Evoe, Bacchus! Hail, Paen, Hail!
Whom in sacred Thebes, the Mother fair
She thy one once Zeus to bear.
All the stars danced for joy
Mirth of mortals hailed thee, Bacchus, at thy birth!

The Male Principle is reborn from the Mother into new life, in the tradition of the Kouretes. This is a birth-song, celebrating the Mother and Her full-grown Child. The Korybantes lead the chariot of the Goddess and this man-Child across the heavens (this is the Horned Selene and Her Son). The Satyrs, brothers to Kouretes, performed the Goddess revelries as well, as fertility aspects of Nature. The Dithyrambs brought in the aspect of the sacred Bull, and maintained into bitter patrarichy the Son of the Goddess as the Sacred Bull, Male Principle of the Universe. It was the custom of the Dithyrambs to lead young men (the Sons) through town with a live, festively garlanded bull. All these acts were culturally diverse, yet focused on the same sacred image — that of Mother and Child.

In springtime, O Dionysus
To Thy holy temple come
To Elis with Thy Graces
Rushing with Thy Bull foot come
Noble Bull, Noble Bull!

Dionysus is a god of the people. An intruder into Hellenism, he represents the early religious instincts, now revived. He is a gentle New Year God, who loves wine, women, men and the dance. His worshippers were a very distinguished people of the mountains (Thrace, for the most part), not easily conquered. The Satyrs, traditionally worshippers of a Nature-god, were the attendants of Dionysus. It is only later, in the patrairchal Greek mythology, that Satyrs become horse-men, beings to be feared "because they rape women."

The Greeks were very quick with mythological justifications for their own hatred and prejudice against the conquered people of the Old Order. As happens in   cultural wars, the conquered people were told to reject all that was natural and familiar to them, and to adopt the "new" ways and religion. They were made to feel evil, dangerous, ugly, lacking breeding, but in possession of superior (unnatural) sexual passion and prowess. They were forced to deny their religion, and taught to fear that which was once beloved. Satyrs were represented as fearsome in order to prevent the instant alignment of women's sympathies with the Nature religions. It didn't work. Dionysus was recognized by women as the brilliant Son of the Mother, and the women attached themselves readily to his worship, taking all manner of unheard of privileges as the "Mad" Meneads.

The women who followed the gentle, fun-loving, nature-god, Dionysus, were not, strictly speaking, the counterparts of Satyrs, since the latter implies a strict genetic code — Thracian Mountain Men. Meneads were neighborhood priestesses, whose task it was to foster good luck in the community, and to officiate at community events. Meneads were the women who altered their consciousness in their nature-worshipping rituals. The resultant Sacred Madness, achieved not necessarily with wine, but with "Amanita Muscaria," fermented mare's milk, ivy, laurel leaves, peyote, etc., was affected to commune with Nature, to see Her secrets and be one with Her. Other names for these "mad" priestesses were: Mimallones, Klodones, Bassadirs, Thyiads, Potniades, names attached as well to the Goddesses worshipped in religious ecstasy. Artemis is thus addressed: "Menead, Thyiad, Phoibad, Lyssad; Mad One, Rushing One, Inspired One, Raging One."

Patriarchs found it difficult, indeed, to digest the "excesses" of these women, to tolerate their freedom to rave and go out at night. For the most part they allowed it only because of the threat of magical and powerful retribution if any man interfered with Women's Mysteries. One legend tells of how Penteus, ruler of an entire kingship, was literally torn apart by his own mother and sisters, because he violated the sacredness of the women's worship. This served well in the culture, to remind the new patriarchs that to pry into women's affairs always angers the Female Principle, causing Her to turn into Her Death-aspect, regardless of the rank or status of the offender.

125

Plutarch relates a story he heard from Klea, a High Priestess of
Delphi. There was a definite religious war against the nature-religions,
and the tyrants had taken sacred Delphi. Attendants of Dionysus, the
Meneads, wandered into the city following their revels, not knowing the
city was in enemy hands. They went to the temple as usual to rest and
sleep. Still under the influence of their ritual, and unaware of danger,
the Meneads slept, while the women of the city formed a circle of protection around them. In silence, the women of the circle waited until the
Meneads woke, then attended to their needs and guided them stealthily
out of the city to escape detection by the soldiers and patriarchs. What
a testimony this is to women's solidarity and women's religion.

Salii

Just as the Kouretes served Rhea with their shields, so did the initiates of the Salii serve their Goddess, Themis. Tradition called for initiates into the Salii to leap a ritual fire and to roll flaming wheels down
mountainsides. The priestesses of Themis would attend to each boy by
anointing his five points, thus assuring him of immortality. Then he was
presented with his toga, shield, and weapon, and received into the frater-
nity of the Salii. These rites were held at a cross-roads, sacred to Hecate.
Rites of passage were held in the sacred temples of Hecate, because of
Her importance as a Goddess of Transformation.

The Salii were actually considered aspects of the sun, sun-priests
serving the Triple Moon Goddess. Salii priesthoods performed their
rituals during the month of March because although the Romans devoted
this month to Mars, the time was earlier and more traditionally held to
be the month for the Rite of Passage for Boys. It was on the 17th of
March that Roman boys assumed the ritual toga according to much
more ancient traditions than Hellenism.

On the 14th of March there was a festival known as the Mamuralia,
followed by the festival of Anna Perenna the next day. This is the time
of year when the cycle of seasons is at the point of completion and continuation (Vernal Equinox, March 21st). During the festival of Mamuralia, an old man of the community would dress in goat skins and be led
through the town while members of the community ritualisitcally purified him with white rods, symbolically driving him from the city. This
signified an exorcism of the past, communally, and the opening up,
psychically and physically, of the new. As soon as the Old Year had
been thusly expelled, the New Year God was introduced, and everyone
rejoiced, wishing each other a healthy and happy new year.

More traditionally, this Old Year was a woman rather than a man.
Her name was Anna, and she would pass herself off as a young bride in
order to marry the New Year God. She is, like the Male Principle, representative of both the old and the new. In any case, there was much

merry-making during these festivities surrounding Nature's "Holy Marriage."

Sons and Lovers

The Son and Lover of the Goddess bears thousands of names, very much like his Mother and Bride. He is called: Dionysus, Bacchos, Iacchos, Bassareus, Euios, Zagreus, Thyoneus, Braites, Lenaios, Eleutherus, Bromios, Pan, The Horned One. These names evolved from religious cries into proper names.

Today we associate the name Dionysus with the wine-god, but the other names point to a more distant past, that of the Earth-born Demetrius, son of Demeter. The intoxicant of which he is made Lord is one of barley, oats and wheat, rather than grapes, which were used much later. He is earth-born rather than sky-born, and he is of the Mother rather than the late-comer father. The name, "Braites," here is of great importance, since it means "grain prepared for the making of the beer braisyum," a kind of heady mead, drunk in worship of the Earth. To degrade this ancient earth-god, the Sacred Son, into a god of drunkeness from whatever alcoholic beverage is to discount the Force as manifest in the Male Principle of the Universe.

> Appear, appear, whatso thy shape or name
> O Mountain Bull, Snake of the Hundred Heads
> Lion of burning flame!
> O God, O Beast, O Mystery, come!

The Male Principle, examined far enough back into antiquity, reveals itself as the "lord of all that is wet and gleaming," and when invoked by the ancient priestesses, emerges out of the Ocean as the Sacred Bull. This basic interpretation is somewhat complicated by the fact that the Mother is the Waters, and the Moon Goddess governs all that is wet and gleaming. She it is who regulates the weather, and causes the Ocean to heave with tidal ebb and flow.

The image of the Bull echoes the crescent horns of the Moon, and male and female worshippers often wore horns during rituals, in honor of this connection — a symbol of the origin of the Moon Goddess and Her Son. The image of the same Bull, as representative of the ancient Goddess religions, is clearly discussed in the Bible, when Moses finds the people making a "golden calf" and dancing around it. Thus we see that it was the Old Religion which he was trying so hard to defeat, in order to bring in the complete monotheistic worship of the "Father."

The essence of the male god is his transformation. He is born of Semele, the Earth, Moon, and Water Triad, and as a child is worshipped by his mother. In this new-born nature, he is also worshipped by priest-esses of the Goddess. (Does it remind you of Xmas?) Through many names he grows to Manhood, and fertilizes the Mother (who remains eternally Virgin). When he gets old he is driven out, or ritualistically torn asunder, and recycled back into the Life-Force, out of which he rises again every Spring as the Beloved Child. This is the magic of rebirth. The ecstasy of life is the form of worship of this very ancient Son.

> O glad, glad on the Mountains
> To swoon in the race outworn
> When the Holy fawn skin clings
> And all else sweeps away
> To the joy of the quick red fountains
> The blood of the hill goat torn
> The glory of the wild beast ravenings
> Where the hilltop catches the day
> To the Phrygian, Lydian mountains
> 'Tis Bromius, leads the way!

THE SPELL TO THE FORCE

Self Dedication for Young Men

Time: New Moon
Take the white candle and carve your name on it with something sharp, a rose thorn is traditional, but a clean nail, or personal pen will do. Take some aluminum foil and make a safe place on it for the white candle and the blessing incense. Pick a lovely flower that you see the force manifest in, and place it in the middle, representing the force.

Now anoint your candle with Protection oil, moving your hands always upward from the middle and not forgetting to anoint the two ends as well. Light blessing incense on the charcoal and when the air is filled with the smell and your mind cleared from fear say:

> Appear, appear, whatso your shape or name
> Oh mountain bull snake of hundred heads!
> Lion of the Burning Flame! Oh force, Pan, beast, mystery come!"

Light your white candle now saying:

Blessed be thou creature of fire!

Watch the flames a while then say:
    Happy am I, on the weary sea
    Who has fled the tempest and won haven.
    Happy whoso has risen free
    Above his striving! Happy I, with the mothers blessings!

Take oil and anoint your forehead:

    Blessed is my mind to think of life;

Anoint your lips: Blessed my lips to speak of life!
Anoint your breast: Blessed be my breast formed in strength and beauty!
Anoint your genital area: Blessed are my genitals, to stimulate life!
Anoint your feet: Blessed are my feet to walk in your path!
    When you have performed this, let the candle finish all the way down; you can burn more incense if you like, but you can save it for other spells. Go home, it is done. Now you are a Kouretes.
    It is best to perform this in the woods or outside if you can wrestle some privacy for yourself.

ACCEPTANCE OF MANHOOD
    This ritual is based on the research of Jane Harrison.

    Enter the temple purified. The teacher guide, Kouretes or Bacchoi, anoints the young man's forehead with gypsum and pitch, erasing the past, and making them pure souls again. As the men enter from the corner of the South, the direction of passions and summertime of life, they are dressed in armour, wearing shields of leather or actual metals. Bronze shields are traditional. Upon the shields are the symbols of Kouretes: the snake of rebirth, the Gorgon head to frighten away evil spirits, and inscriptions of power. In other cases, the family seal may be drawn upon the shield.
    The Kouretes priests invoke the four corners of the universe with their athalmes pointed toward the appropriate watchtower. In the corner of the North, Rhea, the Great Mother, is seated dressed in rich, russet robes. She holds a newborn baby, which can be either male or female. It will be the baby's initiation as well, as the magical wealth is bestowed upon the earth through the Goddess's womb.
    The Kouretes guide says, pointing to the East:

Hail to thee, powers of the East! All Wise Eagle, Great Ruler of Tempest, be present, we pray thee, and guard this circle from all perils approaching from the East. Universal Soul, Force of all beginnings, bless this circle here with your powers of protection!

The Kouretes, pointing his athalme to the South, says:

Hail to thee, powers of the South! Mighty Lion, fiery one, passionate one, come bless this circle from all peril approaching from the South! Bless the sons who are gathered here to initiate the Kouretes!

The Kouretes says, to the West:

Hail to thee, powers of the West! Mighty Serpent, ruler of the Deep! Guardian of the bitter sea, come and protect us from all peril approaching from the West! Give us your blessings and knowledge as thy gift!

The Kouretes says, to the North:

Hail to thee, powers of the North! Black Bull, Mighty Horned One! Ruler of the Mountains and the Valleys, and all that lies beneath them! Protect us from all peril approaching from the North! Bless us with your strength, that all of us will grow!

When they are finished, they face the High Priestess, who stands up, acknowledging their salutes, holding the child aloft with both hands, she addresses them:

The Goddess Demeter welcomes her sons . . . lead in now the Protectors of life . . .

The Kouretes of the North says:

Demeter brought forth Pluto, and kindly was the birth of him whose way is on the sea and all over the earth. Happy, happy is the mortal who thus meets him as he goes. For his hands are full of blessings, and his treasure overflows.

The Kouretes approaches the child, placing barley and wheat at the Goddess's feet in sprinkles, and thrown at the sky as feeding the birds. The Kouretes from the South says:

But the child was hunted much too soon. Angry flew the news that Demeter's son will one day inherit the bountiful earth, and the new

130

Gods grabbed for him and tried to cause him harm. They searched
for him under every bush, saying: 'Baby, baby, don't cry.'

The Kouretes act out this scene. They encircle the Goddess, holding their shields aloft. The Goddess approaches each corner with the baby,
hiding him under her clothing. She yells: "NO!" to each corner as the
appropriate Kouretes try to get the child away from her.

To accompany this, one should start playing the drums, and the
cymbals, and the Kouretes of the watchtowers should get into role-playing
the "meany". They should shout things like: "Give me the child, and I
will eat it right away!", or "Give me the child, and I will send it to war!",
or "Give me the child, and I will make it toil, and toil, and toil!", or
"Give me the child, and I will make it sick with poisons!"

After one such round, the Goddess Demeter returns to her throne,
and calls on the powers to help:

Come, oh Dithyramb, flowers of me, come, my children, come!
Come, oh Kouretes, come, oh Bacchoi, come, Bromios, come. And
coming with thee, bring the holy hours of the holy spring!

The new Kouretes take the child gently from Demeter, saying:

Demeter, Earth Mother, all life originates from thee, Semele, gift
giver, bringer up of wealth and kin. We protect thee from malice,
and destruction of mind and body. The scared child is well with us.
We thunder our shields above!

They place the child on the ground, on a piece of silk, and begin the
dance which is like a wardance, imitating the defense they would put up if
any danger approached. Here imagination can reign. Sword dances of
ethnic origin, wand dances, and leaps over the child, and each other.
While so occupied, the older Kouretes are placing toys into the child's
reach: the cone for fertility, the rhombos (or Bull-Roarer) to invoke the
rain, and the golden apples of Aphrodite for health and happiness.

The young Kouretes are preoccupied until it is too late. The old
ones have taken the child and mimicked tearing him limb from limb.

To demonstrate this, the child gets smeared with white gypsum
and pitch, like the grown-ups, and Demeter receives him again, and hides
him under the silk. She says:

The most important shortcoming of sons is hubris, excessive pride.
Vigilance must be where there was myrth alone.

The new Kouretes says:

We hear you, Holy Mother!

Demeter says:

> An important thing to remember is that rebirth comes through
> understanding of the heart.

The new Kouretes says:

> We pledge ourselves to you, Holy Mother!

K: To be a Kouretes you must treasure life and the carriers of life,
women.

Youth: I searched my heart. I pledge to life and the carriers of life,
women.

K: To be a Kouretes you must cooperate with your brothers. Pan is
not violent. Pan is grace, songs, and creativity.

The rhombos is now twirled, and the drums now drum, and the
silk is removed, and the child is whole again! The Kouretes now lift the
child on their shields, and sing the ancient song of spring:

> Io, Kouros, Most Great, I give thee hail! Kronios Lord of all that is
> wet and gleeming, thou art come at the head of your sacred priests!
> To . . . (fill in the place where the ceremony is taking place, i.e.
> New York, Los Angeles) . . . for a year and a day, oh march and
> rejoice in the dance and song that we make to thee with harps and
> pipes mingled together, and sing as we come to a stand at your well-
> fenced altar. For here the shielded Nurturers took thee, a child im-
> mortal, from Rhea, and with noise and beating feet, hid thee away.
> Death powers found thee, and lured you away, and tore you
> limb from limb with your mother's body bedecked in pain, until you
> were all over the earth. But she of eternal force, made you whole
> again by the dawn of all dawns.
> And vigilance is bidden to us now,
> And love is bidden to us now,
> And honor is bidden to us now.
> And the Horai began to be fruitful year by year, and Dike to possess
> mankind, and all wild, living things were held about by wealth-
> loving peace!
> To us, leap for full jars, and leap for fleecy flocks, and leap for
> fields of fruit, and for hives, bring increase! Leap for our cities, and
> leap for our seaborn ships, and leap for our young citizens, and for
> goodly Themis, justice for all!

After this ritual ends, the Kouretes kiss the Goddess on the cheeks, and she kisses them back. The four elders thank the spirits for participating with the rite, and sound the gong. The last words are from Demeter. She says:

> I know you now as children no more, the Nurturers are sacred, effective, and beloved by the gods.

ACCEPTANCE OF MATRIARCHAL MANHOOD.

Modern.

More often then not you don't have a temple for the Goddess in your friendly neighborhood. So what to do? There is a mother and son, and they need a bonding, on a new level, as young man and mother. This relationship is the basis of our society. If this is a positive experience, less men would hate women. Today, all puberty rituals are done by men for men, without women being invited to it. They perform a "separation from the mother ritual," not the young man pledge as a responsible adult in creation and protection of life. They misunderstand the acceptance of manhood, as if it was enough to reject your origins to be a man. Manhood means acceptance of responsibility for Life. This pact has to be done with a woman who represents the Force of Life. Cutting women out of manhood rituals is like presenting the apples without ever honoring the tree who brought them forth. The tree and the apple forever have a deep connection of continuity. In matriarchal rituals this is rememberd again.

Time: In March sometime when there is a new moon.
Place: Indoors or outdoors. Since there is honoring feast connected
            with it, use your common sense and you will know where.
Celebrants: Mother and her son, general family and friends and affinity
            group, tribe.

The group forms a circle and harmonizes with a deep humming, without straining, just like a beehive. Then the mother picks up her incense

133

burner and goes around in the circle from the inside, smiling, welcoming the friends assembled; she has an opportunity to purify everybody with the fire and air and earth mixture in the burner, as she lets the smoke enfold them. She puts down the censer. Everybody pays attention to her.

Mother of the child:
>We are gathered together here today in the name of Life. I'd like to present my son . . . (name) . . . to the community. He is 13 (12 to 40 actually; Kouros means flower of youth, some people hold up better than others). He has grown into a fine young man. (Mother can have a little speech here if she likes, something about how she feels about the Goddess, her child, Life in general, etc.)
>
>Then an older man (father, brother, etc.), acting as Kouros would step out and call the name of the young man. He steps forward facing him.

Kouros:
>Are you prepared to accept manhood, and what it means in life?

Youth:
>Yes, I searched my heart. The child that I was is distant to me now. A new being is emerging from the child that I was.

Kouros:
>Do you know the meaning of that emerging? It is the natural voice of Pan, the male principle of the Universe.

>A group of other youth come, and together, the youth joins them, and they read the invocation to the Kouretes. The youth and the group answering each other.

Kouros:
>To be a Kouretes you must treasure Life and the carriers of Life, women.

Youth:
>I searched my heart. I pledge to life and the carriers of life, women.

Kouros:
>To be a Kourutes, you must cooperate with your brothers. Pan is not warlike. Pan is love.

Youth: I searched my heart. I pledge to seek a flow of cooperation and avoid aggression.

When they finish, they leap, physically, when the words call for it.
At the end of this, the Kouretes face the mother of the youth as the youth
says,

> "Thank you for the opportunity of my life. I knocked on the door
> and you let me in. I was hungry and you nourished me. I was lonely
> and you loved me. Thou art truly the Goddess manifest among us.

Mother replies:

> Farewell the child, who grew so well from my womb to childhood.
> Welcome the young man who will return to me as friend and ally
> in all Lifes enterprise (presents him with ring). Receive this ring as a
> reminder that while you are gone, our connection forever remains.

This acceptance ring is a silver band. It can be quite thin or thick,
as taste and money allows. The silver is for the powers of Moon, who
controls waters connection and life in general.

After this, more singing and much feasting comes. The mother is
honored along with her son.

EPILOGUE TO THE KOURETES

We received some complaints from Dianic sisters about changing
our manifesto slightly concerning men. "We are opposed to teaching
our magic and our craft to men until the equality of the sexes is reality."

Dianic tradition is a teaching tradition, and from early times on
we taught both sexes of the young. This is a natural way to contribute
to society and make money. What we mean by our manifesto is we
would not be adverse to teaching parts of the usual craft curriculum to
men, such as medicinal herbalogy, because more healers means that
we are all better off. Philosophy is another craft we would definitely
teach both sexes, since if there are more thinkers there are more ideas.
Dances, sports, songs are yet another way to spread Goddess consciousness without divulging Womens Mysteries to men. Ritual work is what
we would never teach men, not even after the ERA is a reality.

Let me tell you a story. This summer (1980) I attended my first
Pan Pagan festival. There in the midwest, next to the emerald-colored
lake pagans were about to have their first Women's Circle, an unheard
of experience for the dominating duality traditions that assembled. The
Goddess told me to get help to insure the safety of the Women's circle.
I asked the very few gay men who called themselves the Fairy Circle to
station themselves around the Woman's Circle in a radius of 49 large
steps and guard us, let no man pass their line.

This proved to be the best idea I had in a long time. As the beautiful and moving Woman's circle got underway, with 66 priestesses participating, from across the lake some kids sighted a glimpse of us through the leaves from a small hill and called their daddies. The daddies watched for an hour working themselves up to a white froth, then charged down on us with big rods fully intending to beat up the naked ladies who in their opinion broke God's law.

Instead of beating up the women the Fairy Circle stopped them and they dealt with their rage. From the Pagan side, there was a man who was so threatened when his wife and daughter joined the Circle, that he came to disrupt us and pull out "his" women. The Fairy Circle again stopped him, and we managed to have a wonderful Dianic ritual in spite of all the male ruffled feathers.

So ten years later things are not as bleak as they used to be. There will be natural allies to the Dianic Women. Nonhomophobic men who respect the Goddess and Her privacy and gay men who search for Her can act as temporary Dianic Priests and help the women to guard their religious rituals. By the way the Dianic priests did exist, and their function was exactly this, help the women create the circle and then LEAVE and GUARD from the outside against other men.

This measure can be taken only when the men are trustworthy (only you know that) keep their backs turned to the Woman's circle and not ever look back no matter what they might hear, and meditate on their own souls in the service of the Lady.

THE SONG OF AMERGIN . . . a round of the year

Words Celtic Translated Robert Graves and by Chris Carol. Music Chris Carol c 1979

To my mother, Gwendolen
Lady of the White Circle.

INTROITUS

Gone is our history, burned to ashes;
Our poetry forgotten as time passes;
Return deep memory, root of our dissention;
Nurture the tree of present invention.

Gone are our dignities, gone our powers;
Once in freedom we blossomed as wild flowers;
Life moved among us, like a loving mother;
Sharing her wisdom, we cared for one another.

Without our mother, how shall we start living?
Without our mother, how shall we seek beauty?
Without our mother, how shall we die peaceful?
Without our mother, how shall we be reborn?

BETH-Birch
I AM A STAG OF SEVEN TINES

Welcome, welcome, welcome all ye here;
Welcome, welcome, welcome in the year.

Dark is the night and chill the winter wind,
Crisp the snow on the barren furrow;
Bring in the Yule Log, make the fire bright,
We shall wish for a warm tomorrow.

Over the fire the branches dangle
Of holly bright that is King tonight;
Red is the berry, green the prickle,
The sacred mistletoe glowing white.

Now we may feast and pass the Wassail Cup,
Sing the ballads with joy and mirth,
Soon we shall sleep and dream the night away,
Gather strength for the Spring's rebirth.

On the earth, in the air,
Thru the fire, by the water;
I am STRENGTH the first month's daughter.

LUIS-Rowan

I AM A LAKE ON A PLAIN

All on a plain there stands a lake,
A magic mirror doth it make;
And gathered on a wintry night,
Ye may behold a wondrous sight.

For in that lake reflected are
The Lady Moon and Morning Star;
Across the sky they journey on,
And to her son she sings this song.

Cradled in my loving arm,
Your dreams unmarred by fear of harm,
Swift be your ride in the heavenly Boat,
As on the Milky Way we float.

Where turns the Crown of the Northern Wind
A silver island shall you find
And on that isle a castle white
Wherein is peace and calm delight.

Inside that castle's silver wall
There stands a dark majestic hall,
And in that hall a Lady fair,
The end of all desire is there.

So slumber deep thou Heavenly Twin,
And so thy journey soon begin;
For they who in Lobe's flames will die,
Shall rise again, I promise thee.

On the earth, in the air,
Thru the fire, by the water,
I am **BREADTH**, the second months daughter.

NION-Ash

I AM A WIND OF THE SEA

In the moonlight, the crystal bright
Of our manes is glowing clear;
Dragon stones stand alone
138

On the sand as we draw near . . .
Wave on wave, wave on wave,
Wave on wave of the sea mares rave;
Tides are high as we ride by,
Embrace the tide and with the sea mares ride.

Foaming, frothing at maddened mouth,
Hooves churning in the brine,
Tails flailing, ranting, raving,
We gather line on line.
Wave on wave, wave on wave,
Wave on wave of the sea mares rave;

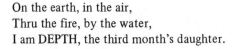

At the spring tide, swell with pride,
Embrace the tide, and with the sea mares ride.
Mighty now, we too must bow
To Time's mightier hand;
Comes the ebb tide, we subside,
And graze the golden sand . . .
Wave on wave, wave on wave,
Wave on wave of the sea mares graze;
One and all heed Rhiannon's call,
Embrace the tide, and with the sea mares ride.

On the earth, in the air,
Thru the fire, by the water,
I am DEPTH, the third month's daughter.

FEARN-Alder

I AM A TEAR OF THE SUN

Weep, weep for the sparkling stream,
Weep, weep for the great oak tree;
Weep, weep for the bright blue sky,
Weep for the memory.

Weep, weep for the sacred grove,
Weep, weep for the peaceful years;
Weep, weep for the fruitful field,
Weep for our present fears.

Weep, weep for the endless fight,
Weep, weep for the vengeance night;
Weep, weep now with all our might;
Weep for our birthright.

On the earth, in the air,
Thru the fire, by the water,
I am CLARITY the fourth month's daughter

The Legend of the ROLLRIGHT STONES.

Once there stood in this sacred place an alder grove, beside the stone
circle. The alder buds spiralled on the twig in the dance of life; the
flowers bursting green sang of the mystery of the waters; the red bark
sang of the flames of fire; the brown twigs echoed the color of earth . . .

　　　The circle now lies silent, each dewdrop a tear of the sun, sorrowing until the prophecy shall unfold . . .

　　　That when the labyris is laid to the alder and her blood is shed,
then shall the King Stone move, and the dance begin anew.

SAILLE-Willow

I AM A HAWK ON A CLIFF

I am a hawk on a cliff
Poised before the fray
In the dance of death, dance of life,
The hunter and the prey.

Flashing feathered streak, wicked beak,
Swift as the eye can see,
Straining every nerve, downward swerve
In glorious artistry.

Bright the open sky in my eye,
But blood is on my breath,
Thunder shakes the sky, as I fly,
In all of life is death.

On the earth, in the air,
Thru the fire and water,
I am SKILL, the fifth month's daughter.

UATH-Hawthorn

I AM FAIR OF FLOWERS

I am fair of flowers,
Blossoming today,

Scent of women's sweetness,
Sprig of magic May.

Snowdrop white in beauty,
First of all the flowers,
Winter cannot bow thee,
Nor the darkness hours.

Sunlike shines the crocus
In the lengthening hours,
Wind and rain caress thee
Thru the springtime showers.

Crimson bloom the roses
Fragrant past belief,
Scent the summer breezes
Bringing sweet relief.

Fairest of all flowers
Crown our roundelay,
Scent of women's sweetness,
Spring of magic May.

On the earth, in the air,
Thru the fire, by the water;
I am BEAUTY, the sixth month's daughter.

DUIR-Oak

I AM THE ONE WITH CROWN OF FIRE

She is awakening
(Magic is afoot)
She is arising;
She is dancing;
She is glowing;
She is radiant;
She is brilliant;
She is beauty;
(Turn back the wheel lest we burn)
She is splendor;
She is shining;
She is setting;
She is fading;

She is dying;
She is peaceful;
(Magic is afoot.)

On the earth, in the air,
Thru the fire, by the water,
I am MAGIC, the seventh month's daughter.

TINNE-Holly

I AM AN AVENGING SPEAR

I who heal may also hex,
The good enhance, the evil vex;
I am an avenging spear.

The rich and powerful know no fear,
Tho' the seasons change thruout the year;

But I'll speak up and make them hear;
I am an avenging spear.

For peace and love we ever yearn,
But some do wrong and never learn;
This time it won't be us that'll burn;
I am an avenging spear.

I'm tired of promises, tired of the lie
Of a better life after I die,
We'll take what's ours and touch the sky;
I am an avenging spear.

What goes up must soon come down,
So wipe your tears and mend your frown
Their time is up, go claim your crown,
I'm an avenging spear.

On the earth, in the air,
Thru the fire, by the water,
I am VENGEANCE, the eighth month's daughter.

COLL-Hazel

I AM A SALMON IN A POOL

Swiftly flows the river
From the mountain to the sea,
The rapids as they flow
Teach me what they know
Of strength and grace and speed,
And flashing as I go
I ever learn and grow.

Gently winds the river
Thru the plain down to the sea;
The still and silent pool
Makes a wise one from a fool
With depth and calm and peace
And flashing as I go
I ever learn and grow.

On the earth, in the air,
Thru the fire, by the water,
I am KNOWLEDGE and the ninth month's daughter.

MUIN-Vine

I AM A HILL OF POETRY

Hey the gift, Ho the gift,
Hey the gift of the living.

Queen of the dawn, Queen of the clouds,
Queen of the planet, Queen of the star;
Queen of the rain, Queen of the dew,
Queen of the welkin, Queen of the sky;
Queen of the flame, Queen of the light,
Queen of the sphere, Queen of the globe;
Queen of the elements, Queen of the heavens,
Queen of the Moon, Queen of the Sun.

On the earth, in the air,
Thru the fire, by the water,
I am ECSTACY the tenth month's daughter.

GORT-Ivy

I AM A BOAR

I am a boar on this high place
In the first fresh frost
On autumn's face;
The hunters call to sound the chase
But I am bold
I will run this race.

For many moons we roamed this land,
Where others fell
I learned to stand;
The old and great join in the dance
Courage and cunning are my inheritance.

On the earth, in the air,
Thru the fire, by the water,
I am VALOR, the eleventh month's daughter.

NGETAL-Reed

I AM A SOUND OF THE SEA

Calmest cold of deepest deep;
Sinuous swishing of sea snake sidling;
Baleful bark of sorrowing seal;
Shrill shreiking of temerous tern;
Bounding breaker on ragged rock.

On the earth, in the air,
Thru the fire, by the water,
I am TERROR, the twelfth month's daughter.

RUIS-Elder

I AM A WAVE OF THE SEA

I am a wave of the sea,
Rolling on forever onward,
Gathering strength
Pausing for none.

Sunbeam riding on the ocean wave,
Firefly riding in the sky,
Amazon riding on the ocean beach,
Old moon riding up on high;
Everything is beautiful
In the earth and sea and starry sky
Old moon fades and young moon grows
Our life will never die.

On the earth, in the air,
Thru the fire, by the water;
I am FLOWING, the last month's daughter.

ENDING

I AM THE WOMB OF EVERY HOLT;
I AM THE BLAZE ON EVERY HILL;
I AM THE QUEEN OF EVERY HIVE;
I AM THE SHIELD TO EVERY HEAD;
I AM THE TOMB TO EVERY HOPE;
BLESSED BE MY NAME.

PRACTICING WITH OTHERS
ABOUT WITCHES AND SABBATS

The word "Sabbath" of Hebrew origin, actually means "bride." Sabbat rituals of Pagans relate often to the Goddess as Bride, Virgin, Maiden, Nymph and Crone. "Sabbath" also means "day of teachings," and the Sabbat Day for us becomes the time of the teachings of the Sacred Bride, the Great Goddess.

How women observe the Sabbats depends upon which tradition they choose to embrace, and is colored by the ancient cultural cradle from which a particular tradition derives. In my own tradition of Classical Witchcraft, much emphasis is placed upon the psychic condition of the women involved. Thus, certain practices, such as drawing the circle, invoking/banishing, purification, consecration, invoking the Four Corners, unifying and toasting are integral to a Sabbat ritual. As Classical practices, such rituals have come down to us through the ages; therefore, their power is cumulative and they are reinforced further by acting them out in the Classical manner. However, our strength is our diversity and creativity of our gift. I do not necessarily conduct Sabbats according to my book, but according to what happens naturally at the Sabbat site. (See details in Holy Book of Womens Mysteries Part One.)

The High Priestess of a Sabbat circle is the female elder. She, as a manifest representation of the Goddess-on-Earth, is one focus of the event. In ancient times the High Priestess was totally devoted to a spiritual lifestyle, serving the aspect of the Goddess of her choice. This was possible only within the safety of matriarchies, however. Later on, the High Priestess became one with the people she served, and the separation between clergy and laypeople disappeared.

The High Priestess of a circle today must accept the major responsibility for keeping the energy level high and flowing. There is no easy way this skill may be taught, so in order to learn it, we give the task of being High Priestess to women who feel thay are willing and able to tune into this delicate mechanism of women's hearts. This important sensitivity to the group energy is the responsibility of the leader. A Sabbat that is boring is a Sabbat where the vital energy was allowed to drop. When the women enter the circle on Sabbat, a certain rhythm is established, and that must be respected and renewed as needed, throughout the Sabbat celebration.

A Priestess is aware of a coming Sabbat long before the actual day of the ceremony. She and other various coven sisters may meet in advance to share ideas and plans for the coming holy day. Responsibilities for preparation may be shared in this way: the gathering of ritual tools; the collection of the essential elements, such as clear water, salt, barley and flour, incenses, Goddess-images; the pre-planning of the ritual itself; making arrangements for flowers, altar decorations, garlands and crowns.

Actual rehearsals are needed only when one is not familiar with all this and improvisation cannot quite be depended upon. Still, even with a rehearsal, you must allow for the moment to teach you. Stay flexible and don't become obsessed with structure or pre-planned ideas. This is the facilitation of a supreme religious experience, not the production of an off-Broadway play. Do, however, try to set up a central phone number women can call for special questions (What color candles? What time? Can a friend come along?)

In our continuing studies we have learned that wine, which figures so prominently in my own tradition, is actually a late-comer as a Sacred Draught, and that before the invention of male gods, the libation was a barley drink mixed with honey. Another priestess, named Hygeia because of her specialty, advised us not to allow meats at Sabbats. Thus, we become educated to the importance of conscious feasting.

The admission of new people to Sabbats can be risky, and must be done according to some pre-plan or pre-established concensus. Our coven is an open coven, but we do screen new people, asking them to meet with one of the facilitating priestesses before Sabbat. We rarely have to turn anyone away. Our policy has been to make the Goddess-consciousness available to as many women as possible, but we are not ignorant of the fact there are those who would harm us.

On the evening of Sabbat, all participants should take a purifying bath or shower, to promote a clean, unruffled state of mind. Each woman should anoint herself with her favorite oil, and dress comfortably. Ritual clothing is fun and spiritually energizing to make and wear, and free-flowing gowns are delightful, but always dress for comfort in any case. There is nothing spiritual about freezing in a place "wild and lone."

Before entering a Sabbat circle, all members spend time meditating while lining up — in order of birth, oldest to youngest — to be admitted to the circle. The Priestess receives each woman at the door to the circle, generally set at the East gate, although that gate may be moved to suit comfort, convenience and/or theme. The Priestess who purifies entering sisters must also be purified "from all anxieties, all disappointments, all preoccupations other than the Mother." Only then can she convey the same to her sisters.

Our coven has used naturally salty sea-water for this purification blessing, but others mix salt with water, blessing the mixture with their athalmes in the name of Diana. Using this water, the Priestess anoints each woman in the following order: blessing the forehead, that the sister may be free to think of Her; the eyes, that she may see Her beauty; the lips, that she may speak Her names; the breasts, created in strength and beauty; the genitals, to create life and pleasure as She brought forth the Universe; the feet, to walk always in Her paths.

This encounter works well when the members number 20 or less, but when the number of celebrants is any higher, it is a good idea to make arrangements to hasten the procedure. This is because those who are waiting often get cold or restless, energies drop and gladness is diminished. One of our solutions born for a circle of 60+, was to use five priestesses as gate-keepers. As each celebrant came to the circle, each of the priestesses would purify her with a different element: water, incense, candle fire, barley, and words of blessing and welcome.

In this way each woman felt she was being concentrated on. Auras picked up the smoke as the incense encircled their bodies, so the deep minds were awakened. The candle burned away, from the front and the back, all the fears they carried with them. The barley, simple and beautiful, fell on their hair or was placed in their mouths to help them visualize the plenty of the earth. The words of blessing and welcome encouraged each one to participate as free and conscious souls.

There are many ways to facilitate this, but the essential thing is to let the feelings flow. Let no one read from pieces of paper by flashlight; let no one pontificate too long, lest the flow be interrupted. Let there be simplicity, sincerity and humor with which to educate. A priestess should never fight for attention. As the representative of the Priestess-Goddess, Hecate, the High Priestess must have control over the circle at least until it has been properly sealed. After that, the real work begins.

Once the circle has been closed, the energy must be raised. This is psychic work of the highest importance. Communication lines must be open. Trances are possible; sisters must be committed to the protection of women in trance rather than disturbed by their uniqueness, worried about validity, or laid to waste by a last moment attack of Judeo-Christian guilt about being, without question, in the midst of witches.

The hum we use to unify and raise power is a low, centering sound, never strained. If the top of the head is vibrating with the sound, the hum is a good one. Allow the hum to flow for awhile before any variations are attempted, because it clears the vocal cords by gently massaging them against each other. This makes the mucous fall away, but simply swallow as necessary rather than clearing your throat.

When the time is right, allow the hum to break into different patterns of humming, then into different patterns of sound — names of the Goddess may form in your mouth, so sing them out. Listen, too, to the tapestry of sound created in the circle. Embroider on it. Communicate with the collective sound without jarring it. The leader of the group must know when to stop participating so that she may begin using the energies thus raised to begin the invocations.

The celebrants should always keep humming, or being in vibration, and the sound should continue even as the High Priestess invokes the Four Corners of the Universe, then invokes the Great Goddess. The energy will be a presence, like air, through which will be channeled omens and psychic communications. Sudden animal noises — the whinny of horses, baying of dogs, hissing of serpents or hootings of owls — are frequent omens, and should be received as gifts.

After the blessing of the foods and the invocation of the Goddess, whether by the Witch's Chant, Great Charge, or Charge to the Star Goddess, we traditionally allow a space of time for Her response. During this time the humming may stop but the channels are left open while circle members sink into themselves for inner listening. Feed the vibration which centered you as a group and allow it to come through each woman in the form of insights, words and sentences, names, pictures, whatever. These may be expressed quietly and personally, under the breath. Often, however, this period results in a deeply meaningful psychic feeling, shared communally by the circle. A heatwave may spread through the group or a collective spinal tingling may affect each celebrant. Shouts or "unearthly" sounds may be made by one of the sisters or by some force not visible. When this occurs, one must be respectful and stand by, since such signs have been asked for and it's not a good idea to back out of a magical experience.

During one of our earliest coven celebrations, held during Full Moon, we all heard Pan. He was obviously coming to us from out of the mountains. Being frightened, overly concerned and generally inexperienced in such matters, I stepped in to ask the Horned Consort to withdraw, since we were Dianics. He did. I would not act that way today.

At another ritual being held outdoors in a mountainous and remote area, we suddenly heard the humming of another full coven, seemingly coming out of the mountain adjacent to ours. The sound was so clear and loud that it drowned out the voice of a newly ordained High Priestess. It was a warning to us. Moments later, eight police cars pulled up and arrested 38 witches for candle-burning (a fire hazard, they said).

So, when the spirits speak, take heed. The message could be one of love, warning or challenge. Interpretation is up to you. We have no books which educate us as to the moral code of the spirits. If a sister is frightened, she may draw the banishing pentagram into the air and the spirit will leave, but it may be the last time she hears a spirit communicate with her.

Another important factor here is the evolutionary level of the spirits coming through. Those who come through an open channel within a magically drawn, spiritually consecrated circle are highly evolved and helpful. Trust that. Spirits invoked haphazardly, for fun, or at random, may very well be any being without a body who happens to be passing by. Such beings love to play games with mortals; love to baffle them and gain their attention. They are not to be taken seriously, and they are not to be toyed with. Circle spirits are manifest through serious psychic work within a sacred circle.

The highest way to make spirits manifest during Sabbat is known as tele-transportation. This may be done by holding hands in a circle, in the dark with only candles burning. Work this ritual magic before feasting, since eating causes the body's blood to serve the stomach rather than the mind. Fasting for a full day before this ritual helps greatly to prepare for the serious work to be done.

After raising energy and unifying, and opening the channels of communication, the Priestess asks for a spirit by name, calling for it to bring something to the circle. My mother once asked for, and received, a dove in her circle. Others have received green boughs in the midst of Winter.

Ask the visiting spirits what can be done for them on this earthly plane. Especially receptive sisters may perceive the answers. For example, a spirit may want her grave tended, candles burned for energy or healing of another, or a promise that someone will look after a loved one left behind. Such worries may be holding the spirit back even though she desires to move on. Be prepared to be helpful to the spirit invoked.

If the visiting spirits are happy ones, the sisters may ask questions. Although spirits know mostly about the world of the dead, they can also see the living — though the living don't generally see them all the time.

If there is a need for healing, call upon the evolved physician spirits; for love, call upon loving women souls because love is a powerful vibration lasting far beyond death; for luck, seek the Goddess only; for general help in personal affairs, talk to spirits of family members who have passed on, provided they are advanced. And, if the need be the influencing of government, invoke spirits who had a political orientation while living. Mothers such as Susan B. Anthony and Elizabeth

A communal festival (September 21st)

Cady Stanton are very much alive in spirit. Also, discover spirits living in your particular area.

Be sure to burn incenses at all times while communicating with spirits, making certain the censer is replenished as necessary. Ask a friend or circle member to assist in this. Incense is the food for the spirits. It tranquilizes them and makes them quite agreeable. Working with invoked spirits is a full and whole tradition, upon which most of South American Witchcraft and African Voo-Doo Craft depend.

Working in Sabbat circle with the elementals, the spirits of fire, earth, air and water, is less of a personal experience in that there may not be instant manifestations or miracles, but things do get done, none-theless. I practice this form of earth-magic, and sometimes my spells take years to come in, but when it's a grand goal, it's worth waiting for.

My standard spell at Sabbats for years was the rebirth of Goddess-worship. I visualized and projected the divine, organic organizing of groups of life-oriented women, springing up like weeds all over the world. It took me several more years to find out that wide-spread, conscious cultivation of the family of the Mother Goddess had begun the same year (1971) I began those spells. I weep for joy when the confirmation of Her powers becomes manifest to me.

Most of the spells in my books depend upon manipulation of elementals and the vibrations from the names of the Goddess. Study-ing the many guises of the Goddess makes a versatile witch. Her names are power. The more names a sister knows, the better her magic will be, as she opens up more and more channels to the Cosmic Mother.

Letting go of spells after they have been done is yet another skill. Casting circle/spell remnants into a body of moving water, or burying them in the womb of the earth, and not looking back, is an obvious act of letting go. A spell can only become reality when the physical mind lets go of it.

151

Finally, when the Sabbat circle feels the first waves of fatigue, it should be concluded shortly with thanks to invoked spirits and Goddesses. Be careful not to over-tax any Sabbat circle. Members could have heavy dreams as a result, and be depleted rather than energized. A good Sabbat rebuilds energy, not exhaustion. Signs of a good Sabbat are still evident the morning after, when celebrants wake up feeling light-hearted and vital. The rewards are infinite.

Celebrating the holy Sabbats, observing the Wheel of Life, is a deep bonding act among sisters and brothers. At Sabbat we meet as Children of the Goddess — one people, one soul. On these pages I communicate practices of my own heritage, the Dianic tradition — Women's Mysteries — where men are not included. Other traditions, equally beautiful and exciting, include males and females in the circle; others balance out the sexes very carefully; others observe men's Mysteries, acting without women but worshipping still the Source of all life, the Great Goddess. Thus are we all different yet the same.

The Dianic descriptions can be adapted for use in mixed circles, however, a strong trinity of priestesses is usually needed to carry it out. This is because some males approach such circles as some sort of personal costume party, rather than serious worship of The Lady. Teaching men to go against their inherent "male privilege," which is totally suspended while in worship, is no small task. There were and are successful exceptions. Men who turn out to be sons and lovers of the Goddess are not remotely interested in a power struggle or the priestesses present. They are, through arduous study and deep desire, role models of the matriarchal men, the priests, the Kouretes. They become protectors of the young and supporters of their sisters. May their numbers increase.

Sabbat celebrations in the Dianic tradition foster the reclamation of our sweet womansouls. This reclamation is universal and will coil around this globe like the sacred Snake of the Goddess of Rebirth. So Be It!

INITIATION OF THE SHAMAN DRUMS

Shamanism in my own country was the dominant pagan ministry. Both sexes could become shamans, usually by a natural selection. You had to be born with an extra bone in your body (a tooth at birth would qualify) or have a very high degree of mediumship displayed at an early age. Shamans were "stolen" by other shamans at seven years old, and taught the shaman ways. Other times a person would be unconscious for two weeks during some sickness, and when she recovered she would report her lessons given to her on the astral plane. This chant is one of those "lessons." The shaman would take her drum under the full moon and chant this over it beating it as the feelings dictated it. The drum from then on becomes her direct line to her guardian spirits; whenever she would play her drums, they would respond to her with help.

INVOCATION TO THE FIRE MOTHER

Blessings! Blessings! Blessings!
You are the white nights fire blessing!
You are the Queens pure blessing!
You are my sixhumped white Mare!
My sixeyed speckeled tiger!
Thirty headed Fire Mother!
Forty headed Virgin Mother!
The cooker of the raw things!
The thawer of the frozen things!
The fanner of the green flame!
Robed in Green whosshing silks
She who decends on seven slopes
She who dances the seven dances
She who plays the seven games!
You are the Mother of the Triple Flame
Woven pearly horns upon thy forehead
You are the keeper of the stone hearths!
Thirty headed Fire Mother!
Forty headed Virgin Mother!
Immaculate Purity!
All wise scientist Mother!
Let our eyes see no evil
Let our hearts know no evil
Descend holding the white flame aloft
Descend encircling six times
Descend blowing forth blue flames
Be our Mother on whirl . . .
Be our father oh swirl . . .

DIANIC ORDINATION RITUAL

When a woman studies a year and a day with a coven she is entitled to be initiated. When the new initiate has worked, helped facilitate circles of the coven a year and day she is entitled to be ordained. A specialty is required for her, and there are many.

You can be ordained to be priestess of teachings, healings, management, prophesy, scriptures, poetry, weather, fire, water, earth. Examples: I am a priestess of teachings and ritual, a therapist friend of mine is priestess of healings, another is priestess of herbology, etc.

Time for ordination is the same as Initiation, Candlemas (February 2nd). After your coven initiates the new members, the ordination follows. The tools of the craft are collected from the women, to be given back to them during the ceremony. Ordination is kind of acknowledgement of the magical works well done, and a group blessing on the individual who achieved it.

The new priestesses are called by their magical names (Medea, Penthesilea, Ea, Circe, etc.). These names signify the guardian spirits the women have chosen for their path.

All stand in a circle and hum. Feel for the jelling of the soul-group; when meditation is deep enough the High Priestess speaks:

> We are the continuation of long lines of ancient women who were dedicated to the Goddess of Life. Tonite we are lucky enough to have new priestesses to be ordained. In the Dianic tradition we have initiation and ordination; we leave the individual free to choose their own process and excellence. Within our coven we like to recognize the contribution of new sisters.

Four ordained priestesses stand at the four corners of the Universe in the circle, each invoking their own favorite goddesses they see with the four elements. An example:

Priestess of the east:
Come great teachers of the East priestesses of Isis, shaking your sacred tambourines, come Ishtar, Come Lilith!

Priestess of the south:
Awake and fly to us teachers of the south, Firesouls, winged like cherubs, sun Goddess Arinna, oh come!

Priestess of the west:
Awake and rise to us oh lovely Goddess of the west, come to us Love, come to us Aphrodite, on your shell float to us Tiamat, Queen of the Dolphins.

Priestess of the north:
Gather together your gifts oh Goddess of the north! Foodmother, greenmother, come teach us all your ways.

High Priestess:
The temple is created. The goddess is here.
Who are the priestesses seeking the recognition of the teachers?

—it is I, Circe (Diana, Melusine, Etoine, etc.) answered by the women one by one.
—Come Circe to be presented to the Universe.

In the middle of the circle the High Priestess steps out touching the new woman's hands without touching. She holds her hand palms open feeling the radiation from the other. They turn to the east:

—I, Medea present to you Circe, a priestess of . . .(list specialty) . . . who has completed her ministry with us. Bless her oh Goddess of beginnings with new powers, new energy, new ways of communications.

By "presenting", I mean the H.P. is turning physically and gently the body of the new priestess with her arms held in Goddess position. Now she is turned to the south:

—I High Priestess of Dianna, Medea, present Circe to you oh Firemothers. Infuse her with your vitality, give yer your passion to accomplish all the works she is to do. Bless her with magnetism, endurance and fierce power.

Turned again:

—I Medea, High Priestess of Dianna, present to you Circe, oh guardians of the West. To bless this new priestess with your love. Let her heart be glad in your service, let her soul warm hearts of others and let her ally always be you, Aphrodite.

I Lady Medea present to you Circe, oh Goddess of the North, Foodmother and fooddaughter, bless this new priestess with nurturance and information, powers of organizing and powers of just and fair conduct. Blessed be.

Then take a small bottle of oil (I used 'Priestess'); anoint the forehead saying:

I purify you from all anxiety, I purify your eyes to see her ways, your nose to smell her essence, your lips to speak of Her and I anoint your breast for courage and beauty, your genitals for pleasure and happiness, your feet to walk in her path. Finally I bless your palms (touching the inside of her hands) to do the Goddess' work.

Turning to the magical tools gathered at the beginning of the ceremony holding your hands over it bless it thusly:

All the tools you used and loved, bless them all with the Goddess love.

Now hand over the ring, putting it gently on her finger, her cord to wind around her waist, her wand to hold in her hands, and knife to invoke the powers and a necklace for immortality put around the ordained priestess' neck. When all this is completed you all say:

It is done. The Goddess blesses her new priestess.

The new ordained priestess can now offer a few words of statement, or just meditate to herself, and participate in the ordination of the next woman following herself.

Celebrating and feasting follows, with laughter and music and stories about how these women found the Goddess and how and when they first felt they were called to serve her as priestess.

PRACTICING "SOLO"

To practice "solo" is something all witches do, usually in greater number than those who act as part of a coven. "Solo-witching" is something that should be an integral part of one's daily life. It is true that many covens have come into existence of their own "organic" accord in the last few years, and that phenomenon is largely due to the natural tendency of women to explore spiritual needs and feelings with each other. The woman who is lucky enough to find like-minded women to commune with still needs to work at her private altar, just as does the woman whose private altar is her sole spiritual expression. At her altar, every woman is her own priestess.

Often women's homes already have a special space set aside where valuables, family pictures, jewels, oils, and other personal momentos are kept. The woman is usually not conscious of the fact that, by natural inclination, she has created the beginnings of an altar. A solo-witch deliberately elaborates on this special space, making it more practical for her purposes by removing all objects but those which aid in her meditations.

The most important difference between coven-witching and solo-witching is the attitude of the practitioner. In a circle of women (or men and women if a "mixed" coven) the witch is usually dependent upon facilitating priestesses, responsible for guiding the ritual toward the most appropriate rhythm, content, and intensity. In her own home, the woman is totally dependent upon herself to create a psychically conducive environment in which to do work. She has a responsibility to establish a "temple" space in which to act and interact. This process is not quite as easy as showing up for coven celebrations of Sabbat. A home space needs to be "cleaned out," telephones unhooked during ritual, visitors discouraged, interruptions ignored. It is also important to gather all the tools of the Craft in one place and to take a ritual bath of purification before doing any altar-work.

The purpose of coven-craft is to build and strengthen the natural female bonding between Sisters as it occurs on a Divine level, while solo-practicing serves to enhance and enlarge a woman's personal power over her own life and circumstances. To do both is to be a practicing priestess. To do either is a matter of Divine choice.

Witches who are fortunate enough to be able to conduct their worship rituals in the natural environment of the out-of-doors have little or no need for extensive preparation or stringent precautions, but an urban solo-witch has need of both, as well as an active imagination, in order to transcend the pervasive vibrations of the city. Rural witches have the luxury of choosing a natural setting in which to worship: groves, meadows, lakes, rivers, woods and hills are excellent temples which provide contact with Nature at Her most elemental. City witches may find they have more need for E.S.P., use of the fifth dimension, and ancestral spirits to provide contact with those same elemental forces.

Solo-witching is a constant exercise in ingenuity, but secrecy regarding your work is still one of the cornerstones of witch-wisdom and power.

Knowing when to keep quiet about an issue is equally as important as knowing when to struggle for one. Love-spells, in particular, are never disclosed to anyone, but it is a good practice in general to avoid telling other people what you have done at your altar. If you know a strong priestess of divination you could check with her in regard to your spells, and she could perhaps suggest an approach or alternative spell. Doing this is not breaking secrecy. Secrecy adds intensity to your work and acts as the vessel in which to hold your spell. Breaking secrecy can damage or ruin a spell.

In covens, secrecy is not as imperative, and the collective-consciousness holds the spell as securely as the vessel of secrecy. A witch does not, however, tell uninitiates about coven work or ritual (unless you are teaching).

Witches' tools become doubly important in the practice of solo-witching. For example, your red cord, perhaps woven with coven members in a Circle, can be used to cast a protective circle around your private worship space at home. It will provide you with a "natural centering" space, and will serve you fully as well as a magic Circle drawn on a sacred mountaintop.

Such witchy tools as athalmes and swords, worn openly, will ward off attack. Pentacles on necklaces are important because they are recognized by the dead and spirits who respond easily to such symbols. This is one of the strengths of ancient symbology — signs are a part of the collective consciousness, whose universal language is symbolism.

Having a special chalice or altar-cup is very important, and this chalice should not be used for any purposes other than your sacred rituals. Try to have incense in the altar space as much as possible. The altar censer or thurible can follow you anywhere, and be a part of daily activities, indoors or out, at worship, work, or recreation. It should be regarded as a very good friend.

It is best not to cut corners when practicing solo-witching. The witch's home is a temple, and there is an on-going maintenance job to be done; purification as well as cleaning must take place. Purification of psychic space can be aided by keeping sacred herbs in the corners of the house (Angelica is traditionally used for peace and harmony, for example), and candles burning in fireproof jars. Additionally, taking good care of houseplants is an excellent idea. These plants are much more than decoration — they are co-workers. This applies to house pets as well. When addressing Athena, Diana, Brigid, Cerridwen, or Artemis, it is helpful to involve cats, dogs, owls, snakes, or some other representative of the animal queendom.

Bless your entire house at New Moon or Full Moon by walking around it three times, carrying a thurbile of burning incense, preferably Frankincense and Myrrh. Invoke the Goddess Vesta and the Muses to assure good times, creativity, and security of your living space. Throw the circle of invisibility around your home, and pronounce it invisible to all evil. This is particularly important for witches practicing in urban areas where the high crime-rates inherent in patriarchal society are of special concern. Witch-sense decrees that we take no chances or short-cuts in the areas of self-protection and self-preservation.

"Targeting" is a very important concept in the art of solo-witching as the process of choosing the intent and ultimate target of your spell. Solo-witches must be particularly cautious about throwing spells of reversal or attack, or hasty revenge based on assumptions. Spells thrown in anger are capable of going much too far and may be heartily regretted later. Personal power ill-directed can be a frightening thing. Before using your powers to throw reversal spells, it is best to sleep on the issue for at least one night, but preferably three, and to ritualistically strengthen and purify yourself before taking any action.

Harm is most often corrected by inevitable karmic Law, and you may not have to involve yourself in a situation at all. Hexing the inno-cent is punishable by the gravest of consequences: your hex returns to you ten-fold. For these reasons, most wiccans studiously avoid hexing and concentrate instead on a fair and karmically just outcome. Forget the "how" and allow the witch-Goddess, Aradia, to take care of the problem. Chances are good that a perfect solution will be arrived at when a witch gives the Goddess free space in which to act, without trying to limit Her by providing specifications born of a finite mind.

Specifically, "targeting" must be done only with a conscious com-mitment and a background of research. Generally, spells should be de-vised in such a way that they remain open and flexible.

Panic-witching for a solo-practitioner occurs when a spell doesn't seem to work. It is true that some do and some don't, but we must remember that karmic "debts" and "assets" accumulate over lifetimes, and provide the landmarks for today. Engagements, appointments and commitments may have been made previously, but may remain hidden in the subconscious. A witch might be actively pursuing one particular solution or individual only to miss a karmic "appointment" with some-one very important.

It is possible to "stall" your karma, but best if you don't because sooner or later the inevitable must occur. Spells which don't work are valid in the sense that an answer has been provided. Sometimes it is necessary to stop throwing a spell in order to await the inevitable Cosmic intervention. The Goddess will make Her plans known to any witch able and willing to listen. Letting go of a spell is not easy, especially if it has become an obsession, but it is never healthy or desirable to nurture an obsession anyway. The key to this is Will. Meditation and maintaining a "white" altar will help.

Solo-witching encompasses the entire lifestyle. It means consciously cooking healthy foods for yourself and your loved ones, and it definitely means not eating much red meat. A witch should take care to provide the physical body with the best care possible: natural sources of vitamins for health, and exercises to strengthen muscles and develop the body are good. The practice of Kundalini Yoga is traditional for many witches, since it originated with ancient women and the concept of serpent-power as power of the Great Goddess. But there are many different disciplines you would enjoy. Sports, games, dance — all offer spiritual-physical exercises.

Avoid slavery of any kind at all costs. A slave-witch is not much good. The Goddess insists on the total freedom of Her worshippers, and often demands full nudity at the altar in order for us to prove the concept. Only "free" beings are able to feel comfortable when uncovered. The naked female or male body represents Truth rather than lewdness, and is important in rituals as a signification of the purity of the prayers. Slavery of course doesn't disappear when we take off our clothes, so the work is social consciousness. Affecting social change becomes a religious activity when it's done against slavery of your economic, spiritual well being.

A solo-witch would do well to subscribe to some king of pagan publication, or to purchase pagan reading materials for the home. These will provide support, encouragement, and motivation for continuing practice of the Craft. Constant education and knowledge-exchange provides fertile ground for growth and development of a creative witch.

It is also imperative that solo-witches keep a meticulous Book of Shadows, which contains in detail the work performed at the altar. This Book is not only a yardstick for measuring how much growth and change has taken place, or how many spells worked in certain ways, but also as a document of practical witch-lore for the benefit of future generations. The Book of Lights and Shadows is the witch's prayerbook.

Solo-witches, as any other people, may be found everywhere, They belong to every profession, age-level, economic status and ethnic group. Some are conscious, some are not. Some acknowledge affinities with the psychic world, while others exhibit completely unacknowledged potential. There are witches who are politically conscious, and who see connections between religion and politics which have existed since time-immemorial. Some witches are involved in the psychic workings of people in the here-and-now, while others are "backyard" pagans who love a good celebration with friends and neighbors. Many males prefer solo-witching, while women tend to become involved more easily in a group.

Among the ethnic groups, blacks and latinas as well as Europeans and Asians are the most practiced magicians. Ethnic minorities have not been able to afford to give up their magical rituals and practices, but use them instead to preserve their genetic souls. Among whites it is only oppressed groups, such as women, which resort to magic. Men often pray to a patriarchal god in one form or another. Women pray most often to a Blessed Virgin, the Queen of Heaven, Queen of the Moon, whose serpent indicates She is the ancient Great Goddess, Dia Anna.

Finally, don't hold back as a practicing solo-witch, but create and give birth to as many new spells, chants, rituals, challenges and endeavors as you can. Designate creativity as a major focal point in this life, and make a conscious effort to walk the five-points of the sacred Pentagram: the "top" point of the Life Force, connected with sexual energies; the "right side" point of individuality and survival, indicative of the principle that we belong and survive in our ecological niche; the "left side" point of the Self as Divine Spark, cultivated through devotions, meditation and rituals; the "left bottom" point of passion and an excitement for life which balances the "right bottom" point of power, natural in origin, learned through development, strong as a foundation for standing or building on. The solo-witch who keeps all this in mind will certainly thrive.

TEN YEARS LATER –

MY GODDESS MINISTRY

To belong to a witches coven is still very scary, elusive as well as dearly desirable to many women. I would like to share my experience of ten years of high priestessing. I wasn't born a polished priestess, I grew with my coven. When I started coming out as a spiritual feminist the term was considered contradictory. Religion and politics were not seen as one and the same. Women thought of politics as leaflets, petitions, or even guns, speeches, rallys, etc. But religion controls the inner woman, her thoughts which then govern her actions, so you can't get away from the fact that the Inner Woman is Revolution. I made a decision to add my talents and heritage to the struggle to liberate the religious woman inside, and help her create a faith system which ultimately serves her and her children.

Ten years later it is becoming more obvious for the rest of us that with all our victories of the seventies we failed to woo away the masses of women from the male dominated churches; it's still 90 percent females who support ANY church today (Mormons, Catholics, Jewish, Protestants, Presbyterians, Methodists, Baptists, Born Agains, etc.). Why? It's because women have a greater spiritual need than men. Yet men capitalize on this instinct and set themselves up to govern women through religion. When we break the stronghold of men on women in religion, we can consider the revolution of women won. Everything else will be evolution compared to religious indoctrination.

What do we need to offer women to make it easier for them to satisfy their religious needs and leave the male glorifying churches?

Results. Space. Peace of mind. High self-image. Universal meaningful work. Love and acceptance.

Do they get all this from male churches?

Patriarchy has invested heavily in nice buildings to go to and sit in quiet, at least women are safe for a while from the male sexual harassment.of the streets. They have incense in some churches (stolen from the Old Religion) pleasing to her senses, they have confessions which give her relief and some acceptance, they have activities where they can find friends, some churches even reach out to gays, without changing the basic concepts of christianity, namely the all powerful male god.

For this she had to donate her money, women always supported churches with labor and donations, she has to subjugate her sexuality; but most women don't really care about that, they are not into heavy sexual experimentation, they only want peace. They get to sing songs with other women and feel like living in a community.

Can we give women all this and more?

Feminist women's religion cannot promise large cathedrals to worship in, women find themselves poorer than ever in this century. But we can promise to build up the inner temple which is portable, and we all have one. This alone will keep us busy for a while. We can recapture the culture, the rituals, the songs, the feeling of community. We can have the incense and candlelight which makes religions so attractive, we can have peerless poetry of divine inspiration, we can have dances, pomp and circumstances.

What is required from women to get all this?

A willingness to study is a must today when so much has to be reclaimed. Women's religion can be orally transmitted, but there are few who are able to do this. The media is not ours, yet; our books are self published (for the most part), our resources are limited. The responsibility to study and follow up is required most certainly. Ten years of my teachings made me exhausted often, and I cry out in desperation saying to a new woman who is demanding from me to tell her all in one breath. I can't help you if you won't read! Only 3 percent of Americans read today, the majority of those are women. Women read naturally more than men. So we are in hopeful shape, but we must make this conscious devotion and continue to READ.

Donating money is a must. Nothing is free in revolutions; our spending power is the only one that as women and consumers we always had. Conscious consumers, putting price on sacred things is new to us. The world was trying to sell us deodorants and washing machines, never our own good graces. We must pay each other, and learn to trust each other with our monies, to make a flora of information possible. I am not talking about adoring one leader and ignoring the others. In my personal experience this is not even a problem. I have not seen anybody adored. Nobody is getting kissed on her silk slippers like the male gurus are. But somehow we went overboard with this fear of creating hierarchies amongst ourselves to the point of completely ignoring an internal honor system without which we are mute in dignity. We are mute because we have no way to say Thank You. We are only saying: Gimmiee, gimmee that Old Time Religion. But we must make it graceful and more honorable for it is ourselves we honor in religions, and nobody else. For example: there are several pagan festivals in the country where the feminist religious presence would be invited and needed. I cannot afford to travel to them, because it would come out of my personal pocket, and I have not grown rich and affluent in the past ten years spreading the faith. Yet strategy-wise, it would be very good if I had a travel fund for the Goddess. Not millions but some funds that pay air fare, publicity, accessability.

So how do you begin?

First of all you gather together and meet for a year and a day doing nothing else but study and read, rearrange your heads. You also may stop reading men authors for a year; did you ever do that? It is a great way to cleanse your mind! Saturate yourself with lore about the Goddess, and try to observe the eight sabbaths even if you just sit in a circle and light a candle for each of you.

I have described in detail the Sabbath proceedings and given the traditional poetry in my Holy Book of Womans Mysteries Part One; there you get a lot of guidance. What I also repeated almost every chapter is that this religion is improvisation. There is no one way to contact the Goddess. This religion is not a One-Book religion, like Christianity, and not a one matra religion like the Krishna cult, but a body of knowledge which revels in variety, in creativity, and in joy. It is a pleasure oriented religion, where kisses and pleasures are seen as sacraments.

Who shall lead the rituals?

Let's look at what specific "jobs" are to be done concerning a Goddess ritual? You need a group, more than three is a coven. You need to invoke the Goddess from the four corners of the Universe so that you can share this with four women right away. You need a recitation of the traditional Great Charge, or Invocation to the Star Goddess, or some other poetry appropriate to the season. This is yet another woman who can do this well, a woman who likes to recite poetry, by heart, who has passion for it. Then you need a High Priestess, who is in charge of the communal energies' rise and fall. This is the trickiest job of them all.

How can I teach you to listen to the communal energy? The best way is when you are all doing the hum, the vibration which we use to raise power/maintain energy with. This is done by all in the circle, and it is not a drone. It is a hum, put out on the outgoing breath; if the top of the head vibrates you are doing it right. This is the barometer for the leader to feel if the group is "cooking" or "sleeping." Your instinct will tell you which.

Don't be overdemanding. There are lulls in the energy flow and that's okay. But for example, if the women shuffle their feet and look all about themselves, while the women with their chalices go unheard, ignored, you stop the circle and get to doing something that gets back the attention to the sacred work at hand.

"The energy is dropped. Let's raise it again sisters!" you can say.

Group leaders need a repetoire of songs and power raising dances, chants, improvisational techniques. I have been trained by an improvisational theater, and I have many such natural skills. Those of you who don't, look into it. Second City School of Improvisation was my teacher. Viola Sills wrote a whole book about it. It is good for circle training. You just use the essence from it, not verbatim of course. (Viola never dreamed she was training a pagan priestess and not an actress. There is a big difference).

Examples: 'The Goddess is Alive!' You cry when you feel her presence (never when she isn't activated). The people answer 'Magic is afoot! Athena is alive!' You continue, 'Magic is afoot! Dianna is alive! Magic is afoot.' Encourage the women to contribute names of goddesses they know about. This makes them think and have no time to be bored.

Then when you run out of goddess names you substitute your own. 'All that is alive is the Goddess.' So then each woman gets to say her own name and the group blesses her with the response. 'Z is alive! Magic is afoot!'

Example 2: If you are outdoors you must dance to keep warm. Standing in one place is boring and unhealthy. So you do the traditional spiral dance. you face outward and leading the group in and out make snaky patterns all around the altar singing a song that all know (see this book for songs).

You can do it until it feels you have had enough; then all fall down to the ground tumbling and laughing; you can gather them again to stand still now that they had a good exercise.

In the beginning try to find a mountain and climb it for warm up exercise. It is spooky at first, ladies foraging out alone into the night, but it will increase your feeling of personal freedom. Meet on mountain tops if possible. My coven and I practiced at least seven years almost exclusively in nature. In any weather. But of course southern California is balmy even when it's wet. You can tell how the gentle Goddess Religion originated from the mediterranian areas, the cradle of high culture and good weather.

Indoor celebrations are harder to maintain high energy in. There is the distraction of familiar surroundings, less space to dance in. The blessing of the indoor practice is that you can be skyclad, which is certain to make any space appear ancient and natural. Skyclad celebrations are very special again because there is an extra freedom lived out, which is not permitted by present day society. Ladies worshipping themselves in the buff.

Be always crowned. If you wear clothes, one pagan act you can always do, and that is to make youself a green crown, a wreath, with flowers and green things. This is our symbol: we are Goddesses. Wear only your bracelets and necklaces, and rings, gowns wands, silver knives, and red girdles, and always wear flower wreaths upon your head and you are transformed into an ancient symbol of the Goddess.

As a priestess you must give yourself permission to do this as soon as possible. In patriarchy, adoring yourself with Revlon products is encouraged. The entire cosmetic industry mythically started from ritualistic adornments which Goddess people spent a lot of energy on. The painted faces they found in Egypt, the rouges in Crete, those were ancient sacred ritual tools, later to be degenerated into making ourselves desirable to men. We must take back vanity's mirror as a sacred tool of women in worship. We are beautiful for ourselves and our sisters too. We are beautiful because nature is beautiful. Women are nature. This fact becomes very clear on a skyclad sabbat.

How do I do it?

Sabbaths psychically begin a couple of days before the Dabat date. First we have to come up with a safe place to go to. This takes phone calls, organization, carpools arranged. Advertising published in our 'Themis' newsletter.

When the group assembles at the Feminist Wicca, they are already crowned, bejeweled, ritually clear. No other talk is disturbing the meditation but about the colors of candles involved and women thinking over what they want out of this sabbat.

I show up usually around 8 p.m., thirty minutes before leaving time. I greet people, we embrace, kiss a lot and tie up the loose ends. There is a collection for the church namely the Susan B. Anthony

Coven No. 1. It is explained that we need to continue publishing and raise funds for a permanent site (sigh).

I am looking at the women, see new faces, see some old friends, distribute the maps, last call to get on the road in a caravan.

When we arrive I take in the new site, and decide where the altar is to be set up. We make a large circle holding hands and also counting heads by running numbers from one another saying our number: 1, 2, 3, 4, 5, 6, 7, 8, etc.

I like to contemplate what that number means when I begin. We appoint the youngest woman present to be Nymph. Her job is to keep an eye on the chalice when passed around, and refill it with wine when needed. She is getting excited, she has never nymphed before. Another young woman laughs gleefully in the corner. I am glad I don't always have to be the youngest! We choose our Crone — the oldest woman in the Coven. She simply Queens, and all her wishes are served.

We appoint the priestesses who will invoke the four corners of the universe. Once upon a time, way back in the early seventies, I had circles of sixty or seventy women, but I had to do everything myself; all the corners, all the dismissals. Times have changed, praise the Goddess Durga. Priestesses ordained are present now to volunteer for corners. I usually take north. The priestesses assume their positions at their posts.(East, South, West and North).

In the meantime, there is last call to the bathroom. Nobody is allowed to leave the circle during rituals. This is most serious. A woman can have enough discipline to stay within a circle for about an hour. If there are dire cases, we can do emergency opening the gates symbolically as to honor the women's experience which is held in common; being in a closed circle.

Make sure all the food you brought is in the circle; everything you need later. Children are not required to follow the same rules. A small child wandering among the women is not breaking circle.

Drop your clothing and put it in the corner memorizing it. You will want to be able to find your belongings after sabbath.

Now we form a circle one more time and breathe together in and out. When the breathing is synchronized, you start the hum. The witches hum is our chanting basis. It is improvisational and can be produced by all, by simply vibrating the vocal chords gently together, without strain. When the top of the head vibrates you are doing it right. Sound unifies the body. The group becomes an entity, a thought form, a vibration, with sometimes intensity, sometimes a lull, but always moving. The bodies of women are undulating, there is sway to the circle. This vibration is kept up all during the magic work.

Priestess of the East picks up her place with arms stretched facing outward to the direction of the east, raising her voice above the general level of hum and invokes the Goddess. The women turn to her and say Blessed Be after she is finished. Now south, and west, and north. Back to east, otherwise the circle 'leaks'. It is an old custom. Just do east twice. (For details see Holy Book of Womens Mysteries Part One.) Then the Crone says "The circle is closed, the Goddess blesses her women."

This is when the serious power raising shall happen. A tapestry of sound can be weaved, a prayer in sound, not words. Oh, I've heard some moving power raising sounds in my time! Singers who flew with their voice straight to the moon. Choruses of women in temples of old come alive. The temple descends on us, and we are transported to the presence of our divine creativity.

You don't actually interfere with that energy. You don't stop it, it stops sometimes and you will listen to when. Then come to the middle of the circle and explain the holyday. Informal speech, not some formal churchy sounding preaching. Let there be humor anytime it wants to happen. Respect without formality. Pick up the sacred chalice and pour the finest wine you have and place it on the altar. Bless it with your hands, then hold it aloft to the moon if you are outdoors (insight: the catholics hold up the holy ghost over their chalice just like the full moon lands and sits in my chalice at esbaths).

The first cup is yours: 'Goddess of all Life! We welcome you and ask you to join in with us in our celebration' Libations on the ground if you are outdoors, just a sprinkle with your fingers on the altar if indoors. Then pass it woman to woman, from east to south, and each toasts the Goddess for their own reasons. This is usually an acknowledgement of the sacred designs, like — 'Thank you goddess for fulfilling my plea last sabbath and giving me this new opportunity to love!'

When the chalice goes around once, depending on the mood of the group, which may have been standing a long time by now, take some time and stretch everybody, make the body warm again. "Breath of Fire" exercise is fast and efficient for a quick warm-up. Then you can send the chalice around one more time for those who want something to help them this season. Sometimes the women are too many to do it twice, so in that case have the women both praise the goddess and ask her a boon at the same time.

Now rekindle the incense burner, put on some very fine quality incense, and recite either the Great Charge (usually the Maiden) or the Invocation to the Star Goddess (my favorite). All listen within for guidance.

You may choose to chant more songs, but it's well now that you bless the food and wine and sit down for a feast. You feed somebody else saying 'May you never hunger,' and offer a drink saying 'May you never thirst." This way you are free to eat and drink to your hearts content.

After the first munchies usually entertainment is in order. Women sing songs they have written or like, poetry gets read. Informal behavior during performances enhances the party atmosphere.

For watching this flow of energy there must be one person in charge and another tuned in to her. Everytime it was "everybody" High priestessing, the circle fell apart. Responsibility can be rotated, of course, and create a great training ground in your coven for all women.

Just before the high energy wanes (you must stay tuned in even through the partying) get up again and thank the spirits (East-North-West-South-East) for attending. Hail and Farewell!

MASIKA'S BOOK OF LIFE

A HUNGARIAN HERITAGE

Introduction

My mother, Masika, was the result of an immaculate conception, the facts of which are strange, yet true. Grandmother lived outside of the small town of Jaszentandras on a farm used for livestock and various farming. Throughout seven months of the year that Masika was born, Grandmother had no idea that she was with child. She had not been fertilized by a man, and she menstruated regularly every month. She did begin to put on weight, however, and when her back began to hurt a little she went to the doctor for a check-up. To everyone's astonishment, Grandmother returned home with my mother, all wrapped up in a baby blanket. At birth, Masika lacked nearly everything necessary for a healthy baby, and weighed a mere 170 dekagrams. Truthfully, no one expected her to survive.

This baby, however, showed extraordinary endurance, and an old woman, Victoria, who worked in Grandmother's house, adopted Masika almost as her own. Constantly vigilant, Victoria kept a close watch on Masika, cooking very special foods for her while nursing her into health. Victoria was a very well-known witch from Transylvania.

From Victoria, my mother learned all the arts of witchcraft: how to bless and how to curse, how diseases are cured with natural herbs; how to understand the language of animals; how to read cards and omens; how to speak with spirits.

168

One time mother became seriously ill, and doctors were imported from the capital of Budapest to heal her, but nothing they did made her any better. The illness spread to mother's eyes and kidneys. She was at her end.

Late one night, as Masika lay dying in bed, she awakened to find Victoria in her room. The old woman's hands bid Masika to keep silent as she brought two containers into mother's room—one filled with thirteen eggs, the other empty. Then Victoria pulled open the curtains of the window, allowing the Full Moon to shine brightly into the room. "The time has come," she said, as she took Masika's nightgown off and sat the child in the bright beams from the Moon. Mother's skinny little body trembled in the cold and Victoria began her cure.

One by one, Victoria took the eggs from the basket, stroking each one gently and fully over a part of Masika's body. She left not one inch untouched. The eggs were then placed in the empty basket after they had been used. Victoria prayed constantly as she did this, chanting rhymes for power and healing; mixing sweetly the Pagan with the Catholic, according to Universal Imagination.

"I am going to take this illness away from you," promised Victoria. She then went home to build very special nests, placing the healing eggs in them. Later, she cleverly left them in various places on the dirt roads of the countryside, as if they were stray nests left by some wandering hen. Daily she visited the nests, watching to see how many of the eggs were still there.

Then one day Victoria whispered to my mother, "Only two nests are left, and when they have been picked up, you will be well."

The physicians from Budapest just looked on, waiting for the child's death, but instead, Masika's fever broke. "All the nests are gone!" Victoria told Masika on another day, and mother got up that day and walked, acting fully cured. Years later my mother said that she had been healed because she believed Victoria more than she believed any other human being.

There were occasional nights in Masika's childhood when Victoria would lift her out of bed and walk a long way in the dark with her. They would march steadily through thickets and bogs until they reached a grove, thickly shaded from the eyes of outsiders, where other people of all ages were assembled around a fire. Masika remembers such groups gently singing of ancient shamen, who could be evoked when people in trouble needed help. Sometimes, at the end of a song, the members of the group would spit into the fire so that it sizzled. They invoked Boldogasszony, the Glad Woman, Great Lady of the Hungarians, and Special Mother to our nation. Although the State and its religion attempted total domination of the peasants, so that no one dared miss a Sunday at the Church, underneath the Hungarian "subas" (sheepskin coats) the hearts beat Pagan.

169

Victoria excelled in telling moon-tales. "There are mountains there," she would say, "and valleys, but not one flower, not one tree grows there. This is the land of the sad, sad spirits who are searching for peace. Lady Luna flies sorrowful through her once-blooming realms. She perches on the edges of the Moon and looks out from there into the great starry Universe, thinking about the Golden Times — when waters and trees, flowers and beings lived there with Her. But today it is the Land of the Dead." Thus did the old Transylvanian weave her tales.

Victoria could not even write her own name, but she was often seen carving signs on a willow branch with her knife, after which she would wrap the branch up and send it to someone — a witchy letter.

For fourteen years Masika lived in the same house with Victoria. During this time Victoria constantly taught my mother all she knew about everything. She spent time teaching Masika how to recognize the marks of death around people. Masika recognized such marks, invisible yet touchable, when visiting one day. "We shall not see this woman again until her burial," Masika informed my Grandmother, and soon the woman suffered a fatal heart attack.

Such incidents brought Masika quite a bit of attention from her family. "How does the child 'know' such things?" they wondered, agreeing eventually that it must have been coincidence. However, Masika's knack for prophecy grew, and her accuracy was amazing. The family, however, was concerned about this strange child, and especially about Masika's habit of talking to spirits all the time, giving the impression that she was forever talking to herself. Eventually, Grandmother took my mother to the nerve-doctor.

The doctor spent an entire morning with this 14-year-old, skinny tomboy. During the examination Masika told the doctor, "There is a woman standing beside you, and she is one you loved very much. It is too bad you cannot see her, for she is very beautiful."

Describe her to me," demanded the surprised doctor.

With complete accuracy, Masika then described the doctor's mother — the hairdo, coloring, clothing, and single red rose she wore over her breasts (the one the doctor had given her at the last good-by). Masika knew it all. The doctor was impressed. His diagnosis of my mother's condition was that she had an overly-sensitive nervous system, inclined to neurasthenia; a nervous system able to sense what the average nervous system cannot.

"She is by no means ill," the doctor reported to the family. "My advice is to ignore her when she makes these predictions, and when they come true, make nothing of it, but act as if it is the most natural thing in the world. Do not act surprised by her or afraid around her. She will grow out of it."

The family tried to follow these directions. The unexpected became

170

Masika Szilagyi

the routine. For example, on normal days Masika, on her way to school, might turn to someone and say, "My cousin, Miklos, just stepped on the train to Karcag. He will be here by 11:00." Nobody acted surprised. The family simply told the cook to prepare one more portion for dinner — company was coming. Everyone now knew that Masika was a "seer."

Masika's education at the hands of Victoria continued. When reading the cards for someone, the old woman would include the younger one, teaching her to do what Victoria could do.

"They think I watch the faces of the cards alone," confided Victoria. "The pictures serve only to take my mind away so that I don't see the lamps, the furniture, or the person whose cards lay before me. I only listen; and I hear, very clearly and deep inside me, the story which the person must hear from me. Then I speak aloud what I have heard within." Victoria believed that card readers had an obligation to refrain from passing into a deep trance in order to rise above immediate circumstances, allowing the inner voice to flow undisturbed.

Victoria taught Masika to bless, to attract, to suggest. If Victoria wanted to see somebody, she would repeat her "special names" a few times, encouraging my mother to say the names too, as she did. Then she told mother to mentally get her coat on, open the door, walk through the streets to the home of the chosen visitor, and ring her bell. "Then," directed Victoria, "take her by the hand and don't let go, but lead her home to us. Mentally open the door again and let her in. Gaze into her eyes very deeply and say, 'We are expecting you! Come and visit.' " This spell worked in three days, and Masika had fun "bewitching" reluctant boyfriends with her new-found charms (when working this on persons a great distance away, expect a letter or phone call rather than personal visit, unless the finances of the person are abundant).

A few years ago I visited Masika in Budapest. I found her in her studio creating masks of ancient witches and shamen and folklore figures. She was a happy woman. She was finally able to build her own house, in which there was room for her art as well as her family. Since she constituted one part of the mere 2% of artists who are women in my country, I was very proud of her. I asked, "Are you still practicing witchcraft?" Mother was taken by surprise. "How would I have the time," she answered. "I am much too busy. Besides, I gave all that up long ago."

The next day we were outside looking at Masika's garden, and she compalined to us about the high-rise that was being constructed across the street from her beloved new home. Intended as a new college for international students, the edifice stolidly blocked Mother's otherwise-perfect view.

"So what?" I shrugged. "Why don't you brush up on some of your powers and erase a few stories from that building?"

"No, I gave that all up," Masika replied seriously, but I could see her eyes sweeping the top two stories of the building with new perspective.

Then, about the time when the first star, Venus, became visible, and the Moon was rising in a crescent over Budapest, my mother got up from her studio workbench and washed the clay from her hands. Walking deliberately to the garden, she stopped and faced the high-rise, crossing her thumbs over each other and stretching her arms out to the Moon. She whispered the names of four Hungarian shamen, one for each of the corners of the Universe. Then she waited, motionless. Soon a small wind woke up and began to rustle the leaves of the Rosemary in Masika's garden. "They are here," noted Masika, with satisfaction.

"My curse upon this building ahead of my view," she said. "Curses into each of its four corners so that they crack. Curses into each molecule. A curse upon the whole edifice, that it may fall! This is my wish. Do it for me, spirits!" Then she returned once again to the house, washed her hands once more and set about preparing dinner.

Nearly a full Moon cycle went by. I had forgotten Masika's emphatic curse until my brother (who was also aware of it) brought me an interesting item from the newspaper. The article told of problems with the new college building across from Mother's house. It seemed that cracks had inexplicably appeared in the walls and foundations, and sewer water had flooded the basement. Moreover, the corners of the building appeared to be out of alignment. The building's engineers had been thrown in jail. Building a faulty structure in Hungary was a politically punishable act.

"That crafty witch," I laughed, as my brother looked at me warily.

Soon after, the construction workers and engineers removed two floors from the building — just enough to remove the block from my mother's view. Feeling a little guilty about the episode and her obvious part in it, Mother decided to make it up to the students who moved into the college. She began leaving slightly imperfect or cracked ceramic art pieces in her yard. The students appropriated every one and held a successful fundraiser with the treasures.

Clairvoyance in the Family

My step-father, Imre, was a physician who came from a long line of healers, and who was the seventh son of a seventh son. He was a sensitive of the good sort. His life was completely possessed by the fates of his patients, and he stayed in touch with them even after they left the hospital.

One night, as Imre was sleeping at home, we were all wakened by the sounds of his yelling and screaming. We found him sitting bolt upright in bed, frantically pointing at his forehead. Mentally, he was back at the hospital.

"Try it on the temples, Zoltan, try it on the temples!" he yelled, obviously calling to a doctor at the hospital who was not noted for his brilliance. Then Imre flew into a rage, yelling, "Damn you! You've killed that patient with your incompetence!" He fell back against his pillows.

Masika woke Imre, demanding to know who had died. "One of my patients on the children's ward," groaned Imre. "Zoltan was on duty and failed to give the child a blood transfusion."

The next morning Masika accompanied Imre to the hospital, where the porter took off his hat to my father as he entered — a signal that there had been a death during the night. Imre questioned Zoltan directly, acting uninformed because he didn't want to have to explain how he had "seen" all that had occurred the night before. Zoltan became very nervous at Imre's probing, and attempted to convince Imre that he had done everything possible.

"Did you try on the child's temples," prodded Imre.

"Oh, I tried that, yes. I tried everything!" Zoltan lied.

Imre threatened to have Zoltan's license taken away, and Zoltan finally confessed to everything. Imre fired Zoltan from the city's hospitals, anyway.

Another time, when Imre was operating on a surgical patient, a colleague noticed that tears were streaming down his cheeks onto his white mask. Concerned, he asked if Imre was all right. Continuing with the operation, Imre paused only briefly to say, "My father has just died." Then he finished the work successfully and went home to find a telegram announcing the sudden death of his father.

Imre's mother also possessed this ability to "see." She was a curious woman, a teacher by profession, whose great sorrow in life was that her husband slept around with various patients in town. As a protest, she refused to leave the house for many years. I would visit her often in her home, and she would tell me, "Little Joy, why don't you go down to Maiu Road? Five yellow roses just opened up on the right-hand side. Pick them for our table." I would obey and find the five yellow roses just opened, exactly where she said they would be.

The day after the death of her husband, Imre's mother received an urgent call from the school in town. The regular teacher was ill and they needed a replacement immediately. This amazing woman, who hadn't left her house in 20-years, suddenly picked up her purse and a few books, and left to teach school as if she'd done it every day. She taught as a regular teacher for the next ten years.

And then, of course, there was my mother. A German airplane once crashed in the vicinity of Masika's farm home. She spoke with the wounded soldiers, ran home for first-aid, and returned with her father to administer it, only to find that there was no plane, no crash, no wounded soldiers. This was before WWII had begun, and Masika's father rebuked her strongly, saying, "You must need a cold shower, saying such things!"

Exactly one year later, at the same place, Masika again witnessed the crash as she had seen it earlier. She convinced her father to go with her, after he threatened her with the spanking of her life if she'd made it all up. This time, however, it was all — even the war with Germany — horribly true.

"Hey, do you know I was talking to Mrs. Y. last night," Masika might remark one morning as she told us about her latest dream. "I had a few jokes with her before I remembered to ask why I was talking with her when she wasn't dead yet. So Mrs. Y. tells me, 'Oh, haven't you heard, Masika? I passed away last Tuesday.' So, what do you think about that?" Talking to the dead was Masika's favorite nighttime entertainment.

Often she would call up other people after breakfast, to relay messages she had received the night before. "Hello, this is Masika. I talked with your mother last night, and she said she is in favor of you sending her granddaughter to college. And one more thing, she said there is some money in the hollow pickle jar in the basement. You'll have to look through the rubble to find it, but she wants you to use it." A normal beginning to a normal day in my mother's house. And Masika was always right.

Fortune-telling was a specialty Masika practiced a lot, sometimes simply for her own entertainment. While riding on a crowded bus in which there was no seat for her, Masika would address a rider lucky enough to be seated: "Hmmm. You are going to see about that new job. You have an appointment with Mr. Kieuz's firm. Well, don't worry, you will get a job with that firm, but not the job you are applying for today." Usually, Mother not only received a seat on the bus as a result, but the eager attention of a busload of passengers, reluctant to disembark until they had had their fortunes told.

The Hungarian Olympic team used to visit our home before each Olympic Games to have Mother tell them how best to use their energy and how to win the most medals. Behind the Iron Curtain, winning is a political must and failure is not safe. Masika would read the cards and then tell the competitors what to watch out for, what to do and where to go, and even which foods to avoid. After the 19th Olympic Games in Helsinki, in which Hungary won sixteen gold medals (unheard of for a small country), the winners returned to our home and gave Masika a trophy for her help.

Masika's most spectacular achievement probably was speaking ancient Egyptian while in a trance. Only some university language professors could understand her during these times. It is believed that Masika was once an Egyptian priestess of Hathor, the Maiden Goddess of Egypt. Masika thinks she must have gone against the rules of her order by consorting with men, and that she was removed from the order as a result. The Order of Isis would have been a lot easier on mother's karma, perhaps, since the Mother Goddess does consort with men, but such are the Fates.

Masika belonged to several psychic groups, the first of which was the so-called "Paris Nine." She was still very young at the time, an art student who joined as the group's only female member, and who became the group's Medium. When she returned to Hungary, she belonged to another secret society, in which they practiced tele-transportations, quite a difficult thing to do.

From such a fertile Hungarian Pagan field, come the following "Books," grown from religious, ethnic, cultural and individual roots unlike any other, and indicative of my own roots.

Book of Superstitions

1. If you receive good news or are healed of disease, don't say, "Thank heaven, I am healed," or "Thank heaven, I have money," or things of this nature, because the evil spirits get jealous and mess up your good fortune. If you said something like this by mistake, knock on wood three times with your left hand, moving from the bottom to the top of the wood.

2. If your dog is sitting on her hind legs and howling, it means that she senses death and announces the approach of the Death Queen, Hecate, whose sacred animal is the dog. This could concern anybody who belongs in the house, or somebody on a journey to the house.

3. If you are travelling to visit someone without an appointment, and a bird flies across your path, forget the visit — the person will not be home.

4. If a bird shits on you, you will have good luck all that day if you don't wipe it off until the following day.

5. If your nose itches, you will have adversities.

6. If you bang your elbow into a corner, an unexpected visitor

will soon arrive. If the elbow hurts a lot, the visitor is from far away.

7. If you place a loaf of bread, bottom-up, on a table, there will be fights in the home.

8. If salt is spilled from its container, let the one who upset it clean it up. Otherwise poverty will strike the house, bringing great fights over money issues.

9. If your left palm is itching, money is coming to you; if it's the right palm that itches, you will soon spend money.

(NOTE: Masika doesn't really have too many superstitions. She says that this sort of thing is really for the Christians rather than witches, and that witches have too much studying to do to bother much with superstitions.)

Book of Dreams

1. If you dream of stepping in animal excrement, that means good luck. If you dream about stepping into human excrement, that's an omen of bad luck. Dreams of stepping into your own excrement usually are omens of disgrace. If you dream of somebody else stepping into excrement, it means money will come to you.

2. If you walk in mud in your dreams, it means illness. If the mud reaches your heart, death is near.

3. If you step next to mud in a dream, you have escaped illness. If you step out of mud, your escape will be a lucky move.

4. If you feed strange children in your dreams, it means gossip which is adverse to your own life.

5. If, in a dream, you brush your hair and lose many strands, troubles are coming. If you see white hairs as you comb your hair in your dreams, the one you love will leave you.

6. If you dream of getting a haircut, shame is coming to you.

7. If someone braids your hair in dreams, it means a journey is coming for you.

8. If somebody in your dream cuts off all your hair, leaving you bald, you will die a violent death.

9. If you dream of bathing in clear waters, your life will take a turn for the better. If the waters you see are dirty and muddy, troubles,

illness and sadness are ahead. (*author's note: my experience has been just the other way around, but dreams are shaped by many variables, not the least of which is the dreamer and her culture.*)

10. If you dream of swimming in a river whose currents are taking you further and further from shore, it means that the plans you are making will be difficult to achieve. If you dream of reaching the shores, it means that you shall overcome all difficulties.

11. If somebody is trying to drown you in your dreams, you have a strong enemy who envies your luck.

12. If you dream of taking a trip by train, car or ship, it means you are lagging behind in your work or plans.

13. When you dream of pushing through a tunnel that is dark, it is a birth memory.

14. If you dream of going for a walk while wearing a hat, it means your sex life isn't very active.

15. If you dance in your dreams, it means you are doing far more than is necessary.

16. If you cry while you dream, it means you will have a light-hearted day.

17. If you dream of lovemaking, it means you are not getting enough physical pleasure when you're awake.

18. If you are chased by wild animals in your dreams, it simply means you ate too much dinner.

(NOTE: on the whole, only dreams which occur at dawn are fit for prophecy because the rest of our dreams are likely to be the product of stomach action, and they may interfere with true psychic messages.)

Book of Cures

(My heritage boasts a wealth of healer-women. The following is but a sample of Masika's particular folk-lore remedies and does not constitute a modern compendium of either diagnostic or treatment techniques. — ZB)

1. Sickly child: When your child is skinny and pale, yawning more than playing, perform this 13-apple cure. Stick one iron nail in each of 13 apples. Place these apples out in the window to keep them fresh. Wait seven days, then take the nail out of the first apple and let your child eat the apple in two portions, after meals. Follow this up with the other apples, always eating each apple in two sittings, after meals. Replace the apples already eaten, thus feeding your child iron-reinforced apples throughout the winter. This will strengthen the bones, increase vitality, weight and stamina.

(Masika's Note: Isn't it wonderful how the ancient witch cures

spoke to the need for adequate iron in the blood, far ahead of the medical doctors who had not yet learned even to read blood-counts, or wash their hands?)

2. Eye-care: If your eyes begin to discharge, gather Chamomile flowers and throw them in boiling water. If it's summer, use only fresh flowers. Boil the flowers for five minutes, then let steep for ten minutes, letting the mixture cool at room temperature. Using a clean white cloth cut into strips, wash your eyes with the liquid, then throw the cloths into the fire and burn them. Use each piece of cloth only once, and when you throw the third piece into the fire say:

Queen of the Flames,

Mighty Mother of Fire,

Take away the sickness from the eyes.

Protect me from illness!

Do this three days in a row, both in the morning and at night, and your eyes will be free from disease.

(Masika's Note: This cure has existed at least 350 years. The doctors then had no idea of bacterium, but the witches, by throwing the used cloths into the fire, prevented reintroduction of bacteria into the eye. And who taught the witches? Other witches.)

3. Beautiful-woman's skin care: clean your skin carefully every night by washing it in lukewarm water and using a mild soap or fresh flowers to scrub the face. When your skin is clean, take the fresh urine of a pregnant woman and rub it on your skin. The next day, cook chicken soup (without paprika) and strain all the fine fat from the top. Using just a little of this, rub it well into your skin every night. Every Tuesday and Friday, lean over a hot tub of boiled Chamomile tea and let the vapors open your pores. The chicken fat is for use every night just before retiring. On Saturdays, when you wash your face, use Rosemary leaves to scent the water. Mint may also be effectively rubbed into the skin.

(Masika's Note: In these Old Days, vitamins were not yet discovered — only in the 20th century did scientists discover that the urine of pregnant women is loaded with vitamins, and is used today in the manufacture of many medicines. This skin care might sound laborious and disgusting to the squemish, but it is still practiced with fine success in the country.)

4. Love Potion: Go to a tree which has Spanish flies swarming around it. Using your LEFT hand, pick up three handfuls of flies. Count them, marking every third one for your will. Kill them so that their bodies remain in one piece. Dry the flies slowly, taking off the hardest parts of their bodies and powdering the soft parts. Put this powder into hard liquor and let it stand for three days, then strain it and give a very short drink to the one you desire. Do not give her more than

one drink, or the one you desire will become ill — the kidneys and the bladder could be harmed from too much of this drink. Do not be bashful after giving this drink, if you were not bashful about preparing it.

(Masika's Note: Love must be easier than this. If you have to go through all this simply to share sexual pleasures with someone, maybe you should reconsider your lifestyle. I give this recipe for curiosity only.)

5. Backaches: If your back hurts very badly and you can only walk while stooped over, this is what you can do to get better. Prepare a clay bench for yourself, built with three rows of bricks — plaster it all around and make the surface as smooth as polished wood. It's good to build this in a place which is protected from the elements in all seasons. When it is completed, lie on the bench on your back. Have your helpers hang red-cloth sacks filled with fine sand from your ankles. Do the same to the shoulders, hanging the red-cloth, sand-filled bags down from just above your head as you lie on the bench. Do this every day for about an hour, and use the bench afterwards whenever you want. Be careful and wise. Backaches can appear to be gone, but when you catch a cold or get otherwise weak, it may come back again. If you cannot build this clay bed for yourself, put a strong, heavy board in your bed and sleep on that.

6. Cold Sores: If your mouth has broken out with something nasty, it usually means you have eaten the wrong thing. Smear the sores thickly with your ear's wax on a swab. This makes it go away faster than any other salve the pharmacies can give you.

7. Advice to Men: When a young man has pimples, it's advisable for him to sleep with women. But when that's impossible, take large leaves of the Comfrey plant and wash them thoroughly (this is important since dogs love to urinate on Comfrey and dog urine is terrible on your skin). Thusly prepared, the Comfrey leaves are ready to put on the face overnight. The leaves work best when crushed in a cloth with a hammer, because then the juices are more available for absorption into the skin. This cure works for young women as well, of course, but women are not advised to sleep with men for their own skincare purposes.

8. Arthritis: This is a very old cure, and a rather painful one. Soak your body, the joints in particular, in hot water, so that you feel warmed all the way through. Prior to soaking, gather a bunch of fresh, so-called "stinging" Nettles, and soak that in a large bowl, with a small amount of vinegar added to it. Let your helper take out a bunch of the Nettles, after your bath, and strike them against your skin, paying special attention to the joints, the back, and the knees. It is a stinging and painful cure, but the ancients swore by it.

9. If you have a boil, do not touch it, scratch it or bother it. It will go away. If your rheumatism bothers you during the Winter, when all the Nettles have been frozen, mix strong paprika with some chicken

fat and apply it to the hurting joints. It will bring new, healing blood to the parts that need it. This cure is sold today in pharmacies, in heat-producing salves.

10. Earaches: If you have an earache, chop up a bunch of red onions. Put some cream on your ear and then stuff your ear with the finely chopped onions. Lay on your good ear so that the vapors from the onions have a chance to cure the earache. Lay with this onion cure for at least one hour, but overnight if you can manage it, as that would be more effective. Repeat treatment daily until the earache is gone.

11. If you have a headache, grind up some Horseradish. While you grind, inhale it, which will make you sneeze. Put some apple cider vinegar on the Horseradish and eat it slowly. Of course, don't do this on an empty stomach, it shocks the system. Let it steep in the vinegar for ½ an hour for more potent effect.

12. At childbirth, the umbilical cord should be cut with a freshly sharpened, Birch-handled knife. This knife is made by the pregnant mother while she is expecting. She dresses the knife up into a baby hat, and nobody is allowed to see it until the moment when the midwife needs it to cut the cord. This practice of hiding a new knife and keeping it clean in baby clothing was one way the ancient's used to assure good hygiene.

13. If your lot is good, such that you have gotten fat, and the dark blood in your face is making you look purple, watch out! You could get a heart attack. Before this happens, call your local healer and let her bring three leeches. Take off all your clothing and lie down on your back for the treatment. Let the leeches be put on your ass or your arms, but never on any major arteries!! They will relieve your condition, used properly. The leeches suck the blood until they get enough, then they fall off. If you desire to have them fall off earlier, put some salt on each one and they will fall off. During the course of one month, you should only have five such treatments, allowing a day in between treatments.

14. The wound which will not heal was, and still is, a medical threat. Scientists are still lost as to a cure. But in the olden times, wounds, in general, were not considered necessarily lethal. If there was a hole in somebody's stomach, the peasants made that person fast and pray for three days. Only milk was allowable to be taken internally. Then the healer-woman would prepare a drink with a mild solution of copper sulfate in lukewarm water and have the sick person drink that. This made the patient vomit up everything from the bottom of the stomach, including ulcerous tissues, and the copper sulfate acted as a disinfectant on the freshly cleaned lining of the stomach. This was especially effective in early days because they didn't operate, and this was an excellent way to remove sick tissues from the body.

15. In olden times, fresh wounds were treated and dressed by putting spiderwebs or mildew (which we know today, contain penicillin). If there was an inflammation or infection somewhere on the body, one remedy was to slice a ripe tomato and place it on the sore with a large Comfrey leaf. All this was then tied to the body with red cloth. In treatments such as these, the bandage was often red, the color of vitality, and was considered important to the cure. Yellow was also a popular color in healing spells, being the color of the Sun. In transferring a sickness away from a patient, the curing objects were often left for others to pick up and take away, but such tools were distinguishable by their yellow cloth, yellow leaves, or yellow flowers. Those of the Wicca never picked up strange monies or nests, or eggs, or any strange items found on country roads, especially if they contianed a yellow object. This always meant a transfer-cure.

16. If you have a weak stomach, or have stomach pains often, here is a treatment that has worked for many. Take three healthy potatoes and grind them slowly to a pulp. Let stand for 15-minutes, then strain them into a cup — it will look like juice. Drink the contents of the entire cup before breakfast, then go back to bed. Toss and turn, lying on your stomach, your back, and your sides, so that the juice gets to coat all the stomach. After this, eat some breakfast. This helps the stomach endure the input of the day's food.

(Note: This last recipe was a major item in the charges against a healer-woman during a witchtrial in 1570.)

These very recipes have been modified and refined into what is modern medicine, especially in part of the world where healers and physicians cannot afford chemicals. The cures of the witches are still the bases for many preparations sold in Hungary and other socialist countries today. In the Third-World countries, herbs and natural remedies are known from the core of medicinal treatments of the people.

Book of Hexes

To curse as well as cure is the heritage of witches. The feminist politic of the Dianic advocates the hexing of rapists and the cursing of male enemies in self-defense. To hex another child of the Goddess is a tremendous responsibility. Pagans who hex work under the knowledge that is LAW: cursing the innocent brings evil back ten-fold. Masika's curses are intentionally strong, to eliminate any doubt of purpose. Cursing and curses are the gravest of matters, never to be undertaken lightly, and the following excerpts from Masika's Book of Hexes reflect a particularly Hungarian flavor. The power to curse and to hex is, in and of itself, neutral. How it is used depends upon the person. To those who abuse the power comes total devastation.

1. When a chronic disease plagued someone, and they wanted to get rid of it, they were given paper money to sleep with. When the night gave way to morning, and the Moon paled into dawn, a relative took the money from the sick person and put it into a rich-looking purse. The purse was then dropped somewhere, preferably where many people could have discovered it. It was believed that whomever took the purse, took the illness as well.

2. "If you have an enemy who threatens you, defend yourself!" said Masika's teacher, Victoria. "That's the only way to save yourself." Create a clay doll, in the physical image of your enemy. Take a strand of your enemy's hair, and a piece of clothing from the enemy. Put all these on the doll, and call out the name of your enemy 13-times. Do all this without anybody hearing or seeing you. Now talk to the doll. Tell the doll that . . .(name) . . . is very bad and evil, and then that . . . (name) . . . must be transformed. Talk to the doll for 13 consecutive nights, telling it all of the sins and transgressions of . . . (name) . . . against you. Stand the doll up facing you, as you do this, either on a piece of white or a piece of black stone. Both colors are significant colors of Death. Allow your anger to swell, then plunge a rusty nail directly into the heart chakra of the doll, into its throat, etc. Let your anger show; experience the anger you feel about this person. When you have tired yourself out with this hexing, ask the Just and Merciful spirits to help you by calling out this person to the happier realms of bodiless existence. On the 13th day, when you have stuck the doll to death and your anger is climbing to the very heights, take the hairs on the head of the doll and tear them apart. Place the doll in the death-position, on its back, with arms crossed on the chest. It is done.

If you cannot get hair or clothing from the enemy, then get his handwriting on a letter (even an envelope will do), roll it up, put it into the middle of the doll, and on the 13th evening (using Waning Moon throughout), cut it into pieces with a sharp scissor or hack it with a sharp

183

hatchet. Then put the pieces together and arrange the doll on its back in the death-position. This last move is most important.

   3. Victoria also believed in the following hex: Get a photograph and put it up on an empty wall. Pick the heart and keep sticking pins into it for 13 nights, preferably at midnight. One needs to concentrate longer for this hex, but it will yield results. For the full 13 days, the pins re-main in the photograph. Then, burn the image and spit into the fire as She consumes it. Bury the ashes as if it was the enemy.

From Mother's Book of Sorrows

   My mother and I come from a long line, or great circle of witches. I am the last branch on an 800-year-old family tree, although I consider myself first on the tree of the New World. Ever since I can remember, Mother has kept a book about the witch-burnings, intending to pass it on to me one day. It was not easy getting this book from her. For years she claimed she had lost it, and other times she denied ever having it at all. Finally, just before the completion of this work, mother sent me her book. She called it her "Book of Sorrows" because it deals with terrify-ing accuracy of the tortures, burnings, and murders of witches. I believe it to be a timely and powerful reminder of what was done to women in the name of Christianity not very long ago. Many of the archaic and repressive laws resulting from this period of mass hysteria are still "on the books," and the persecution of the Goddess's children has not stopped to this day. The following is excerpted from mother's Book of Sorrows:

In Hungary, King Kalman declared a stop and full halt to any witch-persecutions, trials and tortures, the year being 1175. In spite of this order the Christian churches still held legal witch-burnings with no interference from the King. The total recorded number of witches burned at the stake was about 10,000 women. Since records were only kept by the churches, the actual number can be understood to be at least ten-fold.

   Victims: anyone performing any pagan act; carriers of herbal lore and cures; midwives, priestesses, prophets; any person with a witch's paraphernalia (chalice, wand) in the home; any woman pointed out by a man who claims he was hexed by her.

   Accused witches were brutally tortured. To press confessions from the poor women, their tormentors would prick their bodies all over with hot needles. If the accused did not cry out in pain she was lost, since the devil obviously had his mark on her. After hours of torture, women were stripped naked and displayed in the middle of the town, usually in chains. The women were then ridiculed and offered as frightening examples of what happens to pagans.

Meanwhile, the executioner would begin the negotiations with the family of the unfortunate victim, soliciting money as a bribe for a fast, death-dealing blow. He met with each family in this way, sometimes taking the last chair or possession from the house. If the victim's family could not meet the demand in some way, the woman was left to die a slow and wretched death.

Often this barbarism provided entertainment for the town. Every cry and scream was discussed by local observers as the Catholic priest held his crucifix high over the woman's burning flesh.

In spite of the intense tortures, the people clung to their old religion, refusing to give it up.

The last witch burned in Hungary was Margit Salka, who lived in Szeged on a small island in the river Tisza. Margit was an herbalist who had learned the skill from her mother. In 1869 she was accused of poisoning a man from the town and, although there was no evidence against her, she was burned to death. She was 30-years-old. Even today her island is called "Witches Island" in her memory.

The following is excerpted from an accounting of one particular witch-"trial" of Erzsebet Galantai, in February of 1761:

Judge: Do you confess that you made love potions and let the young men from Csongrad drink of it so that they all became enamored of you?

Erzsebet: No. I know nothing of such a drink.

Judge: Do you confess that sitting on a wand you flew up and became a bird;

Erzsebet: No, I don't.

Judge: Do you confess that you spat upon the wheatfields and thereby caused a great drought?

Erzsebet: No.

Judge: Do you confess that you gave birth to twins and then buried them alive?

Erzsebet: It is true that I gave birth to twins, your Honor, but they were dead. I had to bury them, otherwise I would be suckling them, since my milk is oozing after them.

Judge: You had better admit to the rest of the charges or you will be tortured.

Erzsebet: I cannot, your Honor, because I have not done these things.

Erzebet was then given over to be tortured. The sadist men could do anything to her that they wished. The priests were eating lunch and dinner while the poor woman screamed from pain. The torturers poured hot water into Erzsebet's mouth through a sieve, and she finally confessed to everything. At that point she was sentenced to death.

Erzsebet had to dig her own grave. Then she was put in a casket that had the head-end sawed completely off. When they placed her in the casket, her face was looking through the hole into the ground, and the rest of her was buried alive. Then the men poked at Erzsebet's face with hot irons until she felt no more. At last, they chopped up her skull so that she could not rise by night to hunt them. All in the of Jesus.

Another case took place in 1550, in Transylvania. The name of the woman was Anna Apor, a Transylvanian noblewoman, whose father was believed to be friendly toward the Turks, and therefore, he was beheaded and all his goods were taken from the family. Later, when the King himself began making pacts with the Turks, it was feared that Anna might get back all her land, so gossip about her being a witch was begun.

Anna's supposed crimes included the charge that she turned people into wolves and dogs. She denied this, of course, stating that she would love to turn herself into a fly and leave her shackles behind. The judge hastily claimed that Anna had lost her "powers" because she had been sprinkled with "holy water" and smoked with incense. The judge further charged Anna with knowing the power of trees and herbs, which Anna acknowledged she did, indeed.

Anna's fingernails were torn out with hot rods. She was stripped naked and her beautiful hair was chopped off. Still she did not confess to being a witch, so they ordered the water "test," in the belief that witches always float and never sink. Again, the whole town turned out as Anna was stripped naked and heavy chains were fastened around her waist. Slowly they lowered Anna into the Tisza. It was December. Anna knew how to swim, even though few women of the period knew how, but she was so exhausted from the tortures that she sank and embraced the cooling waters like a mother.

The judges then declared Anna innocent, and one of them commented that her pain in this life would come in handy in the next world, in front of her "lord." However, Anna was apparently swimming unconsciously, and soon surfaced after all. Her waist was bleeding from the chains. She was immediately judged guilty of all charges. Her death sentence was to burn at the stake, but a Transylvanian uprising occurred coincidentally with her pending execution, and the records show little of what actually happened to Anna. We believe that she died of hunger, forgotten in the dungeon, as the ruling class busied themselves trying to save their property from the revolutionaries. Some say Anna was freed by her people.

There were instances of men also being executed for witchcraft. One such man, a leader of his town, was found guilty of witchcraft and his body was quartered so that each piece could be taken to one of the four corners of the country as a warning to others predisposed to the practice of paganism.

Mother's Book of Sorrows has many "sister-" books all over the world. In France in the city of Tier, only ONE woman was left alive. There were days when hundreds of women were burned, so that the flesh-burning stench would dissipate by the time Christmas was to be celebrated!

The worst persecutions took place in southern France, southern Germany, northern Italy and southern Austria. When the mother or father of a family was declared a witch, the children, up to a year old, were taken as well. Entire families were burned to death because of the fear of paganism. Later on, the Christians softened this stance, and only drove children of convicted parents around the burning pyres three times, flagellating their naked bodies. What cries, what memories must we all carry in our collective unconscious!
Many witchhunts were the direct result of greed over lands and property rather than religious zeal. Whomever pointed a finger at a witch, resulting in her conviction and execution, was rewarded with ten-percent of the murdered woman's goods. The Church received the rest. In Salem, in the United States, the intent was the same. Cotton Mather had adjoining lands to those of Goodie Nurse, and wanted it all to be his. He managed to acquire almost all the property of all the witches hung.

The budding medical profession was also hungry to rid themselves of the herbalists, who rivalled them. To cure was a bigger sin than to curse as a result of this deep jealousy.

The persecution of the witches may be best explained as a desperate attempt, on the part of the new-fangled Christian churches to establish themselves with the peasants and townspeople, and to accumulate wealth. All this took place during a heavy period of warring which went on for decades, and terrible plagues which the Church could not combat. During times of economical depressions, the ruling class often finds an outlet for the people's anger by pointing the finger at minorities in the population upon which anger may be most safely vented. What they do, in essence, is to scapegoat a particular minority in order to save their own tenuous positions, and to divert attention away from their own inept leadership and impotence in the face of real enemies and problems.

This shows what Judeo-Christianity has done to my religion. It indicates the tremendous suffering and pain that is the heritage of Women's Religion. Every woman who embarks on the Path must allow herself to feel the rage of the Millions of women executed. This atrocity must not be allowed to occur again.

Where I come from in Europe, we suffered tremendous losses. Four of my aunts were killed during the Burning Times, but very few, if any, European families cannot find at least one female member who was murdered. These women were killed because they were women. They knew something that the patriarchal religions considered "sinful." They knew how to deliver babies without giving the mother "childbirth fever," how to cure colds, attract good fortune, and heal the body. These women could take care of a community all by themselves. They didn't need the advice of the struggling new medical profession, which was still quite ignorant. They were prime targets for scapegoating.

Thus, a full-scaled political and religious war was waged against the Wicca. Women were tortured, burned, and hanged regardless of whether or not they had ever been to a Sabbat. Women were slaughtered on a massive scale, often without any evidence whatsoever that they were actual witches, priestesses, or pagans. To the eternal shame of the humanoids, nobody stood up to stop this 300-year massacre. Even today there has been no calling for an accounting of responsibility around this issue. Witches are still being scapegoated and "burnt" today. We must move on, and we must not forget. We can not.

GODDESS OF TEN THOUSAND NAMES

Come with me to the Temple, close your eyes, and then open them again. See without limitation of anything else but your own

188

common sense. I show you images of temples, images of the goddesses who were created before us, by Goddess worshipping people. We are not the first ones, and not the last yet. And even if we are the first women who turned to worship themselves and their own creativity in the Goddess, then more glory to us.

I will not attempt to convince you about the authenticity of what you see. You must trust your own eyes, and learn to see. It is important that you see these images without turning your attention to what they were called, classified, or thought to be by archeologists. Archeologists are not witches who yearn to see the Goddess in her many guises. Her guises often mislead them. We don't have allies among many scientists today. The Craft is threatening to them. Their jobs can be in real danger if they start telling the truth. So for those who debate if there was ever a society where women ruled, or just an assumption of women's inherent ability to be superior, is abhorrent; forget it. The temple is for those who are excited seeing her in a different light. The temple can be entered through your mind with a clear affirmation for life. Come now . . .

Images of the Mother Goddess, female principle of the universe and source of all life, abound. This imagery is much more important than we have been told. She lives in clay, in stone, in ancient tools, in modern paintings. She has been changed almost beyond recognition by the patriarchal militaristic forces, but She survives.

Here is a Great Corn Goddess of South America, Lady-Unique-Inclination-of-the-Night. She is shown at birth. Her delivery is without pain, because She knows nothing about a "curse" from a jealous Christian god. Women knew how to lessen the pains, and expel the after-birth, through herbs. They didn't think of giving life as a punishable crime. The Great Corn Goddess gives birth to Herself.

Corn goddess

189

Mother Demeter is often seen sitting on Her throne. The Goddess Demeter is the fertile earth, from where all bounty comes. She is the law-giver, and protector of women.

Kore (means Maiden) is a correspondent of Persephone, daughter of the Earth. She represents all that is above the ground, and is usually portrayed with a sacred flower, or the "apple of dominion" held in Her hand. It is the same apple we see in Mary's hand later on in Christian temples. Same apple Eve sank a healthy bite into, it was always Her apple!

Persephone

Hathor

The Egyptian Maiden-Goddess is Hathor, whose law is change. She wears a headdress with a disc of the sun and disc of the moon as Her crown. Since She invented writing, Her favorite plant is the papyrus, which she usually holds in Her hand. Hathor is the maiden-aspect of Isis. One of Hathor's holidays is a time when everybody gets drunk. Another festival of Her's is when Hathor is angry, and tears patriarchal men apart, and revels in the sea of their blood. She is a passionate goddess.

The Great Goddess Nut comes to us from Egypt also. She is the Universal Goddess, encircling everything. The Sky Goddess and the Earth Goddess are represented as part of Her trinity, and between them is a calendar of planting cycles, considered sacred wisdom to the followers of Nut. The concept of such a depiction is that if you know when and how to plant your food in order to best feed and nurture your body, then you will be able to consistently create food enough with time left over to engage in the creation of beauty. Nut became a symbol for women marching to "Take Back the Night" because she rules the Universe and the Darkness.

Hygeia   *Bast*

Goddess Hygeia always held a boa constrictor as a symbol of her regenerative powers. Statues of her show a real, seemingly familiar, black woman's face. Many artists of the period used the faces of real people in their creative expressions of the Goddess, so we do have some knowledge of what the people looked like. Images such as those of Hygeia probably came from the women physicians who felt their towns should have statues of the healing-aspect of the Goddess in order to stimulate healing in themselves.

The Goddess Bast also comes from Egypt. She is the sun, powerful and able to effect the growth of living things. Generally She was seen as a black cat or lion-headed Goddess, very much involved with dancing and expressions of a pleasure-orientation. Egyptian physicians often were recognized by the symbol of the black cat, who was worshipped for its symetry, its disposition, and because it had such a strong relationship to Bast.

In other areas of the world (Europe), Bast became Diana Lucifera Moon and Sun Goddess. Lucifera appeared a mere century away from the concept of "Lucifer" as a "fallen angel." Lucifera, in actuality, was the Goddess Lucina, brilliant Sun of Healing. Lucifera is the maiden-aspect, usually shown holding the torch of the Sun. Later on, this image recurs in the Statue of Liberty. Here we see the sun goddess, holding up the torch of life, crowned with a crescent.

Kali the Terrible is the Goddess of Death, greatly resented by men because of Her awesome power. This concept embodies the philosophy of the ultimate return of each of us to the One who gave us life — in this case it is not the human mother of our own biology, but her kin-spirit, the Female Principle. Kali always has a young-looking

Lucina

Kali

Asian Athena

Greek Athena

body, very fit, very trim and very powerful. Portrayals often show Her with a beard, a symbol of wisdom and power not at all confined to males. Beards and garishly protruding tongues are aggression gestures.

Black Kali had a very big impact on Indian culture. Many of the ancient temples of the Goddess and Yoni-shrines are decayed and overgrown with grass, but Black Kali still has Her temples intact. Even the Hindus in the Krishna tradition, speaking of modern times, refer to this as the Age of Kali, suggesting that we are in a period of great evil and wickedness. Kali is Goddess of Death and Regeneration, but She is not evil, and she is certainly not wicked or bad. As the Indian representation of Magaera, Kali is often shown dancing on the body of one of the male gods, indicating Her dominance over all life, particularly the Male Principle of the Universe. Skulls hanging from around her neck usually

192

represent the many generations who went before and will follow after, as well as being symbolic of the inevitability of death.

A painting on this vase containing a woman's remains, shows the attitude towards death. The priestesses are instructing the soul of the departed, which is represented by the Ka, or bird. On the other side, the Goddess is beckoning for the soul to reunite with her. None of the horror of Hell, or cruelty of fear is seen here. A calm and almost cheerful passage from life to another life is depicted.

The worship of the Goddess Athena goes way, way back. She is actually an African Goddess, though the Greeks "whitened" her considerably, Athena is credited with the invention of writing, music, spinning, and sciences. She is usually shown holding Her sacred sceptre of rulership in Her hand. Athena in her African aspect, is still very young, but strong. Legend has it that Athena had a best friend called Pallas. Pallas fell from a cliff during their Amazonian games. In her sorrow and love for Pallas, she affixed her image on her breast as a spirit of protection, and her name in front of her own, hence Pallas-Athena.

Here is an Asian Athena, smug in her power, able and spiritual. She holds her tortoise-shell shield, for woman's wisdom is her shield. The tortoise symbolizes that wisdom and endurance are the tortoise's strength. They live for hundreds of years.

Athena is a very important Maiden Goddess. She never consorts with men. In the trinity of the Goddesses, there is always this Virgin-aspect, the maiden as a lesbian Goddess. This is the Goddess of Freedom, exemplified by Athena, Diana, Persephone, Artemis, and Kalisto (some of the more recognizable Virgin-aspect names). In the Goddess pentarch there is a lesbian Goddess as well. This leads us to surmise that the emphasis on sexuality in the matriarchies was placed strongly on pleasure rather than procreation, and that lesbianism was a natural mode of interaction among women (a natural birth control), while heterosexuality was chosen seasonally for the purpose of breeding or attraction for men.

Here are some Yoni priestesses anointing themselves to prepare for their rituals. The intimacy, the freedom that was theirs, contrasts with the lack of freedom of the sisters in the Orient today sharply. They certainly seem lesbian.

Athena is the force binding humans to their societies, giving social feelings. She is NOT a Goddess of war. Patriarchs, of course, demanded that Athena be re-born from a male or the people would no longer be allowed to worship Her in any way. Thus, an artificial "birth" was contrived, and out of Zeus's headache over what to do with all these maiden Goddesses, Athena supposedly sprang, fully armed. Times being so bad for the Goddess and Her people, Athena was fully clothed at Her "birth," rather than being proudly naked as before.

Yoni priestesses   *Proud Aphrodite*

This time we see Athena holding the Goddess of Victory in her hands, because Athena never loses. Once there was an election in Athens to rename the city. The new patriarchs wanted it to be "Poseidon." After the votes were counted, the patriarchs lost because the women turned out in record numbers and voted for their Goddess. This cost the women the right to vote and the naming of their children after the women (changed over to naming them after the fathers). And the institution of marriage was introduced to subdue the women's civil rights.

Athena was widely and reverently respected. Her sacred bird is the owl, and Her mother is Rhea, whose name means "Flow of Life." Rhea was considered to be the Supreme Queen of Heaven – Queen of All.

The Goddess Ngami is from Africa, a Moon Goddess like Diana. The Voodoo tradition is related to Ngami, but the word, "voodoo" simply means "little god." Think of this when you are forced to hear all the negative teachings about Voodoo, and take it simply as a religiously ignorant, racist, ethnic slur against the African Old Religion.

It was Aphrodite, Goddess of Love and Fertility, who actually suffered the worst rape at the hands of patriarchal rule. The Goddess of Death was basically written out and never talked of again, and the Virgin Goddess survived in modified form. But the Goddess of Love and Sensuality, "She-Who-Binds-Hearts-Together," was made a whore and prostitute, deliberate incorporation of all that is "evil" with all that is "female." Her name used to be Marianna or "La Mer," meaning "The Ocean." She is then a Goddess of the Western corner, usually shown holding an urn or seashell, and pointing out Her genitals as the Source of All Life.

194

Aphrodite with Eros   *Guadalupe madonna*

Aphrodite is the Virgin Mary before appropriation by the Christians. Ancient stone statues depict Aphrodite with Her Sacred Child, Eros. The Child is not turned away from Aphrodite, but turned toward Her in a posture of security, familiarity, and tenderness. There is an awareness here that the Child will grow up to be treated differently, unlike modern patriarchal societies where the male children are treated as children all their lives. First, the mothers nurture and care for the modern male, then girlfriends and wives, and finally, daughters.

This image of Mary is so ingenious, in many ways. First of all, the Lady of Guadalupe appeared on the very spot of an earlier Goddess shrine, and requested herself a new temple. When the peasant to whom she appeared asked for a sign to make the bishops believe him, she gave him roses. Roses are always a sacred flower of the Mother, especially red ones. This image is very reminiscent of a vagina. If you squint your eyes, the pagan idea shines through the door of life, and the yoni appears. The emanations are the labia and hairs. The red is the blood coming out, and the head is the clitoris. The blue has always been the mantel of the Queen of Heaven.

Early depictions of Aphrodite show Her to be strong, and sturdy. She is obviously proud. She has all Her muscles and stands strongly erect. In later representations however, we see Aphrodite losing all Her lovely muscles and the bodily strength that goes with it. Because patriarchy found these particular attributes to be distasteful, Aphrodite is modified accordingly over time. She begins to crouch a little at first, to bend over later, and finally to recline. The postures portrayed thus forced Her image to drop from an assertive strength and power to a languid passivity.

Priestesses of Aphrodite served the fertility-aspect of the Goddess, in contrast to the Maiden-aspect served by the Virgins (Lesbians). Priestesses of Aphrodite were known as "holy women," or "Qadishtu," and lived in the temple complex. These women extended the Goddess' Grace to impotent men who were fathering no children. Usually the wives brought the men to the temple so they could be cured of their impotency by lying with a Goddess-manifest, the "sacred woman." Later, when the child of such a union was born, the happy couple would leave a generous gift at the temple for the Priesteshood. These gifts became part of the temple property, passed down from woman to woman, and a factor in the continuing independence of the Priestesses. Very often the "sacred children" were brought up to assume the temple roles of Priestess or Priest, as extensions of the Goddess.

Lilith is an original Jewish Goddess, mentioned only briefly in Judeo-Christian sacred texts and later written out completely. Lilith is the Female Principle of the Universe whom the Jews had to overcome. Generally a religion which is being superceded by another religion, through military might rather than conversion, suffers a reversal. The first thing that happened to the original religion was that it became totally masculinized. The religious names were changed first, and then the functions of the deities were subverted or completely eliminated. This is particularly obvious in the case of Lilith.

Here we see her with the owl, whom she shares with Athena. She is winged herself because, she too is a spirit. On her head we see snakes, a familiar Goddess symbol of regeneration and wisdom.

Lilith was originally associated with life, with the birth process, and with children. She was protector of all pregnant women, mothers, and children.

Crouching Aphrodite

Lilith

Statuesque portrayals of the Three Graces, the Three Muses, the Three Mothers, are familiar to most of us. Their names must be spoken only with great reverence because if they are taken in vain or abused by the patriarchal forces, the Mothers become the Three Furies. Their names are: Alecto, Goddess of Beginnings; Tisiphone, Goddess of Continuation; Magaera, Goddess of Death and Rebirth, whose name means "Schism," or the "Abyss." These three concepts form the cornerstone of Women's Religion. They were later stolen from us and integrated into the Judeo-Christian religions as their own trinity, when the patriarchs were busy masculinizing the Goddess.

This is an Hecation. Here we see the sacred Nymph, the young woman, the Maiden, and the Crone holding together the torch of life, representing the circle of life. Imagine walking by hecations every day. They stood at the crossroad sacred to Hecate, the Three-formed. She is the priestess to Persephone, She is the Witch Goddess. Hecate can change forms, ages, and can rejuvenate and kill. Her chariot is pulled by dragons, and her favorite witch is Medea (whose name means Preistess). Legend has it that Medea didn't die, but Hecate came for her on her chariot, and swept her away.

Due to financial reasons, not all slides mentioned in the article are shown.

Hecation

Trinity by Masika

The Goddess has 10,000 names, shared by women around the world. Her name is Diana, Holy Mother. Her name is Tiamat, Her name is Hecate. Her name is Isis, Inanna, Belili; Her name is Sapasone, Belladonna, the Great Corn Mother; Her name is Alaskan Bear Mother, Artemis, Brigid, Io, Morrigan and Cerridwen; Her name is every woman's name — Carly, Doris, Lily, Catherine, Sharon, Susan. All of the personal names of women derive from Goddess names, as all women without exception are the expressions of the Mother — Goddess-on-Earth-Manifest.

Three-In-One

Patriarchal theology has purposely fortified the misbegotten impression that the Trinity is male and inherent in Judeo-Christianity. In actuality, the concept of a spiritual triumvirate of deities was understood and respected in religions far older than the young Christian upstarts.

Goddess-worshipping people had little use for perfect dualities — in concept, theory or practice — believing, quite accurately, that such a precept by definition was simplistic and limiting. The children of the Goddess saw Her as the Three-In-One. All the Goddesses were either triads (as three-formed) or pentarchs (five-formed), or ninefold (Muses).

The Nymph begins the Thread of Life, the Goddess of Continuations weaves the Thread into a Tapestry, and Magaera, with Her Shears is ready to cut the Thread. The Three are the Maiden, Mother, and Crone, Beginnings, continuations, and endings with continuations, and endings with constant regeneration are thus symbolized.

The Trinity relates to the three major cycles of womanhood; Nymph as pre-menstrual daughter; Mother as life-giving creative force;

198

Sacred nymph

Crone as the post-menopausal wise woman. Each stage of womanhood was worshipped as sacred in itself. All transitions are being celebrated with appropriate rituals.

Here is the sacred Nymph in all her playfulness. She is representing the fun and play aspect of the Female Principle. The perfection of the nymphs just lately has been hailed during the Olympics when Olga Korbut showed her control and skill. She would be considered a sacred Nymph manifested. The Nymph also has a position in the coven. She is responsible for the fun parts: food and drinks, music and songs. In our coven, she makes sure that the chalice never goes dry, and refills it with her wine jug.

The image of the Crone perhaps suffers from the longest abuse and greatest misunderstanding. Every Goddess, Maiden or Nymph has the "terrible" (as in awesome and frightening) aspect, often referred to as the Hag. We see this aspect in abundance on Halloween, and it is true that it is an important part of the female Life-Force. In Her cycles, as in Her rituals, there is the death of something before there is a rebirth. But the Crone must not be discarded as a useless, ugly hag who shrieks and hoots on Halloween. This modern image of our sacred Crone is deliberately derogatory. Reviling that which is feared is typically patriarchal.

The Crone was revered in Goddess religion as the Carrier of Wisdom; She who has lived long enough and well enough to be able to share Her knowledge, thus making "tuition" a little cheaper for the young ones. We don't all have to go through the same problems, since there is such a positive thing as learning from another's mistakes. When a culture discards its elderly, each succeeding generation has to suffer through the same traumas, never learning a thing. Such an attitude keeps us from following the natural flow of information, and it is very sad for our species.

The concept of the Trinity relates to the three phases of the Moon, as well as to the three major cycles of a woman's life. The New Moon brings beginnings, introspection, inner wisdom to make a start; the Moon grows as beginnings are continued and the energy is heightened; then the Full Moon brings fruition, completion, ripeness, and the endings follow to the next New Moon, thus completing a cycle and beginning another at the same time.

The theme of trinities is carried out in jewelry, in necklaces, in braids of hair, in Nature, clothing and art. The Pentarchs, the sevens, the nines, all harken back to this original concept of the Goddess as One, the Goddess as a sacred Trinity, the Goddess as Three-Times-Three, the Goddess as Multiple. (Multi-racial, multi-functional, etc.).

Luna

Some people think that Goddess-worship is merely some cultic Moon-worship, but that is not true. We are not a religion of the Moon, rather we worship what the Moon does; how it affects Earth's magnetic tides and the waters needed by every living thing.

The Moon controls the ebb and flow, the tides of the Ocean; this concept of the Moon as a Controller of Life gave this divinity that manifestation, but it is not the "planet," the "light", the "Moon", per se, that we worship. It is Her awesome power. Without water there is no life, therefore IS life. Because the Moon has this special relationship with the Earth, She receives a lot of attention from us. We respect and revere what She is able to do, we worship the ways in which She influences and manifests life, and we attempt to learn from Her the healthiest and happiest, most spiritually fulfilled way to live. The Great Huntress, Diana, is Goddess of the Moon. She regulates wildlife, menstrual cycles, and conception of babies, and is therefore of particular relevance to women.

Yoni shrine

*13,000 year old
bronze age goddess*

Signs and Symbols

So-called "traditional" religions have developed symbology through the practice of taking the original pagan symbols and integrating them into the newer religion. They have accomplished this over centuries by deliberately misinterpreting and mistranslating ancient records, and by regularly and very consciously writing the Great Goddess out of the picture altogether.

Nothing can be more unnatural than life without the Mother. However, patriarchy succeeded in selling the world the concept of a self-created male — the concept that a Father God created himself. Never in the history of life has there been an instance of a male giving birth to anything, let alone a universe and let alone people. There has never been an instance where humans 'issued' from anywhere other than a mother's womb. That is how it all works, and that is how Life occurs.

This is also why the naked female form is revered in witchcraft as the Source. The Goddess, in statues, pictures and drawings throughout history, is often shown pointing to Her genitals. This is not because She is being coy or coquettish, but because She points to the Source of Life. Naked figurines such as this found all over the world, have been dismissed by archaeologists as very minor parts of fertility cults, lacking in importance. Try to live without fertility and you will find that without it, nothing and no one goes on. Fertility is your food, dinner. Fertility is your pleasure.

Here's one of my favorite ancient Goddesses. She is 13,000 years old. The more abstract a Goddess representation is, the less it appears humanized. Her rectangular arms are symbols of manifestation. The hole in her legs is the universe. When she was created by some loving hands, male gods were worshipped nowhere on this earth. Her breasts are barely indicated, as it is not important. Her femaleness is evident.

The earliest representations of the Goddess portray Her as a bird. She is the white dove, the wise owl, the vulture in Her death-aspect, the sacred heron of Aphrodite. Early Anatolian findings interpreted the bird symbology as signifying a Holy Spirit. This very sacred Spirit gave life, healed, and could be activated in people.

The dove seems to be the one religious symbol left virtually intact. The dove became a national symbol for peace in the 1960's, Picasso's dove is famous, and the dove still represents the "Holy Ghost," who is almost totally devoid of personality. Even as the symbol of Aphrodite, Goddess of Love, the dove has generally survived the bitter ends of patriarchy. (She is widewinged spread in the Vatican on the ceilings). The dove was always sacred to Isis and Dianna.

The religion of the Goddess is joy-oriented, life-focusing; a celebration in music, dance, poetry, singing, and constantly being in tune with the process of promoting Life. The religions which destroyed us had to do something different in the extreme, because otherwise there would be no reason for the people to change. Even the already existing military controls were not as effective as had been thought. Thus, the concept of "sin," newly invented by patriarchy and introduced with religious and military fervor, was reinforced by the reversal of all the positive symbols of the Goddess into negative (in the sense of "sinful", "bad", "evil").

A major and obvious example of such a practice is met in the Tree of Knowledge or Tree of Good and Evil, growing in the mythical Garden of Eden. Originally, wisdom and knowledge as symbolized by a tree from which it comes, was an additional symbol of wisdom and dominion. Very often, a Goddess was depicted holding an apple in Her outstretched hand. In the Adam and Eve story, however, the apple and the Mother Tree are slandered as vehicles of deceit, shame, and a blinding awareness of the naked human form. Western civilization is still paying for this pathological concept.

In actuality, trees are very psychic beings, capable of magnifying the human aura countless times and directing it sky-ward. Joan of Arc had her personal "faith-tree" just outside of town, and when she stood under it she heard her "voices " (they were all female voices too!) Napoleon Bonaparte used to lean against a tree with his spine when he

Yugoslavian goddess   *Hungarian goddess*

was especially fatigued, believing that the tree would renew his energy.
What is true is that it is a very good idea to develop a close relationship
with a tree. People who worshipped the Goddess believed that trees cure
ills, relieve fatigue, and give new energy. They considered it well worth
their time to establish deep and meaningful relationships with trees.
Although this has been touted as tree-worship, it was not. Pagan celebration of the powers of trees was and is for the purpose of paying
homage to the Life-Force as represented by the Tree of Life.

Very often the Tree symbol has four arms, symbolizing the four
seasons and four major Sabbats. In other areas of the world this Tree/
Wheel of Life has eight arms, indicating the eight sacred Sabbats. The
Wheel of Life is today better known and recognized, perhaps, as the
"swastika," but it originally had absolutely nothing to do with such an
absurdity as "white supremacy" or the Hitler demonics.

Statues of Yugoslavian Goddesses have been found painted with
the Wheel of Life and sacred birds. Furrows on the bellies of such
Goddesses symbolized the farms of the worshipper or of her community,
and were used to invoke fertility of the land. Some statues even sport
sensible, brightly striped socks. She is a Goddess who knows how to
dress for cold weather.

This Hungarian great Goddess, which is about 8000 years old is
very dear to me. You can see the drawings of the fields on Her belly.
The diamonds usually mean rain, and her snaky arms, regeneration.
She has a penis head, but it broke off. Fragile things, penis heads, don't
stand the test of time.

Of course, nakedness to Goddess-worshippers has never been
seen as evil or shameful. The body is a temple, a shrine for the God-

dess, and as such is not separate from our souls. We are a unit. We are whole persons. Pagans never promote the separation of body from soul as the patriarchy does. The patriarchal dualism of good and evil, black and white, leading to a law of sin and shame for which there is a promise of redemption, is religious poison. It is a poison which is carried over into the dangerously foolish practices of building nuclear reactors where people are trying to live; of selling over-sugared foods and health-damaging foods and medication; of forcing concrete buildings and roads onto every available space of earth; of poisoning our air and our waters. This is only possible when the people have no concept of their bodies as sacred, worthy of spiritual and physical attention (or the full protection from their own inventions).

Many statues of the Goddess show Her with proudly exposed breasts. In matriarchal society there was no shame about exposing the female breasts, because the Goddess as Female was revered as women were revered. To expose the breasts meant that the woman was like the Mother — like the Goddess. The breasts of the Goddess-images were not shown as erotic symbols, but as wholly indicative of Her female-ness; the Force that gives Life and Nurturance.

This famous 25,000 year old venus of Willendorf is another example of what kind of art people created before the so-called "civilization." I think this seven-inch statue was used to hold in the palm of the hand, while praying to the Goddess of Plenty. She looks abundant. She has it in her to give. She has no face because she isn't human. She is a Force.

In this scene, we see the Woman's Mysteries dance by Cretans. Crete was a last resort and famous capital of Goddess worship. Beauty and jewelry and high culture are what held their attention.

Today's taboos against the exposure of female breasts, while allowing males to freely expose the small anatomical area, has to do with the ancient symbolism. Symbols of nurturance are the most powerful in that they remind men of their dependence upon the Mother — upon the Female. Patriarchy does not like being reminded of this on a daily basis, but the earlier cultures did not mind being faced with the natural facts of life. They knew how the Great Mother worked, and it was considered healthy and fine for women to expose their breasts, taking pride in the fact that they were the carriers and nurturers of living beings. A society in which women have to hide and cover their breasts is a society in which nurturance is neglected (or despised); a society more in touch with suffering and death than mothering. The naked female breasts, as symbol of women's power, deeply frightens men. Breasts are covered for that reason alone, and not because they arouse passion and sexuality.

The same holds true for the vagina as a Goddess-symbol. It is not

Yoni in conception position

out of lewdness that the vagina is made so prominent a feature of many Goddess images, but out of recognition and reverance for the supremely important Source of Life.

Some images of the Goddess show Her as a Toad in the position of conception. Often the Goddess of these images has rounded breasts but no head. There is often a sheaf of wheat shown to indicate that She is a Force, and energy, and to show how the people personalized the Force just a little in order to better relate to her.

Another symbol of note is the depiction of Lilith with claw-like feet. Pagan symbols are composites, and such feet are meant to be very animalistic. Again, She is a Force, She is not human, solely. She has wings and claws and perhaps hair made of snakes. Like the Great Isis, "She is that is."

Accompanying many Goddess images, we find a double-ax or labyris. This is a symbol of female supremacy. It is not a symbol of equality with your children, but of the Life-Force as superior to all.

The penis-headed Goddess may be found in various areas all over the world. She is one way women have found to include the penis into representations of life-orientation, as a part of her sacred creations. The women recognized that all life comes from the Mother, that Her statues and images generally emphasized Her breasts, vagina or belly as symbols of plenty and abundance. The penis was included as well, however, although its importance, as its function, was necessarily secondary.

This bronze mother is 13 thousand years old. She is strong and tender. She stands on a lion, the great Yin animal often accompanying the Goddess. Her head is a penis.

The penis-shaped heads of many of the Goddess images are interesting in that they tend to illustrate how inclusive matriarchal religions were. Men were not excluded, they were sons and lovers. Thus, the actual representations of the Goddess would include the male procrea-

205

tive organ as a part of Her. Some Goddess images have penis-heads, others were made with the penis-symbol as a necklace or belt, but the Male-principle is not forgotten in representations of the human connection with the Female Life-Force.

The premise behind this was that a true religion will benefit people's individual lives, as well as all humanity. Any religion which excludes any part of humanity, therefore, was deemed inferior and a vehicle for political oppression.

The idea of the serpent, as associated with the female gender in particular and evil in general, has been terribly exploited. In the Bible, the serpent is already suffering from bad "PR" as an instrument of Goddess-worship. So, of necessity, patriarchy masculinizes the snake to the point where it represents a "male force" in an aggressive, even phallic sense. They made that up, we didn't.

The snake is actually a positive, healing concept, embodied in much of the Old Religion. The serpent beautifully symbolizes regeneration. It is a wondrous thing to be able to watch a snake which is going through this regenerative process, in which an entire "old" skin is cast off and replaced by the brilliantly colored new skin beneath it. An awesome reminder of the ingenious way Nature has of renewal.

Snakes are not only symbols of regeneration. They had practical usage in ancient times. They were used to keep vermin out of the community sewers and storehouses. Some snakes were specially trained by Priestesses to gather herbs. This is yet another example of how Mother-religions work cooperatively with Nature. Rather than fighting Her elements and life-forms, and treating Her creatures as pests, we put them to work with us. Snakes were thus kept sacred in the temples, and may still be seen in pharmacies and medical centers as symbols of healing.

There is absolutely nothing evil about the snake. This entire projection of the serpent as evil came from the patriarchal projection of all Goddess-symbols as evil, of the Goddess religion as evil, and the assumption that anything women were involved with must be inherently evil.

Spells and Creativity

There is much more to "creation" than making people. There is the creation of harvests, creation of good feelings, good health, of song and art and culture. What is left to us from the matriarchies is mainly in stone, Alexander "the Great" having seen to it that the libraries were burned. Our fore-mothers have linked themselves to us through their enduring pieces of art, carving much of their essence in clay or stone.

206

Goddess-worshippers were constantly being slandered by patriarchs who attacked them as idol-worshippers. We know that Goddess worshipping people created art, not "idols." Worshipping the Goddess as a Force, the people were never guilty of mistaking the representation of the Force for the Force Herself. This is particularly well demonstrated in artistic images of the Goddess without faces. As Goddess-worship developed, we see more varied and detailed representations of the Life-Force. Where She was revered, Her images looked like Her people.

Small clay figurines represent Ishtar, Ashara, Isis, all the Goddesses. These small "idols" were the "abominations" later described by followers of Yah-weh, because they were such an integral part of the Goddess religions. Made by the women, figurines such as this were representative of different aspects of the Goddess, as well as graphic expressions of the women's prayers. They always have at least one and often more, symbols in common.

These are the creations of the people. The clay figurines were made at home and then carried to the temple as a "votive" offering. There was no interest in sacrificing living beings in Mother's worship. The people made religious art because cultivation of creativity was seen as cultivation of the Divine, and, therefore, was regarded as a form of worship. This was understood by everyone. Creativity was spell-casting.

A statue holding a child may have represented prayers for an easy child birth or a needy child in the family. The ones holding their breasts are pleas for nurturance, for sustenance. Fat bellies with carved furrows were petitions for fertility and abundance of food and health. Simple, instinctual, folkart; expressions of needs presented to the Queen of Heaven.

Such statues have been found which are up to 8,000 years old. Large ones, with back-to-back crescents represented a major petition, the crescents being another universal symbol of the Goddess, used by many witches as a sort of "signature" in their work. The meaning of the crescents used in this manner was "She Who Shines For All."

One Goddess image, from a cave in France, is holding the Horn of Plenty. Her hand points to Her belly in a familiar gesture. This was created in a period during which, we are led to believe, cavemen lived to club women over the heads and drag them into caves. That is pure fantasy. In those caves are walls and walls of Art — more than we could use in many centuries. People were constantly creating spiritual images to help themselves cope with life, help themselves understand life, and it was all centered around the Great Goddess.

Yoni-shrines were very special places, built and used by the ancient peoples as temples or worship. Within these shrines Her people

Yoni shrine

would sit or stand, sing, dance, read poetry, or meditate on the Source. Some people even stayed in the shrine overnight in order to facilitate prophetic dreaming. Several of the yoni-shrines show the Goddess in birth position. Imagine going to pray at such a shrine. Imagine any-one failing to develop a reverence for the Mother as Source of all Life if, from the time men were tiny boys, they were taken to such shrines to burn a little incense and thank the Great Mother for giving them life. The female anatomy in many yoni shrines has been closely ob-served. Even the outline of the clitoris is right where it belongs. There was no need for a denial of sexuality among the children of the Goddess, since it was considered a powerful gift that the Goddess gave to her people. When male and female worship at shrines depicting the Source of all Life there is a chance to experience true spirituality. This is where common sense blends with mysticism. You know where life comes from, you have a healthy respect for it, and you build your en-tire life around it.

This natural stone stands in nature, a shrine. You can tell how often the sides were rubbed for good luck. The shape is unmistakenly female.

At this Yoni shrine, people whispered into her middle and burned incense at the door.

A meteorite, you could climb into it, and chant and meditate. This is a natural place to resource.

One particular ritual of the matriarchal women, recorded in a wall painting at Knossos, but generally misinterpreted, was the matriar-chal sport of bull-leaping. The idea behind this was that no one should be hurt in the sport, even though a bull would sometimes trample an acrobat in the excitement. The bull, however, was a sacred animal,

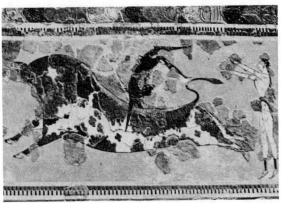

Bull leaping

and never meant to be killed. He signified the Male Principle of the Universe, and was very dear to the Goddess. The entire bull-leaping dance was performed as a ritual, symbolic of the Goddess mating with Her male consort, and exercising gentle control over the raw power of the male animal. Today, the bull-killing that is viewed as such a "macho" sport in Spain, is a direct reversal of this beautiful and ancient ritual. Bull-leaping took much more skill than wounding and killing trapped bulls, and the contrast between the matriarchal ways and patriarchal play could not be made more clear.

The Oldest Profession

Priestessing, not prostitution, is the "oldest profession." Part of Aphrodite's worship called for a Priestess to lay with men to insure their fertility, but that service to the Goddess lasted only one day out of a woman's life and was not, by any wild stretch of the imagination prostitution. Once a woman had done her service, she could spend the rest of her life priestessing in any other way she chose.

Ritual Priestesses often ate sacred mushrooms to increase their physical strength because women of old took their religion very seriously. Celebrating and dancing for three days and nights was not at all unusual.

Ethnic dances of all kinds have come from these sacred dancers and their religious rituals. Sacred ritual dances were taught by Priestesses and used liberally to condition the minds, bodies, and souls of the entire community. This was considered a form of spiritual as well as physical exercise, and is evidenced today in such forms as Yoga and Tai Chi. The law is that which does not move, dies. This holds true for everybody. In the Old Religion it was customary for the people to go to the temple for a ritual celebration or a Sabbat, and to dance and move until they could go home feeling fresh and renewed. All this was a part of the cultural heritage, considered absolutely essential for the well-being of the community.

Basically, a Pagan Priestess in the tradition of the Wicca can do anything from blessing mothers for easy childbirth, to blessing the new-born babies. Women's wisdom included not only the proper blessings, but the proper herbs to administer to the people in need of healing. It was the High Priestess who presided over such rituals as "trysting," the pagan counterpart of patriarchal marriage. Then too, the Priestess was responsible for blessing the fields for abundant harvest, for bringing on rains if there was a drought, and performing the proper spells to rid the town of disease or pestilence.

It was the Priestess who was the "fortune-teller" of the community, well-versed in all manner of divinatory techniques and skills. The Tarot is one such tool of divination, but there are numerable others: "augury," which is divination by omens; sensitivity to the voices of the animals; communication with plant families; interpretation of the stars and planets, the numbers and colors. Whatever the Priestess would touch, the Goddess would touch — the Goddess of Life. So the Priestesses of ancient times were also known to be "Goddesses on Earth," a concept which further separates us from the other religions.

With the marching military advent of patriarchal rule, the spiritual leaders of the matriarchies were an awesome power which had to be dealt with. Priestesses of Athena, Artemis and Diana were promptly hung from Oak trees by their hair, with anvils tied to their feet at the ankles, to force them to renounce Rhea as Supreme Goddess and accept the new male god (Zeus) as omnipotent. Through tortures which have continued to the present day (clitorectomy, electric shock, etc.), these militaristic patriarchs perpetrated the most massive religious and cultural overrule in the history of the planet.

Today, as the influences and results of that patriarchal religious zeal and tradition mount, we see that it has brought us a death-orientation, ecological destruction, etc. TV preachers jubilate over the pending disasters of the world as "proof" for their faith and the end of the world. In the meantime, 90% of all churches are women, the true battle ground for spiritual liberation is in the pews of the temples still.

Here is a relief from the temple of Ephesus again, showing that women can defend themselves. The scene actually is the revenge of Thermadon Amazons on Athens, because Theseus kidnapped their queen. The Amazons existence, so often denied by scientists looks so very real on these statues! Men don't get ideas of defeat by themselves, and certainly don't then put it into stone! But here we have fine examples of womanhood. The Amazons were strong and beauti-

Califia

ful at the same time. Weakness was not seen as feminine.

A local Amazon, Califia, gave us the name California. The story has it that she lived and ruled with her sister and co-queen in the Bajas. They lived an unadventurous life, even though they were prosperous. They kept Griffins (flying mountain lions) and trained them to tear apart any men who might land on their islands. One day Califia decided to go find adventure and help out the Pagans in their fight against the Christians, half way over the world. When she arrived in Turkey, the Christian crusades were on. She whistled for her helpers, the griffins, who proceeded to eat the men of both sides! To make up for this, she promised to lead the troups against the Christians the next morning herself. Here we see that scene. In the battle, she was separated from her sister and got captured. Part of her punishment was that she had to marry men whom she had bested in battle. This was a big disgrace for Amazons. But the women didn't give up. They kept talking about their golden plates and silver chalices, telling the new husbands how much gold they had back in the old country. Greed got to the Christians (bet on it every time!) and they set out to go home to their wive's country, in hopes to clean them out. This never happened, because nobody knows anything about the husbands after they left the harbor. The sisters returned much wiser to Baja, where they reigned in peace, not even missing adventure anymore.

Here is a depiction of the witch burnings.

The original sin was matricide. The toppling of the matriarchies and the rape and murder of the mothers was, and still is, the greatest of all sins. No purging of our culture has occurred since the Inquisition, no purging or public accounting for the sins of the "fathers." A major contribution to the continuing hostility and alienation of males is the

211

Witch burning

deep core of guilt. Men are guilty of matricide, and they are continuing to be guilty of matricide. No amount of purification will take that blemish away. Matricide is punishable by eternal unhappiness and the Goddess pays in different ways. We don't have a heaven and/or hell someplace "out there"; we create both right here where we live.

The punishment for matricide is foul air, poisoned food, ecological disasters (earthquakes, famines, hurricanes, and drought). MAMA is not happy, and She will not take this anymore. She has lots of time. Every 100-million years or so, the entire earth gets re-worked when the Queen decides that this particular spaceship has to change. That is the Law – Change. That which does not change, dies, and even in death, continues to change.

Men harbor this constant, sneaking suspicion that they are wrong after all. As the day of the End nears, they feel their anxiety grow. Sadly, this anxiety is misdirected in their death-orientation, so that they cause the eating of their own young. Kronos eats his own son – the old man sends the young man to die in the war (draft). Young men were and are being used in aggression-expression which is supposed to solve problems. When nations can be convinced that the only solution to differences (usually economical) is to kill the other people, it is apparent that we have nations led by men where thinking isn't happening anymore, and where life-force is no longer healthy.

A very important evolutionary note here, regarding species, us and other beings who are sharing our planet with us; every time the male of a particular species begins to attack the female, that species is on a suicide course. The fact now is that no other male animal attacks the female except the male human animal, and he does so with astonishing violence and regularity. Human males, therefore are hurtling toward a final retribution – the extinction of their species and their planet – a course of self-destruction that began in earnest approximately 2½ thousand years ago.

212

The Fall

The question of how the matriarchies were taken over, destroyed and rebuilt into patriarchal societies remains unanswered. What made men so hostile and angry that they rose up against their own mothers, the life-givers? We still don't know for certain, but there is an obvious probability based upon the fact that not everybody "made it" in the matriarchal cultures — making the problem of power.

Matriarchy was deposed mainly because of our lack of suspicion about our sons. We really did not deal with the possibility that they would find reason to rise up against us and kill us. Imagine living in those societies where it was customary to run around all day bare-breasted and free; where rape was practically unheard of and punishable by death should it ever occur; where women were worshipped by their children if they had any, and worshipped as an expression of the Goddess either way. In such a society there would be no fear that the sons would turn on the mothers, and no one would spend any time and energy building defense systems against anyone, much less the community's offspring.

Matriarchal women had no defense systems. They didn't even have swords, although they did use wands. What they did have was superior sewer systems. What they did have was elaborate baths, beautiful wall-paintings, and exquisite jewelry. They were beauty-oriented, not war-obsessed, and thus were rather easily over-run, sacked in the cruelest sense of the word.

In matrilineal heritage, the superior sires were chosen as mates by matriarchal women. Males who were not selected as mates for some reason or another, were unable to gain any status, property, wealth, or recognition by association with a woman's family. Thus it was that numbers of males who were deemed less than desirable began to ban together outside of the communities. Soon they found that if they could only have their "own" women to breed like chattel, they then could produce their own people, and become more powerful. These males of the outer-communities soon began to do whatever they could to bring women into their possession.

The mythological rape of the Sabines was an example of such beliefs carried out in patriarchal practical reality. Patriarchal soldiers marched into town while the other men were away, they raped all the women, impregnating most of them. The "logic" of it was that if each man could impregnate at least one woman and each woman then bore a child in the next, the original males would have reproduced their numbers and doubled in size. It was a small step from there to the possessing of women, breeding like stock, keeping them pregnant for as long and as much as possible. Soon the patriarchs had their armies (this same right is now defended today by the right to "Life" groups who desire women staying pregnant and poor.).

213

Children of such practices grew up in a totally different power-structure. Women were merely chattel, breeders and servants here. Males called all the shots and violence, brute strength, physical power and aggression became attributes to be admired and worshipped. Within a fifty-year period, then, patriarchs were able to produce entire armies and to continue to escalate such degenerate activities as ransacking cities, raping and murdering women and female children, and theft.

Because history occurs simultaneously, this sort of thing happened all over the world at about the same time. Patriarchs were not a collected and organized group attempting to bring civilization to a "primitive" people. They were hordes of males reacting violently to their positions within matriarchal cities and matrilinear families.

The first patriarchal religions emerged with full knowledge of a culture based on female supremacy. Goddesses and shrines were all around them, after all, and it soon became obvious that the matriarchal identity was not easily squelched. The people of the Old Way simply were not buying the idea of a patriarchal society and death-blood-sacrifice focus. It became necessary for the patriarchs, for the Northern Invaders in particular, to bring in their own god, little "dios." At first it was decided that "dios" should be placed in the temples of the Great Mother of course, since surely it was one of Her sons. Since a spreading military force and pervasive propagandizing by the patriarchs was having such a limited effect upon the Goddess worshippers, it was obviously time to introduce little "dios" to them. Dios thus began as a son of the Mother, but he grew as the patriarchal understanding of power grew and as power over the matriarchies grew.

This jealous male god and son still exist today in great numbers (call them Jehovah, Christ, Krishna, Allah). People continue to worship the Goddess, despite centuries of suppression and a four hundred year long horror known as the Inquisition. The patriarchs have not been able to burn it up, shoot it dead, or torture it out of existence. Goddess worship continues despite the atrocity of world-wide mass murders of women as witches.

Estimates by women historians and scholars today place the number of women exterminated during the witch "trials" at eleven million, and still claim that the estimate is conservative. There are records of certain towns where as many as 400 women were burned to death in ONE day. During this shameful period in the life of the world, no male uprising occurred to stop the murder of women. No husbands, sons or lovers banned together to stop the hysterical slaughter of millions of women. Even in the years following, there has been no one to call for an accounting. No witches have been avenged through trials of accountability such as those for the Jews at Nuremberg. There has been no apparent opposition to the wave of hatred which caused the flesh of the mothers to be burned.

At one point during the Inquisition, the patriarchs were burning or hanging children who were over a year old. At the end of this 400 year period, however, they grew "milder" about the children and spared the ones who were at puberty or younger. But, to teach these children to remember the "sins" of their elders, they were led around the stake at which their parents burned, while the patriarch whipped them. All this horror in the name of the Father God, in the name of Jesus, in the name of Jehovah. I am still filled with rage about this issue, because deep down, I want justice for women.

Epilogue

Judaism and Christianity, Moslem, Buddhism, and Krishna are brothers. Judaism has an inherent back-lash to feminist spirituality built into it. Christianity simply helped itself, through Judaism, to write its own sexist war story. At any rate, both made concerted efforts and succeeded in writing out the Great Goddess, Queen of the Universe, Rhea, Flow of Life. They took special pains to write out everything having to do with the lesbian Goddesses, thereby denying the women a choice of lifestyles.

It is fairly easy to see that Judeo-Christianity is anti-woman and exclusive in its intent. It is not so easy to see this with the Eastern religions who stole religion from the Tara even earlier than the Judeo-Christians did. These have now found that there is a profit to be made from the spiritual poverty of the West. They are now in an excellent position to sell their brand of spirituality to the Westerners (some called New Age).

In the Orient, we find Tara, sometimes shown as the tree of Life. She comes in green, because that is Nature's favorite color, ever young Tara, she comes in yellow for manifesting. Tara comes in white for the blessing. Tara is red for the angry. TARA, and she is black for the death-aspect. Her temples are still standing in India, her worship preceded that of Krishna, the warrior on the chariot. Sometimes Tara is shown pregnant, and that image was taken over by Buddha, with the fat belly.

Death-oriented religions often encourage the killing of other people by promoting the idea that whomever you kill would be forced to serve you in the after-life. Islam is a prime example. Christians too, used to bless their cannons before using them to kill innocent people. Waging war against each other is central to the death-oriented, patriarchal religions (and economy). They revel in wars because that is a time when human suffering becomes very real on a grand scale. Everybody feels bad. At such a time, they are more easily able to attract members and to appear important, offering false "protection."

In times of peace and abundance, a death-oriented religion does not have much of an appeal. During times of peace you cannot attract new members to your religion by promising an end to all suffering and a heaven after death. Peaceful times promotes concerns more oriented toward abundance, prosperity and pleasure — anathema to patriarchs who cannot deliver the goods for the here-and-now.

I am angered by some of the New Age religions which are gaining wealth by selling their liberalized version of religion to Americans who are spiritually starved. A token female leader of a particularly "disciple"-oriented group, now claims that when two women make love, all the energy goes to the devil — we never had such a nasty concept. Witches don't believe in the devil. That entire concept came out of the early patrairchal concept of duality: good/evil; black/white (racism); God/Devil. The Wicca knows better and continues to deal in healthy multiples. This and other patriarchal mythologies were created for the sole purpose of controlling the inner space of the people.

If religious stories are good for the soul, then the believer will control herself — she will police herself into submission. In other words, the most insidious (and cheap!) but effective oppression is an internalized oppression. That can only be achieved when someone goes all the way inside your soul and throws out your self-respect (self-love). This is nothing less than internalized oppression on a spiritual level; foundation for oppression of all kinds.

Why this continues to happen and how we lost the Mother's Religion is not really the point. The point is that it all has to do with a cycle — with a Universal event — and that has to do with the consciousness of a people. Whatever we think, we get. That is the very reason religions are all-important and all-political, and why they will always be that way. Religions can never be left alone while the people argue about whether or not we need it, whether or not it influences us, whether or not we can make it go away by not thinking about it. That's foolish ignorance, actively displayed only through futile debate and verbage.

Just because the religions fed to us so far in the patriarchal scheme have been poison, is no reason for women to reject their spirituality totally. The point is to be wise. To take our powers and to think a way through — to find another way to feed our undernourished spirits. We must find a nourishing, healthy resourcement which will be the basis for our spirituality, which will be the basis for our rebellion against oppression of any kind, and which will be our weapon for awakening and sustaining the Goddess within. And that's the future.

A Year and A Day Calendar

BETH (Dec. 24 — Jan. 20)

Jan. 6 — FEAST OF SIRONA, Goddess of Rivers. Blessing of the waters.

11 & 15 — CARMENTALIA, festival to Carmenta, Roman Goddess of childbirth. This festival was attended only by women who call upon the Goddess to give an easy position for birth.

LUIS (Jan. 21 — Feb. 17)

Feb. 2 — CANDLEMAS, celebration of the waxing light, initiation of new witches.

14-21 — FESTIVAL OF LOVE, celebration of the Goddess Aphrodite.

NION (Feb. 18 — Mar. 17)

Mar. 20 — SPRING EQUINOX, return of Persephone from the underworld to reunite with Demeter, her mother, rejuvenation of the life force in nature.

FEARN (Mar. 18 — Apr. 14)

Mar. 21-25 — QUINQUATRIA, Festival of Minerva, Goddess of Wisdom and inventor of the arts and sciences.

30 — FEAST OF ESOTARA, Goddess of Fertility.

SAILLE (Apr. 15 — May 12)

Apr. 28—
May 3 — FESTIVAL OF FLORA, Goddess of Spring Flowers and Vegetation. Celebration is rather licentious.

May 1 — BELTANE, the maiden goddess comes of age, sometimes celebrated May Eve, April 30.

UATH (May 13 — June 9)

June 1 — FESTIVAL OF EPIPI, Goddess of the Dark. This celebration is always on the Full Moon in late May to early June and is an investigation of the mysteries.

7 — VESTALIA, Feast of Vesta, Goddess of the hearth and home.

DRUIR (June 10 — July 7)

June 13 — FEAST OF EPONA, Goddess of Horses.

21 — SUMMER SOLSTICE, sacred to the fire queen of love and celebration of the Goddess' power over men.

July 2 — FEAST OF EXPECTANT MOTHERS.

7 — NONAE CAPROTINAE, a feast under the wild fig tree and oldest of women's celebrations in Rome.

TINNE (July 8 — Aug. 4)

July 17 — BIRTHDAY OF ISIS.

Aug. 2 — LAMMAS, celebration of Habondia, the Goddess of plenty, of fortune, and of the daughters of the earth mother.

COLL (Aug. 5 — Sept. 1)

Aug. 13 — FESTIVAL TO DIANA, Goddess of the Moon. Women made pilgrimages to Nemi with torches and wreaths to grant children and easy delivery.

21 — CONSUALIA, Celebration of the taking in of the Harvest. There were Chariot races and horse races, entertainment, dancing and singing.

MUIN (Sept. 2 — Sept. 29)

Sept. 8	FEAST OF THE BIRTH OF THE MOTHER.
23	AUTUMN EQUINOX, a witches Thanksgiving, celebration of the harvest.
27	DAY OF WILLOWS, a Ceremony of Fire and Water.

GORT (Sept. 30 — Oct. 27)

Oct. 24	FEAST OF THE SPIRITS OF THE AIR.
26	FESTIVAL OF HATHOR, Egyptian Goddess of Productivity. This celebration occurs on the Full Moon.

NGETAL (Oct. 28 — Nov. 24)

Oct. 31	HALLOWMAS, Witches New Year, celebration of the sacred hag aspect of the Goddess, the destroyer of life, essential for future life.
Nov. 30	FEAST OF THE GODDESSES OF THE CROSSROADS.

RUIS (Nov. 25 — Dec. 22)

Dec. 13	FEAST OF BELISAMA, Goddess of Light.
15	CONSUALIA, Celebration of the sowing of the Harvest.
19	OPALIA, Festival of Ops, ancient Sabine Goddess of Creative Force and Agricultural Fertility.
21	WINTER SOLSTICE, birth of the sun Goddess, Lucina.

THE DAY (Dec. 23)

23	DAY OF LIBERATION, DAY OF THE DIVINE CHILDREN, or DAY OF THE FOOL.

Researched by Ariel Dougherty

CONCLUSION

The Holy Book Part One and Two are but fragments of the grow-knowledge of Women's Spirituality. Yet they have changed lives of women and changed herstory. No longer are Goddess worshippers mocked as silly in the Feminist Movement, no longer are we seen as threatening clouds on the political horizons, but as the very essence of Womens Politics.

Ten years later, there are more covens that can be counted, organically sprung up like wild roses. Women who practice solo have increased, more conferences are planned, more newsletters of the Goddess are born. And so it should be.

We don't pretend that we covered all the areas of Woman's Religion, but we labored in love and we reap love. This book is published when the New Right is organizing against Woman's Rights, and when a new oppressive Christian area is looming over us. Never before was an articulate Women's Religion more needed to maintain us. Never before was our own endorsement in our own behalf more political.

Five years ago when we started working on the Holy Book idea, Janet Roslund found a quote from Florence Nightingale:

> Is it possible to write a mystical book with the essence of common sense? she asked.

I hope with these two volumes, I can answer a proud — Yes, to the sister in the past.

May the Goddess prosper all who follow her Paths, and may we all be free to worship her!

ABOUT THE AUTHOR

Zsuzsanna Emese Budapest was born in Budepest to Masika Szilagyi whose art and beliefs shaped her into the High Priestess she is today. Masika taught her the lore and skills of Hungarian Craft which she enriched by studying independently after she left Hungary after the 1956 Hungarian Uprising.

Ms. Budapest published her first short story when she was but 14, and never stopped writing since. She attended University in Vienna, University of Chicago. Studied improvisational Theater with Second City. All this came together in the late sixties when her witchcraft background started blending with her new found feminism, and her life work direction emerged from both.

Z Budapest became a sought after speaker in the College circuits whose Hungarian charm and soft accent endeared her to thousands along with her message of Womens Religion, a vision inclusive of women and their children.

She published the Feminist Book of Lights and Shadows, (now included into the Holy Book Part One) in 1975, Luna Publication; SELENE, a mystical book for youth, Dianna Press; The Holy Book of Womens Mysteries, a large work collecting the old and the living faith among witches practiced today.

Currently she is supporting herself traveling around the country giving speeches with her ever-changing Goddess Slide Show, reading the Tarot cards to her sisters, ESP and fundraising to publish her historical book, The Holy Book of Womens Mysteries. She is also working on her memoirs based on almost ten years of witchy covens life, called "Like-minded Wimmin". She is busy planning the first Spirituality Conference in Southern California in 1981, sponsored by the Susan B. Anthony Coven Number One, her coven which she has served as High Priestess for a decade.

Z and her coven is publishing *THEMIS*, a newsletter to Dianics dedicated to the Goddess of Social Change.

ABOUT THE ARTIST

Masika Szilagyi was born in rural Hungary to a suffragist mother, Ilona, who founded trade schools for girls, and became a congress-woman, the first in the country. As a youth, Masika was a poet and medium. She wrote poems of invocations in trance states, and sometimes spoke ancient egyptian. Through her poetry she won a scholarship to Paris where she began her studies as a ceramic artist and sculptoress. She continued in Budapest University; erected two statues in the city capital before she was 25 years old.

She went through a lot of hardship during the war and afterwards emerged as the only artist who taught the homecoming maimed soldiers how to paint with their teeth if they lacked arms, and how to throw the wheel with only one leg, etc. She then worked in a factory for exports and finally in 1956 began her career anew and won her first show in Budapest, followed by many annually.

Masika is a folk artist, maintaining Pagan symbolism and Goddess portrayal in all her works as well as honoring peasant rebels and other historical figures. She remained a beloved artist of the people, still reading the palms of those she loved and bringing back rich stories each morning as she communed with the dead in her dreams. She died in 1979, April 19th, to deep sorrow and loss of us all.

Blessed Be!

ORDER NOW!
The Susan B. Anthony Coven No. 1
P.O. Box 11363
Oakland, CA 94611

Bulk orders to bookstores and covens;
minimum 3 copies, standard trade
discount (40%) plus shipping.

RISE OF THE FATES $5.00
HOLY BOOK, PART 1 . . . . 7.35
GODDESS TAPE 6.00

Add 75¢ per item for shipping